BY ELISABETH KÜBLER-ROSS

Elisabeth Kübler-Ross, M.D.

ON DEATH AND DYING

SCRIBNER CLASSICS

SCRIBNER
1230 Avenue of the Americas
New York, NY 10020

First Scribner Classics edition 1997

SCRIBNER and design are trademarks of Simon & Schuster Inc.

DESIGNED BY ERICH HOBBING

Set in Janson

Manufactured in the United States of America

11   13   15   17   19   20   18   16   14   12

Library of Congress Cataloging-in-Publication Data is available.

ISBN-13: 978-0-684-84223-3
ISBN-10:   0-684-84223-8

Acknowledgment is made to Macmillan Publishing Company, a division of Macmillan, Inc., New York, Macmillan & Co. Ltd., London, and the Trustees of the Tagore Estate for permission to reprint the following selections from *Collected Poems and Plays of Rabindranath Tagore:* "Fruit-Gathering," Copyright 1916 by Macmillan Publishing Company, a division of Macmillan, Inc., renewed 1944 by Rabindranath Tagore, "Gitanjali," "Stray Birds," Copyright 1916 by Macmillan Publishing Company, a division of Macmillan, Inc., renewed 1949 by Rabindranath Tagore; and to McGraw-Hill Book Company for "On a Sunny Evening" from *I Never Saw Another Butterfly,* edited by M. Volavkova, 1964.

To the memory of
MY FATHER
and of
SEPPLI BUCHER

Acknowledgments

There are too many people who have directly or indirectly contributed to this work to express my appreciation to them individually. Dr. Sydney Margolin deserves the credit for having stimulated the idea of interviewing terminally ill patients in the presence of students as a meaningful learning-teaching model.

The Department of Psychiatry at the University of Chicago Billings Hospital has supplied the environment and facilities to make such a seminar technically possible.

Chaplains Herman Cook and Carl Nighswonger have been helpful and stimulating co-interviewers, who also have assisted in the search for patients at a time when that was immensely difficult. Wayne Rydberg and the original four students by their interest and curiosity have enabled me to overcome the initial difficulties. I was also assisted by the support of the Chicago Theological Seminary staff. Reverend Renford Gaines and his wife Harriet have spent countless hours reviewing the manuscript and have maintained my faith in the worth of this kind of undertaking. Dr. C. Knight Aldrich has supported this work over the past three years.

Dr. Edgar Draper and Jane Kennedy reviewed part of the manuscript. Bonita McDaniel, Janet Reshkin, and Joyce Carlson deserve thanks for the typing of the chapters.

My thanks to the many patients and their families is perhaps best expressed by the publication of their communications.

There are many authors who have inspired this work, and

7

thanks should be given finally to all those who have given thought and attention to the terminally ill.

Thanks is given to Mr. Peter Nevraumont for suggesting the writing of this book as well as to Mr. Clement Alexandre, of the Macmillan Company, for his patience and understanding while the book was in preparation.

Last but not least I wish to thank my husband and my children for their patience and continued support which enables me to carry on a full-time job in addition to being a wife and mother.

Contents

Preface

When I was asked if I would be willing to write a book on death and dying, I enthusiastically accepted the challenge. When I actually sat down and began to wonder what I had got myself into, it became a different matter. Where do I begin? What do I include? How much can I say to strangers who are going to read this book, how much can I share from this experience with dying patients? How many things are communicated nonverbally and have to be felt, experienced, seen, and can hardly be translated into words?

I have worked with dying patients for the past two and a half years and this book will tell about the beginning of this experiment, which turned out to be a meaningful and instructive experience for all participants. It is not meant to be a textbook on how to manage dying patients, nor is it intended as a complete study of the psychology of the dying. It is simply an account of a new and challenging opportunity to refocus on the patient as a human being, to include him in dialogues, to learn from him the strengths and weaknesses of our hospital management of the patient. We have asked him to be our teacher so that we may learn more about the final stages of life with all its anxieties, fears, and hopes. I am simply telling the stories of my patients who shared their agonies, their expectations, and their frustrations with us. It is hoped that it will encourage others not to shy away from the "hopelessly" sick but to get closer to them, as they can help them much during their final hours. The few who can do this will also discover that it can be a mutually gratifying experience; they will learn much about the functioning of the human mind, the unique human aspects of our existence, and will emerge from the experience enriched and perhaps with fewer anxieties about their own finality.

ON DEATH AND DYING

CHAPTER I

On the Fear of Death

Let me not pray to be sheltered from
dangers but to be fearless in facing
them.
Let me not beg for the stilling of
my pain but for the heart to conquer it.
Let me not look for allies in life's
battlefield but to my own strength.
Let me not crave in anxious fear to
be saved but hope for the patience to
win my freedom.
Grant me that I may not be a
coward, feeling your mercy in my
success alone; but let me find the grasp
of your hand in my failure.

RABINDRANATH TAGORE,
Fruit-Gathering

Epidemics have taken a great toll of lives in past generations. Death in infancy and early childhood was frequent and there were few families who didn't lose a member of the family at an early age. Medicine has changed greatly in the last decades. Widespread vaccinations have practically eradicated many illnesses, at least in western Europe and the United States. The use of chemotherapy, especially the antibiotics, has contributed to an ever decreasing number of fatalities in infectious diseases. Better child care and education has effected a low morbidity and mortality among children. The many diseases that have taken an impressive toll among the young and middle-aged have been conquered. The number of old people is on the rise, and with this fact come the number of people with malignancies and chronic diseases associated more with old age.

Pediatricians have less work with acute and life-threatening situations as they have an ever increasing number of patients with psychosomatic disturbances and adjustment and behavior problems. Physicians have more people in their waiting rooms with emotional problems than they have ever had before, but they also have more elderly patients who not only try to live with their decreased physical abilities and limitations but who also face loneliness and isolation with all its pains and anguish. The majority of these people are not seen by a psychiatrist. Their needs have to be elicited and gratified by other professional people, for instance, chaplains and social workers. It is for them that I am trying to outline the changes that have taken place in the last few decades, changes that are ultimately responsible for the increased fear of death, the rising number of emotional problems, and the greater need for understanding of and coping with the problems of death and dying.

When we look back in time and study old cultures and people, we are impressed that death has always been distasteful to man and will probably always be. From a psychiatrist's point of view this is very understandable and can perhaps best be explained by our basic knowledge that, in our unconscious, death is never possible in regard to ourselves. It is inconceivable for our unconscious to imagine an actual ending of our own life here on earth, and if this life of ours has to end, the ending is always attributed to a malicious intervention from the outside by someone else. In simple terms, in our unconscious mind we can only be killed; it is inconceivable to die of a natural cause or of old age. Therefore death in itself is associated with a bad act, a frightening happening, something that in itself calls for retribution and punishment.

One is wise to remember these fundamental facts as they are essential in understanding some of the most important, otherwise unintelligible communications of our patients.

The second fact that we have to comprehend is that in our unconscious mind we cannot distinguish between a wish and a deed. We are all aware of some of our illogical dreams in which two completely opposite statements can exist side by side—very acceptable in our dreams but unthinkable and illogical in our wakening state. Just as our unconscious mind cannot differentiate between the wish to kill somebody in anger and the act of having done so, the young child is unable to make this distinction. The child who angrily wishes his mother to drop dead for not having gratified his needs will be traumatized greatly by the actual death of his mother—even if this event is not linked closely in time with his destructive wishes. He will always take part or the whole blame for the loss of his mother. He will always say to himself—rarely to others—"I did it, I am responsible, I was bad, therefore Mommy left me." It is well to remember that the child will react in the same manner if he loses a parent by divorce, separation, or desertion. Death is often seen by a child as an impermanent thing and has therefore little distinction from a divorce in which he may have an opportunity to see a parent again.

Many a parent will remember remarks of their children such as, "I will bury my doggy now and next spring when the flowers come up again, he will get up." Maybe it was the same wish that motivated the ancient Egyptians to supply their dead with food and goods to keep them happy and the old American Indians to bury their relatives with their belongings.

When we grow older and begin to realize that our omnipotence is really not so omnipotent, that our strongest wishes are not powerful enough to make the impossible possible, the fear that we have contributed to the death of a loved one diminishes—and with it the guilt. The fear remains diminished, however, only so long as it is not challenged too strongly. Its vestiges can be seen daily in hospital corridors and in people associated with the bereaved.

A husband and wife may have been fighting for years, but when the partner dies, the survivor will pull his hair, whine and cry louder and beat his chest in regret, fear and anguish, and will hence fear his own death more than before, still believing in the law of talion—an eye for an eye, a tooth for a tooth—"I am responsible for her death, I will have to die a pitiful death in retribution."

Maybe this knowledge will help us understand many of the old customs and rituals which have lasted over the centuries and whose purpose is to diminish the anger of the gods or the people as the case may be, thus decreasing the anticipated punishment. I am thinking of the ashes, the torn clothes, the veil, the *Klage Weiber* of the old days—they are all means to ask you to take pity on them, the mourners, and are expressions of sorrow, grief, and shame. If someone grieves, beats his chest, tears his hair, or refuses to eat, it is an attempt at self-punishment to avoid or reduce the anticipated punishment for the blame that he takes on the death of a loved one.

This grief, shame, and guilt are not very far removed from feelings of anger and rage. The process of grief always includes some qualities of anger. Since none of us likes to admit anger at a deceased person, these emotions are often disguised or repressed and prolong the period of grief or show up in other ways. It is well to remember that it is not up to us to judge such feelings as bad or shameful but to understand their true meaning and origin as something very human. In order to illustrate this I will again use the example of the child—and the child in us. The five-year-old who loses his mother is both blaming himself for her disappearance and being angry at her for having deserted him and for no longer gratifying his needs. The dead person then turns into something the child loves and wants very much but also hates with equal intensity for this severe deprivation.

The ancient Hebrews regarded the body of a dead person as something unclean and not to be touched. The early American Indians talked about the evil spirits and shot arrows in the air to drive the spirits away. Many other cultures have rituals to take care of the "bad" dead person, and they all originate in this feeling of anger which still exists in all of us, though we dislike admit-

ting it. The tradition of the tombstone may originate in this wish
to keep the bad spirits deep down in the ground, and the pebbles
that many mourners put on the grave are left-over symbols of the
same wish. Though we call the firing of guns at military funerals
a last salute, it is the same symbolic ritual as the Indian used
when he shot his spears and arrows into the skies.

I give these examples to emphasize that man has not basically
changed. Death is still a fearful, frightening happening, and the
fear of death is a universal fear even if we think we have mastered
it on many levels.

What has changed is our way of coping and dealing with death
and dying and our dying patients.

Having been raised in a country in Europe where science is not
so advanced, where modern techniques have just started to find
their way into medicine, and where people still live as they did in
this country half a century ago, I may have had an opportunity to
study a part of the evolution of mankind in a shorter period.

I remember as a child the death of a farmer. He fell from a tree
and was not expected to live. He asked simply to die at home, a
wish that was granted without questioning. He called his daugh-
ters into the bedroom and spoke with each one of them alone for
a few minutes. He arranged his affairs quietly, though he was in
great pain, and distributed his belongings and his land, none of
which was to be split until his wife should follow him in death.
He also asked each of his children to share in the work, duties,
and tasks that he had carried on until the time of the accident. He
asked his friends to visit him once more, to bid good-bye to them.
Although I was a small child at the time, he did not exclude me or
my siblings. We were allowed to share in the preparations of the
family just as we were permitted to grieve with them until he
died. When he did die, he was left at home, in his own beloved
home which he had built, and among his friends and neighbors
who went to take a last look at him where he lay in the midst of
flowers in the place he had lived in and loved so much. In that
country today there is still no make-believe slumber room, no
embalming, no false makeup to pretend sleep. Only the signs of

very disfiguring illnesses are covered up with bandages and only infectious cases are removed from the home prior to the burial.

Why do I describe such "old-fashioned" customs? I think they are an indication of our acceptance of a fatal outcome, and they help the dying patient as well as his family to accept the loss of a loved one. If a patient is allowed to terminate his life in the familiar and beloved environment, it requires less adjustment for him. His own family knows him well enough to replace a sedative with a glass of his favorite wine; or the smell of a home-cooked soup may give him the appetite to sip a few spoons of fluid which, I think, is still more enjoyable than an infusion. I will not minimize the need for sedatives and infusions and realize full well from my own experience as a country doctor that they are sometimes life-saving and often unavoidable. But I also know that patience and familiar people and foods could replace many a bottle of intravenous fluids given for the simple reason that it fulfills the physiological need without involving too many people and/or individual nursing care.

The fact that children are allowed to stay at home where a fatality has stricken and are included in the talk, discussions, and fears gives them the feeling that they are not alone in the grief and gives them the comfort of shared responsibility and shared mourning. It prepares them gradually and helps them view death as part of life, an experience which may help them grow and mature.

This is in great contrast to a society in which death is viewed as taboo, discussion of it is regarded as morbid, and children are excluded with the presumption and pretext that it would be "too much" for them. They are then sent off to relatives, often accompanied with some unconvincing lies of "Mother has gone on a long trip" or other unbelievable stories. The child senses that something is wrong, and his distrust in adults will only multiply if other relatives add new variations of the story, avoid his questions or suspicions, shower him with gifts as a meager substitute for a loss he is not permitted to deal with. Sooner or later the child will become aware of the changed family situation and, depending on the age and personality of the child, will have an unresolved grief and regard this incident as a frightening, mysterious, in any case very traumatic experience with untrustworthy grownups, which he has no way to cope with.

It is equally unwise to tell a little child who lost her brother that God loved little boys so much that he took little Johnny to heaven. When this little girl grew up to be a woman she never solved her anger at God, which resulted in a psychotic depression when she lost her own little son three decades later.

We would think that our great emancipation, our knowledge of science and of man, has given us better ways and means to prepare ourselves and our families for this inevitable happening. Instead the days are gone when a man was allowed to die in peace and dignity in his own home.

The more we are making advancements in science, the more we seem to fear and deny the reality of death. How is this possible?

We use euphemisms, we make the dead look as if they were asleep, we ship the children off to protect them from the anxiety and turmoil around the house if the patient is fortunate enough to die at home, we don't allow children to visit their dying parents in the hospitals, we have long and controversial discussions about whether patients should be told the truth—a question that rarely arises when the dying person is tended by the family physician who has known him from delivery to death and who knows the weaknesses and strengths of each member of the family.

I think there are many reasons for this flight away from facing death calmly. One of the most important facts is that dying nowadays is more gruesome in many ways, namely, more lonely, mechanical, and dehumanized; at times it is even difficult to determine technically when the time of death has occurred.

Dying becomes lonely and impersonal because the patient is often taken out of his familiar environment and rushed to an emergency room. Whoever has been very sick and has required rest and comfort especially may recall his experience of being put on a stretcher and enduring the noise of the ambulance siren and hectic rush until the hospital gates open. Only those who have lived through this may appreciate the discomfort and cold necessity of such transportation which is only the beginning of a long ordeal—hard to endure when you are well, difficult to express in words when noise, light, pumps, and voices are all too much to put up with. It may well be that we might consider more the patient under the sheets and blankets and perhaps stop our well-meant efficiency and rush in order to hold the patient's hand, to smile, or to listen to a question. I include the trip to the hospital as the first episode in dying, as it is for many. I am putting it exaggeratedly in contrast to the sick man who is left at home—not to say that lives should not be saved if they can be saved by a hospitalization but to keep the focus on the patient's experience, his needs and his reactions.

When a patient is severely ill, he is often treated like a person with no right to an opinion. It is often someone else who makes the decision if and when and where a patient should be hospitalized. It would take so little to remember that the sick person too has feelings, has wishes and opinions, and has—most important of all—the right to be heard.

Well, our presumed patient has now reached the emergency room. He will be surrounded by busy nurses, orderlies, interns, residents, a lab technician perhaps who will take some blood, an electrocardiogram technician who takes the cardiogram. He may be moved to X-ray and he will overhear opinions of his condition and discussions and questions to members of the family. He slowly but surely is beginning to be treated like a thing. He is no longer a person. Decisions are made often without his opinion. If he tries to rebel he will be sedated and after hours of waiting and wondering whether he has the strength, he will be wheeled into the operating room or intensive treatment unit and become an object of great concern and great financial investment.

He may cry for rest, peace, and dignity, but he will get infusions, transfusions, a heart machine, or tracheostomy if necessary. He may want one single person to stop for one single minute so that he can ask one single question—but he will get a dozen people around the clock, all busily preoccupied with his heart rate, pulse, electrocardiogram or pulmonary functions, his secretions or excretions but not with him as a human being. He may wish to fight it all but it is going to be a useless fight since all this is done in the fight for his life, and if they can save his life they can consider the person afterwards. Those who consider the person first may lose precious time to save his life! At least this seems to be the rationale or justification behind all this—or is it? Is the reason for this increasingly mechanical, depersonalized approach our own defensiveness? Is this approach our own way to cope with and repress the anxieties that a terminally or critically ill patient evokes in us? Is our concentration on equipment, on blood pressure our desperate attempt to deny the impending death which is so frightening and discomforting to us that we displace all our knowledge onto machines, since they are less close to us than the suffering face of another human being which would remind us once more of our lack of omnipotence, our own limits and failures, and last but not least perhaps our own mortality?

Maybe the question has to be raised: Are we becoming less human or more human? Though this book is in no way meant to be judgmental, it is clear that whatever the answer may be, the patient is suffering more—not physically, perhaps, but emotionally. And his needs have not changed over the centuries, only our ability to gratify them.

CHAPTER II

Attitudes Toward Death and Dying

Men are cruel, but Man is kind.
TAGORE,
from *Stray Birds,* CCXIX

SOCIETY'S CONTRIBUTIONS TO DEFENSIVENESS

Until now we have looked at the individual human reaction to death and dying. If we now take a look at our society, we may want to ask ourselves what happens to man in a society bent on ignoring or avoiding death. What factors, if any, contribute to an increasing anxiety in relation to death? What happens in a changing field of medicine, where we have to ask ourselves whether medicine is to remain a humanitarian and respected profession or a new but depersonalized science in the service of prolonging life rather than diminishing human suffering? Where the medical students have a choice of dozens of lectures on RNA and DNA but less experience in the simple doctor-patient relationship that used to be the alphabet for every successful family physician? What happens in a society that puts more emphasis on IQ and class-standing than on simple matters of tact, sensitivity, perceptiveness, and good taste in the management of the suffering? In a professional society where the young medical student is admired for his research and laboratory work during the first years of medical school while he is at a loss for words when a patient asks him a simple question? If we could combine the teaching of the new scientific and technical achievements with equal emphasis on interpersonal human relationships we would indeed make progress, but not if the new knowledge is conveyed to the student at the price of less and less interpersonal contact. What is going to become of a society which puts the emphasis on numbers and masses, rather than on the individual—where medical schools hope to enlarge their classes, where the trend is away from the teacher-student contact, which is replaced by closed-circuit television teaching, recordings, and movies, all of which can teach a greater number of students in a more depersonalized manner?

This change of focus from the individual to the masses has been more dramatic in other areas of human interaction. If we take a look at the changes that have taken place in the last decades, we can notice it everywhere. In the old days a man was able to face his enemy eye to eye. He had a fair chance in a personal encounter with a visible enemy. Now the soldier as well as the civilian has to anticipate weapons of mass destruction which offer no one a reasonable chance, often not even an awareness of their approach. Destruction can strike out of the blue skies and destroy thousands like the bomb at Hiroshima; it may come in the form of gases or other means of chemical warfare—invisible, crippling, killing. It is no longer the man who fights for his rights, his convictions, or the safety or honor of his family, it is the nation including its women and children who are in the war, affected directly or indirectly without a chance of survival. This is how science and technology have contributed to an ever increasing fear of destruction and therefore fear of death.

Is it surprising, then, that man has to defend himself more? If his ability to defend himself physically is getting smaller and smaller, his psychological defenses have to increase manifoldly. He cannot maintain denial forever. He cannot continuously and successfully pretend that he is safe. If we cannot deny death we may attempt to master it. We may join the race on the highways, we may read the death toll over national holidays and shudder, but also rejoice—"It was the other guy, not me, I made it."

Groups of people, from street gangs to nations, may use their group identity to express their fear of being destroyed by attacking and destroying others. Is war perhaps nothing else but a need to face death, to conquer and master it, to come out of it alive—a peculiar form of denial of our own mortality? One of our patients dying of leukemia said in utter disbelief: "It is impossible for me to die now. It cannot be God's will, since he let me survive when I was hit by bullets just a few feet away during World War II."

Another woman expressed her shock and sense of incredulity when she described the "unfair death" of a young man who was on leave from Vietnam and met his death in a car accident, as if his survival on the battlefield was supposed to have guaranteed immunity from death back home.

A chance for peace may thus be found in studying the attitudes toward death in the leaders of the nations, in those who make the final decisions of war and peace between nations. If all of us would make an all-out effort to contemplate our own death, to deal with our anxieties surrounding the concept of our death, and to help others familiarize themselves with these thoughts, perhaps there could be less destructiveness around us.

News agencies may be able to contribute their share in helping people face the reality of death by avoiding such depersonalized terms as the "solution of the Jewish question" to tell of the murder of millions of men, women, and children; or to use a more recent issue, the recovery of a hill in Vietnam through elimination of a machine gun nest and heavy loss of VC could be described in terms of human tragedies and loss of human beings on both sides. There are so many examples in all newspapers and other news media that it is unnecessary to add more here.

In summary, then, I think that with rapid technical advancement and new scientific achievements men have been able to develop not only new skills but also new weapons of mass destruction which increase the fear of a violent, catastrophic death. Man has to defend himself psychologically in many ways against this increased fear of death and increased inability to foresee and protect himself against it. Psychologically he can deny the reality of his own death for a while. Since in our unconscious we cannot perceive our own death and do believe in our own immortality, but can conceive our neighbor's death, news of numbers of people killed in battle, in wars, on the highways only supports our unconscious belief in our own immortality and allows us—in the privacy and secrecy of our unconscious mind—to rejoice that it is "the next guy, not me."

If denial is no longer possible, we can attempt to master death by challenging it. If we can drive the highways at rapid speed, if we can come back home from Vietnam, we must indeed feel immune to death. We have killed ten times the number of enemies compared to our own losses—we hear on the news almost daily. Is this our wishful thinking, our projection of our infantile wish for omnipotence and immortality? If a whole nation, a whole society suffers from such a fear and denial of death, it has to use defenses which can only be destructive. Wars, riots, and increasing numbers of murders and other crimes may be indicators of our decreasing ability to face death with acceptance and dignity. Perhaps we have to come back to the individual human being and start from scratch, to attempt to conceive our own death and learn to face this tragic but inevitable happening with less irrationality and fear.

What role has religion played in these changing times? In the old days more people seemed to believe in God unquestionably; they believed in a hereafter, which was to relieve people of their suffering and their pain. There was a reward in heaven, and if we had suffered much here on earth we would be rewarded after death depending on the courage and grace, patience and dignity with which we had carried our burden. Suffering was more common, as childbirth was a more natural, long and painful event—but the mother was awake when the child was born. There was a purpose and future reward in the suffering. Now we sedate mothers, try to avoid pain and agony; we may even induce labor to have a birth occur on a relative's birthday or to avoid interference with another important event. Many mothers only wake up hours after the babies are born, too drugged and sleepy to rejoice the birth of their children. There is not much sense in suffering, since drugs can be given for pain, itching, and other discomforts. The belief has long died that suffering here on earth will be rewarded in heaven. Suffering has lost its meaning.

But with this change, also, fewer people really believe in life after death, in itself perhaps a denial of our mortality. Well, if we cannot anticipate life after death, then we have to consider death. If we are no longer rewarded in heaven for our suffering, then suffering becomes purposeless in itself. If we take part in church activities in order to socialize or to go to a dance, then we are deprived of the church's former purpose, namely, to give hope, a purpose in tragedies here on earth, and an attempt to understand and bring meaning to otherwise inacceptable painful occurrences in our life.

Paradoxical as it may sound, while society has contributed to our denial of death, religion has lost many of its believers in a life after death, i.e., immortality, and thus has decreased the denial of death in that respect. In terms of the patient, this has been a poor exchange. While the religious denial, i.e., the belief in the meaning of suffering here on earth and reward in heaven after death, has offered hope and purpose, the denial of society has given neither hope nor purpose but has only increased our anxiety and contributed to our destructiveness and aggressiveness—to kill in order to avoid the reality and facing of our own death.

A look into the future shows us a society in which more and more people are "kept alive" both with machines replacing vital organs and computers checking from time to time to see if some additional physiologic functionings have to be replaced by electronic equipment. Centers may be established in increasing numbers where all the technical data is collected and where a light may flash up when a patient expires in order to stop the equipment automatically.

Other centers may enjoy more and more popularity where the

deceased are quickly deep-frozen to be placed in a special building of low temperature, awaiting the day when science and technology have advanced enough to defrost them, to return them to life and back into society, which may be so frighteningly over-populated that special committees may be needed to decide how many can be defrosted, just as there are committees now to decide who shall be the recipient of an available organ and who shall die.

It may sound all very horrible and incredible. The sad truth, however, is that all this is happening already. There is no law in this country that prevents business-minded people from making money out of the fear of death, that denies opportunists the right to advertise and sell at high cost a promise for possible life after years of deep-freeze. These organizations exist already, and while we may laugh at people who ask whether a widow of a deep-frozen person is entitled to accept social security or to remarry, the questions are all too serious to be ignored. They actually show the fantastic degrees of denial that some people require in order to avoid facing death as a reality, and it seems time that people of all professions and religious backgrounds put their heads together before our society becomes so petrified that it has to destroy itself.

Now that we have taken a look into the past with man's ability to face death with equanimity and a somewhat frightening glimpse into the future, let us come back to the present and ask ourselves very seriously what we as individuals can do about all this. It is clear that we cannot avoid the trend toward increasing numbers altogether. We live in a society of the mass man rather than the individual man. The classes in the medical schools will get bigger, whether we like it or not. The number of cars on the highways will increase. The number of people being kept alive will increase, if we consider only the advancement in cardiology and cardiac surgery.

Also, we cannot go back in time. We cannot afford every child the learning experience of a simple life on a farm with its closeness to nature, the experience of birth and death in the natural surrounding of the child. Men of the churches may not even be successful in bringing many more people back to the belief in a life after death which would make dying more rewarding though through a form of denial of mortality in a sense.

We cannot deny the existence of weapons of mass destruction nor can we go back in any way or sense in time. Science and technology will enable us to replace more vital organs, and the responsibility of questions concerning life and death, donors and recipients will increase manifoldly. Legal, moral, ethical, and psychological problems will be posed to the present and future generation which will decide questions of life and death in ever increasing numbers until these decisions, too, will probably be made by computers.

Though every man will attempt in his own way to postpone such questions and issues until he is forced to face them, he will only be able to change things if he can start to conceive of his own death. This cannot be done on a mass level. This cannot be done by computers. This has to be done by every human being alone. Each one of us has the need to avoid this issue, yet each one of us has to face it sooner or later. If all of us could make a start by contemplating the possibility of our own personal death, we may effect many things, most important of all the welfare of our patients, our families, and finally perhaps our nation.

If we could teach our students the value of science and technology simultaneously with the art and science of inter-human relationships, of human and total patient-care, it would be real progress. If science and technology are not to be misused to increase destructiveness, prolonging life rather than making it more human, if they could go hand in hand with freeing more time rather than less for individual person-to-person contacts, then we could really speak of a great society.

Finally, we may achieve peace—our own inner peace as well as peace between nations—by facing and accepting the reality of our own death.

An example of combined medical, scientific achievement and humanity is given in the following case of Mr. P.:

Mr. P. was a fifty-one-year-old patient who was hospitalized with rapidly progressing amyotrophic lateral sclerosis with bulbar involvement. He was unable to breathe without a respirator, had difficulties coughing up any sputum, and developed pneumonia and an infection at the site of his tracheostomy. Because of the latter he was also unable to speak; thus he would lie in bed, listening to the frightening sound of the respirator, unable to communicate to anybody his needs, thoughts, and feelings. We might have never called on this patient had it not been for one of the physicians who had the courage to ask for help for himself. One Friday evening he visited us and asked simply for some support, not for the patient primarily but for himself. While we sat and listened to him, we heard an account of feelings that are not often spoken about. The doctor was assigned to this patient on admission and was obviously impressed by this man's suffering. His patient was relatively young and had a neurological disorder which required immense medical attention and nursing care in order to extend his life for a short while only. The patient's wife had multiple sclerosis and had been paralyzed in all limbs for the past three years. The patient hoped to die during this admission as it was inconceivable for him to have two paralyzed people at home, each watching the other without the ability to care for the other.

This double tragedy resulted in the physician's anxiety and in his overly vigorous efforts to save this man's life "no matter in what condition." The doctor was quite aware that this was contrary to the patient's wishes. His efforts continued successfully even after a coronary occlusion which complicated the picture. He fought it as successfully as he fought the pneumonia and infections. When the patient began to recover from all the complications, the question arose—"What now?" He could live only on the respirator with twenty-four-hour nursing care, unable to talk or move a finger, alive intellectually and fully aware of his predicament but otherwise unable to function. The doctor picked up implicit criticism of his attempts to save this man. He also elicited the patient's anger and frustration at him. What was he supposed to do? Besides, it was too late to change matters. He had wished to do his best as a physician to prolong life and now that he had succeeded, he elicited nothing but criticism (real or unreal) and anger from the patient.

We decided to attempt to solve the conflict in the patient's presence since he was an important part of it. The patient looked interested when we told him of the reason for our visit. He was obviously satisfied that we had included him, thus regarding and treating him as a person in spite of his inability to communicate. In introducing the problem I asked him to nod his head or to give us another signal if he did not want to discuss the matter. His eyes spoke more than words. He obviously struggled to say more and we were looking for means of allowing him to take his part. The physician, relieved by sharing his burden, became quite inventive and deflated the respirator tube for a few minutes at a time which allowed the patient to speak a few words while exhaling. A flood of feelings were expressed in these interviews. He emphasized that he was not afraid to die, but was afraid to live. He also empathized with the physician but demanded of him "to help me live now that you so vigorously tried to pull me through." The patient smiled and the physician smiled.

There was a great relief of tension in the air when the two were able to talk to each other. I rephrased the doctor's conflicts with which the patient sympathized. I asked him how we could be of the most help to him now. He described his increasing panic when he was unable to communicate by speaking, writing, or other means. He was grateful for those few minutes of joint effort and communication which made the next weeks much less painful. At a later session I observed with pleasure how the patient even considered a possible discharge and planned on a transfer to the West Coast "if I can get the respirator and the nursing care there."

This example perhaps best shows the predicament that many young physicians find themselves in. They learn to prolong life but get little training or discussion in the definition of "life." This patient regarded himself appropriately as "dead up to my head," the tragedy being that he was intellectually fully aware of his position and unable to move a single finger. When the tube pressured and hurt him, he was unable to tell it to the nurse, who was with him around the clock but was unable to learn to communicate. We often take for granted that "there is nothing one can do" and focus our interests on the equipment rather than on the facial expressions of the patient, which can tell us more important things than the most efficient machine. When the patient had an itch, he was unable to move or rub or blow and became preoccupied with this inability until it took on panic proportions which drove him "near insanity." The introduction of this regular five-minute session made the patient calm and better able to tolerate his discomforts.

This relieved the physician of his conflicts and insured him of a better relationship without guilt or pity. Once he saw how much ease and comfort such direct explicit dialogues can provide, he continued them on his own, having used us merely as a kind of catalyst to get the communication going.

I feel strongly that this should be the case. I do not feel it beneficial that a psychiatrist be called each time a patient-doctor relationship is in danger or a physician is unable or unwilling to discuss important issues with his patient. I found it courageous and a sign of great maturity on the part of this young doctor to acknowledge his limits and his conflicts and seek help rather than to avoid the issue and the patient. Our goals should not be to have specialists for dying patients but to train our hospital personnel to feel comfortable in facing such difficulties and to seek solutions. I am confident that this young physician will have much less turmoil and conflict when he is faced with such tragedies the next time. He will attempt to be a physician and prolong life but also consider the patient's needs and discuss them frankly with him. This patient, who was still a person, was only unable to bear to live because he was unable to make use of the faculties that he had left. With combined efforts many of these faculties can be used if we are not frightened away by the mere sight of such a helpless, suffering individual. Perhaps what I am saying is that we can help them die by trying to help them live, rather than vegetate in an inhuman manner.

THE BEGINNING OF AN INTERDISCIPLINARY SEMINAR ON DEATH AND DYING

In the fall of 1965 four theology students of the Chicago Theological Seminary approached me for assistance in a research project they had chosen. Their class was to write a paper on "crisis in human life,"and the four students considered death as the biggest crisis people had to face. Then the natural question arose: How do you do research on dying, when the data is so impossible to get? When you cannot verify your data and cannot set up experiments? We met for a while and decided that the best possible way we could study death and dying was by asking terminally ill patients to be our teachers. We would observe critically ill patients, study their responses and needs, evaluate the reactions of the people around them, and get as close to the dying as they would allow us.

We decided to interview a dying patient the following week. We agreed on time and place, and the whole project seemed rather simple and uncomplicated. Since the students had no clinical experience and no past encounter with terminally ill patients in a hospital, we expected some emotional reaction on their part. I was to do the interview while they stood around the bed watching and observing. We would then retire to my office and discuss our own reactions and the patient's response. We believed that by doing many interviews like this we would get a feeling for the terminally ill and their needs which in turn we were ready to gratify if possible.

We had no other preconceived ideas nor did we read any papers or publications on this topic so that we might have an open mind and record only what we ourselves were able to notice, both in the patient and in ourselves. We also purposely did not study the patient's chart since this too might dilute or alter our own observations. We did not want to have any preconceived notion as to how the patients might react. We were quite prepared, however, to study all available data after we had recorded our own impressions. This, we thought, would sensitize us to the needs of the critically ill, would enhance our perceptiveness and, we hoped, desensitize the rather frightened students through an increasing number of confrontations with terminally ill patients of different ages and backgrounds.

We were well satisfied with our plans and it was not until a few days later that our difficulties started.

I set out to ask physicians of different services and wards for permission to interview a terminally ill patient of theirs. The reactions were varied, from stunned looks of disbelief to rather abrupt changes of topic of conversation; the end result being that I did not get one single chance even to get near such a patient. Some doctors "protected" their patients by saying that they were too sick, too tired or weak, or not the talking kind; others bluntly refused to take part in such a project. I have to add in their defense that they were justified to some degree, as I had just started my work in this hospital and no one had had a chance to know me or my style and type of work. They had no assurance, except from me, that the patients were not to be traumatized, that those who had not been told of the seriousness of their illness would not be told. Also, these physicians were not aware of my past experience with the dying in other hospitals.

I have added this in order to present their reactions as fairly as I can. These doctors were both very defensive when it came to talking about death and dying and also protective of their patients in order to avoid a traumatic experience with a yet unknown faculty member who had just joined their ranks. It suddenly seemed that there were no dying patients in this huge hospital. My phone calls and personal visits to the wards were all in vain. Some physicians said politely that they would think about it, others said they did not wish to expose their patients to such questioning as it might tire them too much. A nurse angrily asked in utter disbelief if I enjoyed telling a twenty-year-old man that he had only a couple of weeks to live! She walked away before I could tell her more about our plans.

When we finally had a patient, he welcomed me with open arms. He invited me to sit down and it was obvious that he was eager to speak. I told him that I did not wish to hear him now but would return the next day with my students. I was not sensitive enough to appreciate his communications. It was so hard to get one patient, I had to share him with my students. Little did I realize then that when such a patient says "Please sit down *now*," tomorrow may be too late. When we revisited him the next day, he was lying back in his pillow, too weak to speak. He made a meager attempt to lift his arm and whispered "Thank you for trying"— he died less than an hour later and kept to himself what he wanted to share with us and what we so desperately wanted to learn. It was our first and most painful lesson, but also the beginning of a seminar which was to start as an experiment and ended up to be quite an experience for many.

The students met with me in my office after this encounter. We felt the need to talk about our own experience and wanted to share our reactions in order to understand them. This procedure is continued until the present day. Technically little has changed in that respect. We still see a terminally ill patient once a week. We ask him for permission to tape-record the dialogue and leave up to him entirely how long he feels like talking. We have moved from the patient's room to a little interviewing room from which we can be seen and heard but we do not see the audience. From a group of four theology students the class has grown to up to fifty, which necessitated the move to a screen window set-up.

When we hear of a patient who may be available for the seminar, we approach him either alone or with one of the students and the referring physician or hospital chaplain, or both. After a brief introduction we state the purpose and timing of our visit, clearly and concretely. I tell each patient that we have an interdisciplinary group of hospital personnel eager to learn from the patient. We emphasize that we need to know more about the very sick and dying patient. We then pause and await the patient's verbal or nonverbal reactions. We do this only after the patient has invited us to talk. A typical dialogue follows:

DOCTOR: Hello Mr. X. I am Dr. R. and this is Chaplain N. Do you feel like talking for a little while?
PATIENT: Please, by all means, sit down.

DOCTOR: We are here with a peculiar request. Chaplain N. and I are working with a group of people from the hospital who are trying to learn more about very sick and dying patients. I wonder if you feel up to answering some of our questions?
PATIENT: Why don't you ask and I'll see if I can answer them.
DOCTOR: How sick are you?
PATIENT: I am full of metastasis. . . .

(Another patient may say, "Do you really want to talk to an old and dying woman? You are young and healthy!")

Others are not so receptive at first. They start complaining about their pain, their discomfort, their anger, until they are in the midst of sharing their agony. We then remind them that this is exactly what we wanted the others to hear and would they consider repeating the same a little time later.

When the patient agrees, the doctor has granted permission, and arrangements have been made, the patient is brought personally by us to the interviewing room. Very few of them walk, most are in wheelchairs, a few have to be carried on a stretcher. Where infusions and transfusions are necessary, they are brought along. Relatives have not been included, though they have occasionally been interviewed following the dialogue with the patient.

Our interviews keep in mind that no one present has much if any background information on the patient. We usually rephrase the purpose of the interview on our way to the interviewing room during which time we emphasize the patient's right to stop the session at any moment for any reason of his own. We again describe the mirror on the wall which makes it possible for the audience to see and hear us and this allows the patient a moment of privacy with us which is often used to alleviate last-minute concerns and fears.

Once in the interviewing room the conversation flows easily and quickly, starting with general information and going on to very personal concerns as shown in actual recorded interviews, a few of which are presented in this book.

Following each session the patient is first brought back to his room after which the seminar continues. No patient is kept waiting in the hallways. When the interviewer has returned to the classroom he joins the audience and together we discuss the event. Our own spontaneous reactions are brought to light, no matter how appropriate or irrational. We discuss our different responses, both emotional and intellectual. We discuss the patient's response to different interviewers and different questions and approaches and finally attempt a psychodynamic understanding of his communications. We study his strengths and weaknesses as well as ours in the management of this given person and conclude by recommending certain approaches that we hope will make the patient's final days or weeks more comfortable.

None of our patients has died during the interview. Survival ranged from twelve hours to several months. Many of our more recent patients are still alive and many of the very critically ill patients have had a remission and have gone home once more. Several of them have had no relapse and are doing well. I emphasize this since we are talking about dying with patients who are not actually dying in the classical sense of the word. We are talking with many if not most of them about this event because it is something that they have faced because of the occurrence of a usually fatal illness—our intervention may take place at any time between the making of the diagnosis until just before death.

The discussion serves many purposes, as we have found out by experience. It has been most helpful in making the students aware of the necessity of considering death as a real possibility, not only for others but also for themselves. It has proven to be a meaningful way of desensitization, which comes slowly and painfully. Many a student appearing for the first time has left before the interview was over. Some were finally able to sit through a whole session but were unable to express their opinions in the discussion. Some of them have displaced all their anger and rage onto other participants or the interviewer, at times onto the patients. The last has occasionally happened when a patient apparently faced death with calmness and equanimity while the student was highly upset by the encounter. The discussion then revealed that the student thought the patient was unrealistic or even faking, because it was inconceivable to him that anyone could face such a crisis with so much dignity.

Other participants began to identify with the patients, especially if they were of the same age and had to deal with these conflicts in the discussion—and long afterwards. As those in the group began to know each other and realized that nothing was taboo, the discussions became a sort of group therapy for the participants, with many frank confrontations, mutual support, and at times painful discoveries and insights. Little did the patients realize the impact and long-lasting effects many of the communications had on a great variety and number of students.

Two years after the creation of this seminar, it became an accredited course for the medical school and the theological seminary. It is also attended by many visiting physicians, by nurses and nurses' aids, orderlies, social workers, priests and rabbis, by inhalation therapists and occupational therapists, but only rarely by faculty members of our own hospital. The medical and theology students who take it as a formal credit course are also attending a theoretical session, which deals with theory, philosophical, moral, ethical, and religious questions, and which is alternately held by the author and the hospital chaplain.

All interviews are tape-recorded and remain available to students and teachers. At the end of each quarter each student writes a paper on a subject of his own choice. These papers will be presented in a future publication; they range from very personal workings-through of concepts and fears of death to highly philosophical, religious, or sociological papers dealing with death and dying.

In order to ensure confidentiality, a checklist is made of all those attending, and names and identifying data are altered on all transcribed recordings.

From an informal get-together of four students, a seminar has grown within two years which is attended by as many as fifty people consisting of members of all the helping professions. Originally it took an average of ten hours a week to get permission from a doctor to ask a patient to be interviewed; now we are rarely forced to search for a patient. We are getting referrals from physicians, nurses, social workers, and most encouragingly, perhaps, from patients who have attended the seminar and have shared their experience with other terminally ill patients who then ask to attend, at times to do us a service, at other times in order to be heard.

THE DYING AS TEACHERS

To tell or not to tell, that is the question.

In talking to physicians, hospital chaplains, and nursing staff, we are often impressed about their concern for a patient's tolerance of "the truth." "Which truth?" is usually our question. The confronting of patients after the diagnosis of a malignancy is made is always difficult. Some physicians favor telling the relatives but keeping the facts from the patient in order to avoid an emotional outburst. Some doctors are sensitive to their patient's needs and can quite successfully present the patient with the awareness of a serious illness without taking all hope away from him.

I personally feel that this question should never come up as a real conflict. The question should not be "Should we tell. . . ?" but rather "How do I share this with my patient?" I will try to explain this attitude in the following pages. I will therefore have to categorize crudely the many experiences that patients have when they are faced with the sudden awareness of their own finality. As we have outlined previously, man is not freely willing to look at his own end of life on earth and will only occasionally and half-heartedly take a glimpse at the possibility of his own death. One such occasion, obviously, is the awareness of a life-threatening illness. The mere fact that a patient is told that he has cancer brings his possible death to his conscious awareness.

It is often said that people equate a malignancy with terminal illness and regard the two as synonymous. This is basically true and can be a blessing or a curse, depending on the manner in which the patient and family are managed in this crucial situation. Cancer is still for most people a terminal illness, in spite of increasing numbers of real cures as well as meaningful remissions. I believe that we should make it a habit to think about death and dying occasionally, I hope before we encounter it in our own life. If we have not done so, the diagnosis of cancer in our family will brutally remind us of our own finality. It may be a blessing, therefore, to use the time of illness to think about death and dying in terms of ourselves, regardless of whether the patient will have to meet death or get an extension of life.

If a doctor can speak freely with his patients about the diagnosis of malignancy without equating it necessarily with impending death, he will do the patient a great service. He should at the same time leave the door open for hope, namely, new drugs, treatments, chances of new techniques and new research. The main thing is that he communicates to the patient that all is not lost; that he is not giving him up because of a certain diagnosis; that it is a battle they are going to fight together—patient, family, and doctor—no matter the end result. Such a patient will not fear isolation, deceit, rejection, but will continue to have confidence in the honesty of his physician and know that if there is anything that can be done, they will do it together. Such an approach is equally reassuring to the family who often feel terribly impotent in such moments. They greatly depend on verbal or nonverbal reassurance from the doctor. They are encouraged to know that everything possible will be done, if not to prolong life at least to diminish suffering.

If a patient comes in with a lump in the breast, a considerate doctor will prepare her with the possibility of a malignancy and tell her that a biopsy, for example, will reveal the true nature of the tumor. He will also tell her ahead of time that a more extensive surgery will be required if a malignancy is found. Such a patient has more time to prepare herself for the possibility of a cancer and will be better prepared to accept more extensive surgery should it be necessary. When the patient awakens from the surgical procedure the doctor can say, "I am sorry, we had to do the more extensive surgery." If the patient responds, "Thank God, it was benign," he can simply say, "I wish that were true," and then silently sit with her for a while and not run off. Such a patient may pretend not to know for several days. It would be cruel for a physician to force her to accept the fact when she clearly communicates that she is not yet ready to hear it. The fact that he has told her once will be sufficient to maintain confidence in the doctor. Such a patient will seek him out later when she is able and strong enough to face the possible fatal outcome of her illness.

Another patient's response may be, "Oh, doctor, how terrible, how long do I have to live?" The physician may then tell her how much has been achieved in recent years in terms of extending the life span of such patients, and about the possibility of additional surgery which has shown good results; he may tell her frankly that nobody knows how long she can live. I think it is the worst possible management of any patient, no matter how strong, to give him a concrete number of months or years. Since such information is wrong in any case, and exceptions in both directions are the rule, I see no reason why we even consider such information. There may be a need in some rare instances where a head of a household should be informed of the shortness of his expected life in order to bring his affairs in order. I think even in such cases a tactful, understanding physician can communicate to his patient that he may be better off putting his affairs in order while he has the leisure and strength to do so, rather than to wait too long. Such a patient will most likely get the implicit message while still able to maintain the hope which each and every patient has to keep, including the ones who say that they are ready to die. Our interviews have shown that all patients have kept a door open to the possibility of continued existence, and not one of them has at all times maintained that there is no wish to live at all.

When we asked our patients how they had been told, we learned that all the patients knew about their terminal illness anyway, whether they were explicitly told or not, but depended greatly on the physician to present the news in an acceptable manner.

What, then, is an acceptable manner? How does a physician know which patient wants to hear it briefly, which one with a long scientific explanation, and which one wants to avoid the issue all together? How do we know when we do not have the advantage of knowing the patient well enough before being confronted with such decisions?

*   *   *

The answer depends on two things. The most important one is our own attitude and ability to face terminal illness and death. If this is a big problem in our own life, and death is viewed as a frightening, horrible, taboo topic, we will never be able to face it calmly and helpfully with a patient. And I say "death" on purpose, even if we only have to answer the question of malignancy or no malignancy. The former is always associated with impending death, a destructive nature of death, and it is the former that evokes all the emotions. If we cannot face death with equanimity, how can we be of assistance to our patients? We, then, hope that our patients will not ask us this horrible question. We make rounds and talk about many trivialities or the wonderful weather outside and the sensitive patient will play the game and talk about next spring, even if he is quite aware that there will be no next spring for him. These doctors then, when asked, will tell us that their patients do not want to know the truth, that they never ask for it, and that they believe all is well. The doctors are, in fact, greatly relieved that they are not confronted and are often quite unaware that they provoked this response in their patients.

Doctors who are still uneasy about such discussions but not so defensive may call a chaplain or priest and ask him to talk to the patient. They may feel more at ease having passed on the difficult responsibility to someone else, which may be better than avoiding it altogether. They may, on the other hand, be so anxious about it that they leave explicit orders to the staff and chaplain not to tell the patient. The degree of explicitness in such orders will reveal more about the doctors' anxiety than they wish to recognize.

There are others who have less difficulty with this issue and who find a much smaller number of patients unwilling to talk about their serious illness. I am convinced, from the many patients with whom I have spoken about this matter, that those doctors who need denial themselves will find it in their patients and that those who can talk about the terminal illness will find their patients better able to face and acknowledge it. The need of denial is in direct proportion with the doctor's need for denial. But this is only half of the problem.

We have found that different patients react differently to such news depending on their personality makeup and the style and manner they used in their past life. People who use denial as a main defense will use denial much more extensively than others. Patients who faced past stressful situations with open confrontation will do similarly in the present situation. It is, therefore, very helpful to get acquainted with a new patient, in order to elicit his strengths and weaknesses. I will give an example of this:

Mrs. A., a thirty-year-old white woman, asked us to see her during her hospitalization. She presented herself as a short, obese, pseudo-gay woman who smilingly told us of her "benign lymphoma" for which she had received a variety of treatments including cobalt and nitrogen mustard, known by most people in the hospital to be given for malignancies. She was very familiar with her illness and readily acknowledged having read the literature about it. She suddenly became quite weepy and told a rather pathetic story of how her doctor at home told her of her "benign lymphoma" after receiving the biopsy results. "A benign lymphoma?" I repeated, expressing some doubt in my voice and then sitting quietly for an answer. "Please, doctor, tell me whether it's malignant or benign?" she asked but without waiting for my answer, she began a story of a fruitless attempt to get pregnant. For nine years she had hoped for a baby, she went through all possible tests, finally through agencies in the hope of adopting a child. She was turned down for many reasons, first because she had been married only two and a half years, later because of emotional instability perhaps. She had not been able to accept the fact that she could not even have an adopted child. Now she was in the hospital and was forced to sign a paper for radiation treatment with the explicit statement that this would result in sterility, thus rendering her finally and irrevocably unable to bear a child. It was unacceptable to her in spite of the fact that she had signed the paper and had undergone the preliminary work-up for the radiation. Her abdomen was marked and she was to have her first treatment the following morning.

This communication revealed to me that she was not able to accept the fact yet. She asked the question of the malignancy but did not wait for an answer. She also told me of her inability to accept the fact of her childlessness in spite of her acceptance of the radiation treatment. She went on at great length to tell about all the details of her unfulfilled wish and kept on looking at me with big question marks in her eyes. I told her that she might be talking about her inability to face her illness rather than her inability to face being barren. I told her that I could understand this. I also said that both situations were difficult but not hopeless and left her with the promise to return the next day after the treatment.

It was on the way to the first radiation treatment that she confirmed her knowledge of her malignancy, but she hoped that this treatment might cure it. During the following informal, almost social visits, she fluctuated between talking about babies and her malignancy. She became increasingly tearful and dropped her pseudo-gay appearance during these sessions. She asked for a "magic button" which would enable her to get rid of all her fears and free her from the heavy burden in her chest. She was deeply concerned about the expected new roommate, "worrying to death" as she called it that she would get a terminally sick woman. Since the nursing staff on her ward was very understanding, we related her fears to them, and she became the companion of a cheerful young woman who was a great relief to her. The nursing staff also encouraged her to cry when she felt like it, rather than expecting her to smile all the time, which the patient appreciated. She had a great capacity to determine with whom she could talk about her malignancy and chose the less willing ones for her conversations about babies. The staff was quite surprised to hear of her awareness and ability to discuss her future realistically.

It was after a few very fruitful visits that the patient suddenly asked me if I had children and when I acknowledged this, she asked to terminate the visit because she was tired. The following visits were filled with angry, nasty remarks at the nursing staff, psychiatrists, and others until she was able to admit her feelings of envy for the healthy and the young, but especially towards me since I seemed to have everything. When she realized that she was not rejected in spite of becoming at times a rather difficult patient, she became increasingly aware of the origin of her anger and expressed it quite directly as anger at God for allowing her to die so young and so unfulfilled. The hospital chaplain fortunately was not a punitive but a very understanding man and talked with her about this anger in much the same terms as I did until her anger subsided to make room for more depression and, it is hoped, final acceptance of her fate.

Until the present time, this patient still maintains this dichotomy in regard to her chief problem. To one group of people she only relates as a conflicted woman in terms of her childlessness; to the chaplain and me, she talks about the meaning of her short life and the hopes she still maintains (rightfully so) for prolonging it. Her greatest fear at the time of this writing is the possibility of her husband marrying another woman who might bear children, but then she laughingly admits, "He is not the shah of Persia, though a really great man." She still has not completely coped with her envy for the living. The fact that she does not need to maintain denial or displace it onto another tragic but more acceptable problem allows her to deal with her illness more successfully.

Another example of a problem of "to tell or not to tell" is Mr. D., of whom nobody was sure whether he knew the nature of his illness. The staff was convinced that the patient did not know the great seriousness of his condition, since he never allowed anybody to get close to him. He never asked a question about it, and seemed in general rather feared by the staff. The nurses were ready to bet that he would never accept an invitation to discuss the matter with me. Anticipating difficulties, I approached him hesitantly and asked him simply, "How sick are you?" "I am full of cancer . . ." was his answer. The problem with him was that nobody ever asked a simple straightforward question. They mistook his grim look as a closed door; in fact, their own anxiety prevented them from finding out what he wanted to share so badly with another human being.

If malignancy is presented as a hopeless disease which results in a sense of "what's the use, there is nothing we can do anyway," it will be the beginning of a difficult time for the patient and for those around him. The patient will feel the increasing isolation, the loss of interest on part of his doctor, the isolation and increasing hopelessness. He may rapidly deteriorate or fall into a deep depression from which he may not emerge unless someone is able to give him a sense of hope.

The family of such patients may share their feelings of sorrow and uselessness, hopelessness and despair, and add little to the patient's well-being. They may spend the short remaining time in a morbid depression instead of an enriching experience which is often encountered when the physician responds as outlined earlier.

I have to emphasize, though, that the patient's reaction does not depend solely on how the doctor tells him. The way in which the bad news is communicated is, however, an important factor which is often underestimated and which should be given more emphasis in the teaching of medical students and supervision of young physicians.

In summary, then, I believe the question should not be stated, "Do I tell my patient?" but should be rephrased as, "How do I share this knowledge with my patient?" The physician should first examine his own attitude toward malignancy and death so that he is able to talk about such grave matters without undue anxiety. He should listen for cues from the patient which enable him to elicit the patient's willingness to face the reality. The more people in the patient's environment who know the diagnosis of a malignancy, the sooner the patient himself will realize the true state of affairs anyway, since few people are actors enough to maintain a believable mask of cheerfulness over a long period of time. Most if not all of the patients know anyway. They sense it by the changed attention, by the new and different approach that people take to them, by the lowering of voices or avoidance of rounds, by a tearful face of a relative or an ominous, smiling member of the family who cannot hide their true feelings. They will pretend not to know when the doctor or relative is unable to talk about their true condition, and they will welcome someone who is willing to talk about it but allows them to keep their defenses as long as they have the need for them.

Whether the patient is told explicitly or not, he will nevertheless come to this awareness and may lose confidence in a doctor who either told him a lie or who did not help him face the seriousness of his illness while there might have been time to get his affairs in order.

It is an art to share this painful news with any patient. The simpler it is done, the easier it is usually for a patient who recollects it at a later date, if he can't "hear it" at the moment. Our patients appreciated it when they were told in the privacy of a little room rather than being told in the hallway of a crowded clinic.

What all of our patients stressed was the sense of empathy which counted more than the immediate tragedy of the news. It was the reassurance that everything possible will be done, that they will not be "dropped," that there were treatments available, that there was a glimpse of hope—even in the most advanced cases. If the news can be conveyed in such a manner, the patient will continue to have confidence in the doctor, and he will have time to work through the different reactions which will enable him to cope with this new and stressful life situation.

In the following pages is an attempt to summarize what we have learned from our dying patients in terms of coping mechanisms at the time of a terminal illness.

CHAPTER III

First Stage:
Denial and Isolation

Man barricades against himself.
TAGORE,
from *Stray Birds*, LXXIX

Among the over two hundred dying patients we have interviewed, most reacted to the awareness of a terminal illness at first with the statement, "No, not me, it cannot be true." This *initial* denial was as true for those patients who were told outright at the beginning of their illness as it was true for those who were not told explicitly and who came to this conclusion on their own a bit later on. One of our patients described a long and expensive ritual, as she called it, to support her denial. She was convinced that the X-rays were "mixed up"; she asked for reassurance that her pathology report could not possibly be back so soon and that another patient's report must have been marked with her name. When none of this could be confirmed, she quickly asked to leave the hospital, looking for another physician in the vain hope "to get a better explanation for my troubles." This patient went "shopping around" for many doctors, some of whom gave her reassuring

51

answers, others of whom confirmed the previous suspicion. Whether confirmed or not, she reacted in the same manner; she asked for examination and reexamination, partially knowing that the original diagnosis was correct, but also seeking further evaluations in the hope that the first conclusion was indeed an error, at the same time keeping in contact with a physician in order to have help available "at all times" as she said.

This anxious denial following the presentation of a diagnosis is more typical of the patient who is informed prematurely or abruptly by someone who does not know the patient well or does it quickly "to get it over with" without taking the patient's readiness into consideration. Denial, at least partial denial, is used by almost all patients, not only during the first stages of illness or following confrontation, but also later on from time to time. Who was it who said, "We cannot look at the sun all the time, we cannot face death all the time"? These patients can consider the possibility of their own death for a while but then have to put this consideration away in order to pursue life.

I emphasize this strongly since I regard it a healthy way of dealing with the uncomfortable and painful situation with which some of these patients have to live for a long time. Denial functions as a buffer after unexpected shocking news, allows the patient to collect himself and, with time, mobilize other, less radical defenses. This does not mean, however, that the same patient later on will not be willing or even happy and relieved if he can sit and talk with someone about his impending death. Such a dialogue will and must take place at the convenience of the patient, when he (not the listener!) is ready to face it. The dialogue also has to be terminated when the patient can no longer face the facts and resumes his previous denial. It is irrelevant when this dialogue takes place. We are often accused of talking with very sick patients about death when the doctor feels—very rightfully so—that they are not dying. I favor talking about death and dying with patients long before it actually happens if the patient indicates that he wants to. A healthier, stronger individual can deal with it better and is less frightened by oncoming death when it is still "miles away" than when it "is right in front of the door," as one of our patients put it so appropriately. It is also easier for the family to discuss such matters in times of relative health and well-being and arrange for financial security for the children and others while the head of the household is still functioning. To postpone such talks is often not in the service of the patient but serves our own defensiveness.

Denial is usually a temporary defense and will soon be replaced by partial acceptance. Maintained denial does not always bring increased distress if it holds out until the end, which I still consider a rarity. Among our two hundred terminally ill patients, I have encountered only three who attempted to deny its approach to the very last. Two of these women talked about dying briefly but only referred to it as "an inevitable nuisance which hopefully comes during sleep" and said "I hope it comes without pain." After these statements they resumed their previous denial of their illness.

The third patient, also a middle-aged spinster, apparently had used denial during most of her life. She had a visible, large ulcerative type of cancer of the breast but refused treatment until briefly before she died. She had great faith in Christian Science and held onto this belief to the last day. In spite of her denial, one part of her must have faced the reality of her illness since she did finally accept hospitalization and at least some of the treatments offered to her. When I visited her prior to planned surgery, she referred to the operation as "cutting part of the wound out so it can heal better." She also made it clear that she wished only to know details regarding her hospitalization "which have nothing to do with my wound." Repeated visits made it obvious that she feared any communications from staff members, who might possibly break down her denial, i.e., talk about her advanced cancer. As she grew weaker, her make-up became more grotesque. Originally rather discretely applied red lipstick and rouge, the makeup became brighter and redder until she resembled a clown. Her clothing became equally brighter and more colorful as her end approached. During the last few days she avoided looking in a mirror, but continued to apply the masquerade in an attempt to cover up her increasing depression and her rapidly deteriorating looks. When asked if there was anything we could do for her, she replied, "Come tomorrow." She did not say, "Leave me alone," or "Don't bother me," but left the possibility open that tomorrow might be the day that her defenses would not hold up any longer, thus making help mandatory. Her last statement was, "I guess I cannot make it anymore." She died less than an hour later.

Most patients do not use denial so extensively. They may briefly talk about the reality of their situation, and suddenly indicate their inability to look at it realistically any longer. How do we know, then, when a patient does not wish to face it anymore? He may talk about relevant issues as far as his life is concerned, he may share some important fantasies about death itself or life after death (a denial in itself), only to change the topic after a few minutes, almost contradicting what he said earlier. Listening to him at this point may seem like listening to a patient with a minor ailment, nothing as serious as a life-threatening condition. This is when we try to pick up the cues and acknowledge (to ourselves) that this is the moment at which the patient prefers to look at brighter, more cheery things. We then allow the patient to daydream about happier things, no matter how improbable they may be. (We have had several patients who daydreamed about seemingly impossible situations which—much to our surprise— became true.) What I am trying to emphasize is that the need for denial exists in every patient at times, at the very beginning of a serious illness more so than towards the end of life. Later on the need comes and goes, and the sensitive and perceptive listener will acknowledge this and allow the patient his defenses without making him aware of the contradictions. It is much later, usually, that the patient uses isolation more than denial. He can then talk about his health and his illness, his mortality and his immortality as if they were twin brothers permitted to exist side by side, thus facing death and still maintaining hope.

In summary, then, the patient's first reaction may be a temporary state of shock from which he recuperates gradually. When his initial feeling of numbness begins to disappear and he can collect himself again, man's usual response is "No, it cannot be me." Since in our unconscious mind we are all immortal, it is almost inconceivable for us to acknowledge that we too have to face death. Depending very much on how a patient is told, how much time he has to gradually acknowledge the inevitable happening, and how he has been prepared throughout life to cope with stressful situations, he will gradually drop his denial and use less radical defense mechanisms.

We have also found that many of our patients have used denial when faced with hospital staff members who had to use this form of coping for their own reasons. Such patients can be quite elective in choosing different people among family members or staff with whom they discuss matters of their illness or impending death while pretending to get well with those who cannot tolerate the thought of their demise. It is possible that this is the reason for the discrepancy of opinions in regard of the patient's needs to know about a fatal illness.

The following brief case description of Mrs. K. is an example of a patient who used massive denial for an extended period of time and shows our management of her from the time of admission until her death several months later.

Mrs. K. was a twenty-eight-year-old white Catholic woman, mother of two preschool children. She was hospitalized with a terminal liver disease. A very careful diet and daily laboratory measurement were mandatory to keep her alive.

We were told that two days before her admission to the hospital, she visited the medical clinic and was told that there was no hope for a recovery. The family reported that the patient "fell apart" until a neighbor reassured her that there was always some hope, encouraging her to attend a tabernacle where many people had been healed. The patient then asked her priest for support but was told not to go to a faith healer.

On Saturday, the day after the clinic visit, the patient went to this faith healer and "immediately felt wonderful." She was found in a trance on Sunday by her mother-in-law, while the husband was out at work and the small children were left alone without being fed or otherwise attended to. The husband and mother-in-law brought her to the hospital and left before the physician was able to talk to them.

The patient asked for the hospital chaplain "to tell him of the good news." When he entered her room she welcomed him in an exalted mood: "Oh, Father, it was wonderful. I have been healed. I am going to show the doctors that God will heal me. I am all well now." She expressed her sorrow that "even my own church did not understand how God works," referring to the priest's advice not to visit the tabernacle.

The patient was a problem for the physicians since she denied her illness almost completely and became quite unreliable in regard to her food intake. She occasionally stuffed herself to a degree that she became comatose; at times she followed the orders obediently. For this reason a psychiatric consultation was requested.

When we saw the patient she was inappropriately cheerful, laughed and giggled, and reassured us that she was completely well. She went around the ward visiting patients and staff, attempting to collect money for a gift for one of the staff physicians in whom she had immense faith, which seemed to indicate at least a partial awareness of her present condition. She was a difficult management problem as she was unreliable about her diet and medications and "did not behave like a patient." Her belief in her well-being was unshakable and she insisted on hearing it confirmed.

A discussion with the husband revealed a rather simple, unemotional man who seriously believed that his wife was better off living a short time at home with the children rather than having her suffering prolonged by long hospitalizations, endless costs, and all the ups and downs of her chronic illness. He had little empathy with her and separated his feelings quite effectively from the context of his thoughts. He matter-of-factly related the impossibility of having a stable home environment, with him working nights and the children living out during the week. Listening to him and placing ourselves into his position, we were able to appreciate that he could deal with his present life situation only in this detached manner. We were unable to relate some of her needs to him, in the hope that his empathy might diminish her needs for such denial, thus rendering her more amenable to effective treatment. He left the interview as if he had completed a compulsory task, obviously unable to change his attitude.

Mrs. K. was visited by us at regular intervals. She appreciated our chats, which dealt with daily happenings and inquiries about her needs. She became gradually weaker and—for a couple of weeks—just dozed and held our hand, and did not speak much. After this she became increasingly confused, was disoriented, and had delusions of a beautiful bedroom filled with fragrant flowers brought to her by her husband. When she became more clear, we tried to help her with arts and crafts to make the time go by a bit faster. She had spent much of her past weeks alone in a room, with the double doors closed, and few staff people dropped in since there was so little they felt they could do. The staff rationalized their own avoidance by such remarks as, "She is too confused to know" and "I would not know what to say to her, she has such crazy ideas."

As she felt this isolation and increasing loneliness, she was often observed to take the telephone off the hook, "just to hear a voice."

When she was put on a protein-free diet she became very hungry and lost much weight. She would sit on her bed, holding the little bags of sugar between her fingers and say, "This sugar is finally going to kill me." I sat with her, and when she held my hand she said, "You have such warm hands. I hope you are going to be with me when I get colder and colder." She smiled knowingly. She knew and I knew that at this moment she had dropped her denial. She was able to think and talk about her own death and she asked for just a little comfort of companionship and a final stage without too much hunger. We did not exchange more than the abovementioned words; we just sat silently for a while, and when I left she asked if I would be sure to return and bring that wonderful OT (occupational therapist) girl with me, who helped her make some leatherwork for her family "so they have something to remember me by."

Hospital personnel, whether they are physicians, nurses, social workers, or chaplains, don't know what they miss when they avoid such patients. If one is interested in human behavior, in the adaptations and defenses that human beings have to use in order to cope with such stresses, this is the place to learn about it. If they sit and listen, and repeat their visits if the patient does not feel like talking on the first or second encounter, the patient will soon develop a feeling of confidence that here is a person who cares, who is available, who sticks around.

When they are ready to talk, they will open up and share their loneliness, sometimes with words, sometimes with little gestures or nonverbal communications. In the case of Mrs. K. we never attempted to break her denial, we never contradicted her when she assured us of her well-being. We just reinforced that she had to take her medication and stick to her diet if she wanted to return home to her children. There were days when she stuffed herself with forbidden foods, only to suffer twice as much the next days. This was intolerable and we told her so. This was part of reality that we could not deny with her. So, in a way, implicitly, we told her that she was critically sick. Explicitly, we did not do it because it was obvious that she was unable to tolerate the truth at that stage of her illness. It was much later, after having gone through stages of semicomatose stupor and extreme withdrawal, and stages of confusion with delusions of her husband's tender loving care expressed in the flowers, that she developed the strength to look at the reality of her situation and was able to ask for more palatable food and final companionship, which she sensed was not forthcoming from her family.

Looking back at this long and meaningful relationship, I am sure that it was possible only because she sensed that we respected her wish to deny her illness as long as possible. We never became judgmental no matter how much of a management problem she presented. (Granted, that was much easier for us as we were a kind of visiting staff and not responsible for the balance of her diet or around her all day long from one frustrating experience to another.) We continued our visits even during the times when she was totally irrational and could neither recall our face nor the professional role we played. In the long run it is the persistent nurturing role of the therapist who has dealt with his or her own death complex sufficiently that helps the patient overcome the anxiety and fear of his impending death. Mrs. K. asked for two people during her final days in the hospital; one was the therapist with whom she exchanged few if any words at the time, occasionally just holding hands and expressing less and less concern about food, pain, or discomfort. The other person was the occupational therapist who helped her forget the reality for a while and allowed her to function as a creative, productive woman, making objects which she would leave for her family—maybe as little signs of immortality.

I use this example to show that we do not always state explicitly that the patient is actually terminally ill. We attempt to elicit the patients' needs first, try to become aware of their strengths and weaknesses, and look for overt or hidden communications to determine how much a patient wants to face reality at a given moment. This patient, in many ways exceptional, made it quite clear from the very beginning that denial was essential in order for her to remain sane. Though many staff people regarded her as clearly psychotic, testing showed her sense of reality was intact in spite of the manifestations to the contrary. We learned from it that she was not able to accept her family's need to see her dead "the sooner the better," she was unable to acknowledge her own end when she had just started to enjoy her small children, and she desperately grasped at the reinforcement by the faith healer who assured her of excellent health.

Another part of her was, however, quite aware of her illness. She did not fight to leave the hospital; in fact, she made herself quite comfortable there. She surrounded herself with many familiar items as if she was to stay for a long time. (She never left the hospital.) She also accepted our limit-setting. She ate what she was asked to eat, with a few exceptions when she went overboard. She later acknowledged that she was unable to exist with so many restrictions and that the suffering was worse than death itself. One may regard the episodes of excessive overeating of forbidden foods as a form of suicide attempt, in that they would have brought about a rapid demise if the staff had not interfered so vigorously.

In a way, then, this patient showed a fluctuation between an almost total denial of her illness and a repeated attempt to bring about her death. Rejected by her family, often overlooked or ignored by the hospital personnel, she became a pitiful figure, a disheveled-looking young woman who sat desperately lonely on the edge of her bed, clutching the telephone to hear a sound. She found temporary refuge in delusions of beauty, flowers, and loving care which she could not obtain in real life. She did not have a sound religious background to help her through this crisis and required weeks and months of often silent companionship to help her finally accept her death without suicide and without psychosis.

Our own reactions to this young woman were manifold. At first there was utter disbelief. How could she pretend to be so healthy when she was so limited in her food intake? How was she able to stay in the hospital and undergo all those tests if she was really convinced of her well-being? We soon realized that she was unable to hear such questions and proceeded to get to know her better by talking about less painful things. That she was young and cheerful, that she had small children and a nonsupportive family contributed much to our attempts to help her in spite of her prolonged denial. We allowed her to deny as much as was necessary for her survival and remained available to her during her whole hospitalization.

When the staff contributed to her isolation, we tended to be angry at them and made it a routine to keep the door open, only to find it closed again on our next visit. As we became more familiar with her peculiarities, they appeared less strange to us and began to make more sense, adding to our difficulties in appreciating the nurses' needs to avoid her. Towards the end it became a personal matter, a feeling of sharing a foreign language with someone who was unable to communicate with others.

There is no question that we got deeply involved with this patient, beyond the usual involvement of hospital personnel. In trying to understand the reasons for this involvement, we also have to add that some of it was an expression of our frustration at being unable to have the family play a more helpful role for this pathetic patient. Our anger expressed itself perhaps in our taking on the role of the comforting visitor which we expected the husband to be. And—who knows—perhaps this need to extend ourselves under such circumstances was an expression of an unconscious wish that we may not be rejected one day if fate should have something similar in store for us. After all, she was a young woman with two small children—in retrospect I am beginning to wonder if I was not a bit too ready to support her denial.

This shows the need to examine more closely our own reactions when working with patients as they will always be reflected in the patient's behavior and can contribute a great deal to his well-being or detriment. If we are willing to take an honest look at ourselves, it can help us in our own growth and maturity. No work is better suited for this than the dealing with very sick, old, or dying patients.

CHAPTER IV

Second Stage:
Anger

We read the world wrong and say that it deceives us.

TAGORE,

from *Stray Birds,* LXXV

If our first reaction to catastrophic news is, "No, it's not true, no, it cannot involve me," this has to give way to a new reaction, when it finally dawns on us: "Oh, yes, it is me, it was not a mistake." Fortunately or unfortunately very few patients are able to maintain a make-believe world in which they are healthy and well until they die.

When the first stage of denial cannot be maintained any longer, it is replaced by feelings of anger, rage, envy, and resentment. The logical next question becomes: "Why me?" As one of our patients, Dr. G., put it, "I suppose most anybody in my position would look at somebody else and say, 'Well, why couldn't it have been him?' and this has crossed my mind several times. . . . An old man whom I have known ever since I was a little kid came down the street. He was eighty-two years old, and he is of no earthly use as far as we mortals can tell. He's rheumatic, he's a cripple, he's dirty, just not the type of a person you would like to be. And the thought hit me strongly, now why couldn't it have been old George instead of me?" (extract from interview of Dr. G.).

In contrast to the stage of denial, this stage of anger is very difficult to cope with from the point of view of family and staff. The reason for this is the fact that this anger is displaced in all directions and projected onto the environment at times almost at random. The doctors are just no good, they don't know what tests to require and what diet to prescribe. They keep the patients too long in the hospital or don't respect their wishes in regards to special privileges. They allow a miserably sick roommate to be brought into their room when they pay so much money for some privacy and rest, etc. The nurses are even more often a target of their anger. Whatever they touch is not right. The moment they have left the room, the bell rings. The light is on the very minute they start their report for the next shifts of nurses. When they do shake the pillows and straighten out the bed, they are blamed for never leaving the patients alone. When they do leave the patients alone, the light goes on with the request to have the bed arranged more comfortably. The visiting family is received with little cheerfulness and anticipation, which makes the encounter a painful event. They then either respond with grief and tears, guilt or shame, or avoid future visits, which only increases the patient's discomfort and anger.

The problem here is that few people place themselves in the patient's position and wonder where this anger might come from. Maybe we too would be angry if all our life activities were interrupted so prematurely; if all the buildings we started were to go unfinished, to be completed by someone else; if we had put some hard-earned money aside to enjoy a few years of rest and enjoyment, for travel and pursuing hobbies, only to be confronted with the fact that "this is not for me." What else would we do with our anger, but let it out on the people who are most likely to enjoy all these things? People who rush busily around only to remind us that we cannot even stand on our two feet anymore. People who order unpleasant tests and prolonged hospitalization with all its limitations, restrictions, and costs, while at the end of the day they can go home and enjoy life. People who tell us to lie still so that the infusion or transfusion does not have to be restarted, when we feel like jumping out of our skin to be doing something in order to know that we are still functioning on some level!

Wherever the patient looks at this time, he will find grievances. He may put the television on only to find a group of young jolly people doing some of the modern dances which irritates him when every move of his is painful or limited. He may see a movie western in which people are shot in cold blood with different onlookers continuing to drink their beer. He will compare them with his family or the attending staff. He may listen to the news full of reports of destruction, war, fires, and tragedies—far away from him, unconcerned about the fight and plight of an individual who will soon be forgotten. So this patient makes sure that he is not forgotten. He will raise his voice, he will make demands, he will complain and ask to be given attention, perhaps as the last loud cry, "I am alive, don't forget that. You can hear my voice, I am not dead yet!"

A patient who is respected and understood, who is given attention and a little time, will soon lower his voice and reduce his angry demands. He will know that he is a valuable human being, cared for, allowed to function at the highest possible level as long as he can. He will be listened to without the need for a temper tantrum, he will be visited without ringing the bell every so often because dropping in on him is not a necessary duty but a pleasure.

The tragedy is perhaps that we do not think of the reasons for patients' anger and take it personally, when it has originally nothing or little to do with the people who become the target of the anger. As the staff or family reacts personally to this anger, however, they respond with increasing anger on their part, only feeding into the patient's hostile behavior. They may use avoidance and shorten the visits or the rounds or they may get into unnecessary arguments by defending their stand, not knowing that the issue is often totally irrelevant.

An example of a rational anger provoked by the reaction of a nurse was the case of Mr. X. He had been flat in bed for several months and had just been allowed to come off the respirator for a few hours during the daytime. He had led a life of many activities and had taken it hard to be so utterly restricted. He was quite aware that his days were numbered, and his greatest wish was to be moved into different positions (he was paralyzed to his neck). He begged the nurse never to put the siderails up as it reminded him of being in a casket. The nurse, who was very hostile to this patient, agreed that she would leave them down at all times. This private duty nurse was very angry when she was disturbed in her reading, and she knew that he would keep quiet as long as she fulfilled this wish.

During my last visit to Mr. X., I saw that this usually dignified man was furious. He said over and over again to his nurse, "You lied to me," staring at her in angry disbelief. I asked him the reason for this outburst. He tried to tell me that she had put the siderails up as soon as he asked to be put in an upright position so that he could put his legs out of bed "once more." This communication was interrupted several times by the nurse, who, equally angry, stated her side of the story, namely, that she had to put the siderails up in order to get help to fulfill his demands. A loud argument ensued during which the nurse's anger was perhaps best expressed in her statement: "If I had left them down, you would have fallen out of bed and cracked your head open." If we look at this incident again in an attempt to understand the reactions rather than to judge them, we must realize that this nurse also used avoidance by sitting in a corner reading paperbacks and "at all costs" tried to keep the patient quiet. She was deeply uncomfortable in taking care of a terminally ill patient and never faced him voluntarily or attempted to have a dialogue with him. She did her "duty" by sitting in the same room, but emotionally she was as far detached from him as possible. This was the only way this woman was able to do this job. She wished him dead ("crack your head open") and made explicit demands on him to lie still and quiet on his back (as if he were already in a casket). She was indignant when he asked to be moved, which for him was a sign of still being alive and which she wanted to deny. She was obviously so terrified by the closeness of death that she had to defend herself against it with avoidance and isolation. Her wish to have him quiet and not move only reinforced the patient's fear of immobility and death. He was deprived of communication, lonely and isolated as well as utterly helpless in his agony and increasing anger. When his last demand was met with an initially increased restriction (the symbolic locking him up with the siderails raised), his previously unexpressed rage gave way to this unfortunate incident. If the nurse had not felt so guilty about her own destructive wishes, she probably would have been less defensive and argumentative, thus preventing the incident from happening in the first place and allowing the patient to express his feelings and to die a bit more comfortably a few hours later.

I use these examples to emphasize the importance of our tolerance of the patient's rational or irrational anger. Needless to say, we can do this only if we are not afraid and therefore not so defensive. We have to learn to listen to our patients and at times even to accept some irrational anger, knowing that the relief in expressing it will help them toward a better acceptance of the final hours. We can do this only when we have faced our own fears of death, our own destructive wishes, and have become aware of our own defenses which may interfere with our patient care.

Another problem patient is the man who has been in control all his life and who reacts with rage and anger when he is forced to give up these controls. I am reminded of Mr. O. who was hospitalized with Hodgkin's disease which, he claimed, was caused by his poor eating habits. He was a rich and successful businessman who had never had any problems in eating, and had never been obliged to diet to lose weight. His account was totally unrealistic, yet he insisted that he, and only he, caused "this weakness." This denial was maintained in spite of the radiotherapy and his superior knowledge and intelligence. He claimed that it was in his hands to get up and walk out of the hospital the moment he made up his mind to eat more.

His wife came one day to my office with tears in her eyes. It was hard for her to bear it any longer, she said. He had always been a tyrant and kept strict control over his business and his home life. Now that he was in the hospital, he refused to let anybody know what business transactions had to take place. He was angry with her when she visited and overreacted when she asked questions of him or tried to give him any advice. Mrs. O. asked for help in the management of a domineering, demanding, controlling man, who was unable to accept his limits and unwilling to communicate some of the realities that had to be shared.

We showed her—in the example of his need to blame himself for "his weakness"—that he had to be in control of all situations and wondered if she could give him more of a feeling of being in control, at a time when he had lost control of so much of his environment. She did that by continuing her daily visits but she telephoned him first, asking him each time for the most convenient time and duration of the visit. As soon as it was up to him to set the time and length of the visits, they became brief but pleasant encounters. Also, she stopped giving him advice as to what to eat and how often to get up, but rather rephrased it into statements like, "I bet only you can decide when to start eating this and that." He was able to eat again, but only after all staff and relatives stopped telling him what to do.

The nursing staff used the same approach by allowing him to control certain times for infusions, changing bed sheets, etc., and—not surprising perhaps—he chose approximately the same times for these procedures as they had been previously done, with no anger and struggles involved. His wife and daughter enjoyed their visits more and also felt less angry and guilty about their own reactions to this very sick husband and father, who had been difficult to live with when he was well, but who became almost unbearable when he was in the process of losing his controlling grasp on his environment.

For a counselor, psychiatrist, chaplain, or other staff member, such patients are especially difficult as our time is usually limited and our workload great. When we finally have a free moment to visit patients like Mr. O., we are told, "Not now, come later." It is very easy then to forget such patients, to just leave them out; after all, they did it to themselves. They had their chance and our time is limited. It is the patient like Mr. O., however, who is the most lonely, not only because he is hard to take but because he rejects first and can only accept when it is on his terms. In that respect, the rich and successful, the controlling VIP is perhaps the poorest under these circumstances, as he is to lose the very things that made life so comfortable for him. In the end, we are all the same, but the Mr. O.'s cannot admit that. They fight it to the end and often miss an opportunity for reaching a humble acceptance of death as a final outcome. They provoke rejection and anger, and are yet the most desperate of them all.

The following interview gives an example of the dying patient's anger. Sister I. was a young nun who was rehospitalized with Hodgkin's disease. It is a verbal transcript of a discussion by the chaplain, the patient, and me during her eleventh hospitalization.

Sister I. was an angry, demanding patient who was resented by many within and outside the hospital because of her behavior. The more incapacitated she became, the more she became a management problem especially for the nursing staff. She made it a habit while hospitalized to go from room to room, visiting especially sick patients and eliciting their needs. She would then stand in front of the nurses' desk and demand attention for these patients, which the nurses resented as interference and inappropriate behavior. Since she was quite sick herself, they did not confront her with her unacceptable behavior, but expressed their resentment by making shorter visits to her room, by avoiding contact, and by the briefness of their encounters. It seemed that things were going from bad to worse and when we stepped in everybody appeared relieved that someone else was willing to take care of Sister I. The Sister was asked if she was willing to come to our seminar to share some of her thoughts and feelings with us. She appeared quite eager to please; the following discussion took place a few months before her death.

CHAPLAIN: Well, we've talked a bit this morning, about the purpose of the conference. You know that doctors and nurses are concerned how we may more effectively respond to patients who are seriously ill. I won't say you have become a fixture around here, but a lot of people know you. We came down the hall and I think we hadn't gone more than eighty feet and four different staff people stopped to say hello.

PATIENT: Just before you came a housekeeper who was waxing the floors opened the door just to say "Hi." I've never seen her before. I thought this was kind of tremendous. She said, "I just wanted to see what you were like (laughter) because I don't know—"

DOCTOR: To see a Sister in the hospital?

PATIENT: Maybe to see a Sister in bed, or maybe she had heard or seen me in the hall and really wanted to talk and then decided that she shouldn't spend the time. I don't really know, but I felt this out. She said, "I just wanted to say hello."

DOCTOR: How long have you been in the hospital? Just to give us a brief summary of the events.

PATIENT: This time it would be practically eleven days.

DOCTOR: When were you admitted?

PATIENT: Monday night, two weeks ago.

DOCTOR: But you have been here before.

PATIENT: This is my eleventh admission.

DOCTOR: Eleven admissions, since when?

PATIENT: Since 1962.

DOCTOR: Since '62 you have been in the hospital eleven times?

PATIENT: Yes.

DOCTOR: Is this for the same illness?

PATIENT: No. I was first diagnosed in '53.

DOCTOR: Um hm. What did they diagnose you as?

PATIENT: As Hodgkin's disease.

DOCTOR: Hodgkin's disease.

PATIENT: But this hospital has the high radiation machine which our hospital does not. Yet, at the time I was admitted there was a question of whether they had made the right diagnosis in past years. I met the doctor here and within five minutes we confirmed that I did—that I had what I said I had.

DOCTOR: That was Hodgkin's?

PATIENT: Yes. Whereas other doctors have looked at the slides and said I didn't. The last time I was admitted I had a rash all over my body. Not rash, sores really, because I scratched from the itching. I should say I was covered with sores. I felt like a leper and they thought I had a psychological problem. I told them I had Hodgkin's and they thought that was my psychological problem, that I insisted that I had it. When they couldn't feel any more nodes which they had felt in the past that I had had it but they had controlled it at home by radiation. And they said that I did not have it at this time. I said I had it at this time because I felt the same way I had felt before. And he said, "What do you think?" I said, "All of this is due to Hodgkin's, I think." And he said, "You are completely right." So in that moment he gave me back my self-respect. I knew I had met someone here who would work with me on this and not try to make me feel I wasn't ill really.

DOCTOR: In the sense. . . ? (Tape not audible) Well, this was psychosomatic.

PATIENT: Yes, well, it was very clever to think that this was my problem, that I thought I had Hodgkin's. It was because they couldn't feel any of the nodes in the abdomen where a venogram shows them up right away and an ordinary plate or palpitation doesn't show it. It was unfortunate but it was something I had to go through, that's all I can say.

CHAPLAIN: But you were relieved.

PATIENT: Oh, I mean it just, I'm surely relieved because no problem could be solved that I was emotionally ill, until I could prove that I was physically ill. I couldn't discuss it anymore with people or get relief because I didn't feel they believed that I was ill. You see what I mean, I had to almost hide all my sores and I washed out my own bloody clothes and that as much as I could. I didn't feel accepted. I'm sure they were waiting for me to work out my own problems, you know.

DOCTOR: You are a nurse by profession?

PATIENT: Yes, I am.

DOCTOR: Where do you work?

PATIENT: At S. T. Hospital. And at that time when all of this started I had been just replaced as Director of Nursing Service. I have had six months of my master's program and then they decided to put me back in the school to again teach anatomy and physiology, which I told them I couldn't do because they had now combined chemistry and physics and I had taken the last chemistry course ten years before and chemistry is entirely different now. And so they sent me for a chemistry course that summer in organic and I flunked it. It was the first time I flunked a course in my whole life. And my father died that year and the business was broken up, meaning there was conflict among the three boys as to who was going to run the business and it caused bitterness that I didn't know could exist in a family. And then they demanded of me that I sell my share. I had been thrilled to even inherit a part in our family business and then it just seemed like in every way I didn't count, that I could be replaced in my work, that I had to take a teaching job which I didn't feel prepared for. I could see that I had many psychological problems and then all summer this situation was going on and in December when I had the fever and the chills and I was starting to teach, I found it so hard and became so sick that I had to really ask to see a doctor. Even after this time I never went back to the doctor. I was always trying my hardest. I had to be sure that the symptoms were so objective, that it was high enough on the thermometer that I didn't have to convince anybody. Before they would care for me, you know.

DOCTOR: This is quite different from what we usually hear. Usually the patient likes to deny his own illness. But you had to kind of prove that you were physically sick.

PATIENT: Insofar as that I couldn't get care otherwise, it would get to a point where I would desperately need, I would need to be free to lie down when I felt so punk. And just fake and push—

DOCTOR: You can't get any help, professional help when you have an emotional problem? Or are you not supposed to have any emotional problems?

PATIENT: I think they were trying to treat me symptomatically. They didn't deny me aspirin but I felt that I would never get to the bottom of it unless I found out,* and I did go to see a psy-

---

*The patient was being blamed for malingering while she herself was sure that a physical illness was causing the variety of symptoms she had. To make sure that she was right she went to see a psychiatrist who confirmed her conviction.

chiatrist. And he told me that I was emotionally ill because I had been physically ill for so long. And he treated me physically. He insisted that they take me out of work, that I have at least ten hours of rest a day. Gave me huge dosages of vitamins. And the general practitioner was the one who wanted to treat me psychologically. The psychiatrist treated me medically.

DOCTOR: It's a mixed up world, hm?

PATIENT: Yes. And all of the fear I had to see a psychiatrist. I thought he would make me a new problem, but he didn't. He kept them from hounding me, once they got me to him, they were kind of satisfied, you know. And it was a farce because he treated me exactly how I needed to be treated.

CHAPLAIN: By the general practitioner.

PATIENT:—In the meantime I had been radiated. I was receiving some drugs from him but they had stopped the dosage when they thought I had colitis. The radiologist decided the pain in the abdomen was colitis. And so they stopped. They did enough to do some good, but they didn't give me enough to stop my symptoms slowly and insidiously, which is what I would have done. But they couldn't see them, you see, they couldn't feel these nodes, they just had to go by where my pain was.

DOCTOR: So to summarize a bit, to clarify the whole thing, what you are really saying is, when you were diagnosed as having Hodgkin's, you also had a lot of problems. Your father died around the same time, the business in your family was in the course of being dissolved and they asked you to give up your share. Where you worked you were assigned a job you didn't like.

PATIENT: Yes.

DOCTOR: And your itch, which is a very well-known symptom of Hodgkin's, was not even considered to be a part of your illness. It was considered your emotional problem. And the general practitioner treated you like a psychiatrist and the psychiatrist like a general practitioner.

PATIENT: Yes, and they left me alone. They stopped trying to take care of me.

DOCTOR: Why?

PATIENT: Because I refused to accept their diagnosis and they were waiting for me to get common sense.

DOCTOR: I see. How did you accept the diagnosis of Hodgkin's disease? What did this mean to you?

PATIENT: Well, when I first—you see, I diagnosed it when I felt it, and so I went and looked it up and then told the doctor and he said you don't have to think of the worst at first. And yet, when he came back after surgery and told me, I didn't think I'd have more than a year to live. Though I didn't really feel so well, I kind of forgot about it and thought, well, I'll live as long as I can, you know. But since 1960, when all of these problems had started I really have never been well. And there were hours of the day when I really felt ill. But it's now accepted and they have never given me any indication that they didn't believe I was ill. And at home they've never said anything. I went back to the same doctor who stopped the radiation and everything and he's never said a word, except when I developed nodes again and in that case he was on vacation and so when he came back, I told him. I thought he was sincere. There are others who told me sarcastically that I had never had Hodgkin's, that the nodes I had developed were probably on some inflammatory basis. This was sarcasm, meaning we know better than you. We have decided all of this. He at least was sincere, meaning that he had been waiting for something objective all of this time. And that the doctor here told me to remember that this man had maybe five of these in his lifetime to deal with and each is just a little different. I really have a problem understanding all of these things. So he is one who will always call up here and ask the doctor about the dosage and everything. I am afraid of him treating me for long because I don't feel he is adequate. I mean if I hadn't continued to come down here, I don't think I would be alive. It was because we don't offer the same facilities, and also because he doesn't really understand all these drugs. He tries with each patient where here they have tried with fifty before they will try with me.

DOCTOR: Well, what does it mean to you to be so young and have an illness that will eventually make you die? In perhaps a short time?

PATIENT: I'm not so young. I'm forty-three. I hope you consider that young.

DOCTOR: I hope *you* consider that young. (laughter)

CHAPLAIN: For your sake or ours?

DOCTOR: For my sake.

PATIENT: If I ever thought it, I don't think it now because I've watched—last summer for instance when I was here all summer, I watched a fourteen-year-old boy with leukemia die. I watched a five-year-old die. I spent the whole summer with a nineteen-year-old girl in great pain and frustration. And she couldn't be on the beach with her friends. I have lived longer than they. I don't say I have a sense of accomplishment. I don't want to die, I like life. I don't mean that, but I have gotten panicky a couple of times when I felt that no one was around or that no one would come. I mean sometimes in intense pain and things like that. I don't bother the nurses in the sense that I ask for anything I can do myself, which has often made me feel that they aren't aware of how I really feel. Because they don't come in and ask. I mean I could have really used a backrub, really, but you see, they don't come in to me routinely and do what they do for other patients that they think are ill. I can't give myself a backrub. I take the blanket out, I crank the bed down. I do everything else for myself even when I have to do it slowly and sometimes I do it in pain. I think this is all good for me. But because of this they don't, I don't think they really—I think for hours on end, I think someday if I ever started bleeding or going into shock it would be the cleaning lady that finds me, not the staff. Because they just come in, you get a pill, and I get a pill two times a day unless I ask for a pain pill . . .

DOCTOR: How does all that make you feel?

PATIENT: Hm?

DOCTOR: How does that make you feel?

PATIENT: Well, it's all right except in the times when I have been in intense pain or when I haven't been able to get up and no one has offered to take care of me. I could ask for this but I don't think this should be necessary. I think they should be aware of how their patients are. I'm not trying to hide anything but when you try and do as much as you can, again you pay a price for it and see, there's been several times when I've been very ill, when I—from the nitrogen mustard and things like that—a lot of diarrhea, and no one has ever come to check the stools or ask if I've been up ten times. I have to tell the nurses what is wrong. I mean that I have had ten stools. Last night I knew my X-ray in the morning was not adequate because they sent me down to do it with too much barium. I had to remind them that I needed six pills to have the X-ray today. I am aware of these things but I am nursing myself a lot of times. Where at home at least, in the infirmary, they will come in and ask, they really believe I'm a patient. Here I don't know if I've done this to myself, meaning that I'm not ashamed that I've done it. I'm glad that I have done everything I possibly could for myself, but I have gone a couple of times when I have gone into intense pain and the light hasn't been answered. And also because I didn't think they would get there in time, if anything happened. And I felt if they do this to me they do this to the others. And part of my making rounds with the patients in the past years was really to find out how ill they were and then I would stand in front of that desk and say So-and-So needs something for her pain and just waited a half hour . . .

DOCTOR: How did the nurses respond to that?

PATIENT: Well, it varies. The only one I think that resented me very much was the night nurse. There was a patient, you see the night before, a patient had come into my room and just gone into my bed with me. I happened to know the case and I'm a nurse and I'm not afraid. So I put on the light and waited. Well, that night this lady got out of her bed, over the side rail. She should have had a belt on. I said nothing to anybody about this. I called the nurse and she and I took her back to bed. And then that night when a lady fell out of bed, I was in the room next to her so I got there first. You see, I got there much sooner than the nurse did. And then, another young girl, about twenty, was dying and she was moaning out loud. So I couldn't sleep those nights anyway. The policy in this hospital is you don't get a sleeping pill after three o'clock. I don't know why, but it is. And if you felt—If I take a mild chloral hydrate that doesn't give me a hangover the next day, it's only going to help me for now. To them the policy means more than you get another hour of sleep, or two hours sleep. This is a policy here. The non-habit-forming drugs are treated the same way, you know. You can't have—If the doctor orders codeine and a half every four hours, you can't have another dosage 'til five. I mean the concept is you can't have a repeat within four hours no *matter what it is!* Whether it's habit-forming or not. We haven't changed our concept. The patient has pain, he needs it when he has pain. Not necessarily in four hours, especially if it's not a habit-forming drug.

DOCTOR: Are you resentful that there isn't more individual attention? And individual care? Is that where your feelings come from?

PATIENT: Well, it isn't on an individual basis. They just don't understand pain. If they haven't had any . . .

DOCTOR: It's the pain that concerns you most?

PATIENT: Well, it concerns me most with the cancer patients that I've been with, you see. And I resent the fact that they are trying to keep these people from becoming dope fiends when they are not going to live long enough to be one. There's one nurse over on that wing who even holds the hypo behind her back to try and dissuade them. Even at the last minute, you know. She's afraid she could make a dope addict out of someone. This patient isn't going to live long enough. They are entitled to this really, because you can't eat, or sleep, you just exist when you are in that much pain. At least with the hypo you are relaxed, you can live, you can enjoy things, you can talk. You are alive. But the other is that you are desperately waiting for someone to be merciful and to give you relief.

CHAPLAIN: Has this been something that you've experienced ever since you started coming here?

PATIENT: Yes. Yes it is. I mean I've noticed it. I thought it was typical of certain floors because the same group of nurses are on. It's something in us, that we just don't seem to respect pain anymore.

CHAPLAIN: How do you account for it?

PATIENT: I think they are busy. I hope that's what they are.

DOCTOR: What's this?

PATIENT: But I have walked and seen them talking there and then see them go on breaks. And it makes me furious. When the nurse goes on a break and the aide comes back and tells you that the nurse is downstairs with the key and you have to wait. When that person wanted to have her medication even before that nurse went down for her meal. And I think there should be somebody in charge of that floor that could come and give you the pain medicine, that you shouldn't have to sweat through another half hour before anybody comes up. And sometimes it's forty-five minutes before they come up. And they certainly aren't going to take care of you first. They are going to answer the phone and look at the new hours, and new orders that the doctors left. They are not going to do this the first thing, find out if somebody asked for pain medication.

DOCTOR: To come off, do you mind if I . . . switch the topic? I would like to use our time for looking at many different aspects. Would that be okay with you?

PATIENT: Surely.

DOCTOR: You mentioned that you have seen or observed a room with a five-year-old and nine-year-old youngster dying. How do you conceive of this? Do you have a picture, do you have fantasies about this?

PATIENT: Do you mean how do I accept it?

DOCTOR: Yes. You kind of, answered this question partially already. That you don't want to be, you don't like to be alone. That when you are in a crisis, whether this is pain or diarrhea or anything else you like to have somebody come through. That means you don't like to be left alone. The other one is the pain. If you have to die you would like it to be without agony and pain and loneliness.

PATIENT: That's very true.

DOCTOR: What other things do you think are important? That we should consider? I don't mean just with you but with other patients.

PATIENT: I remember D.F., who was driven frantic by the bare walls he looked at in his room, which were very unattractive. And this same nurse who doesn't want to give you medication brought him some beautiful pictures of Switzerland. And we pasted them on his walls. When he died, before he died he asked her to give them to me. I had come in to see him a few times and I made them into pictures because I realized how much they had meant to him. And so in every room, I mean we, this nineteen-year-old girl's mother who stayed with her day after day, she brought me the cardboard and we made them and we put them on. We didn't ask the supervisor's permission but we used this kind of tape that doesn't ruin walls, you know. And I think she resented it. I think there is very much red tape in this place. I know that beautiful scenery can remind, must remind other people of life and living, if not of God. I can actually see God in nature very much. This is what I mean, you wouldn't be that much alone if you had something that would make you a part of life. This meant that much to D.F. To S., she was surrounded by flowers and the phone calls, and the visitors that were allowed to see her, the girl friends that came, and I think that if they had all been sent out because she was so critically ill, it would have bothered her very much. She seemed to be alive when a visitor was with her, even when she was in intense pain. She couldn't talk to them either, you know. I think of her, you see. My Sisters only come once a week and sometimes they don't come at all. And so I have received most of my company from the visitors or the patients I have visited and this has helped me a lot. When I am in tears or depressed I know I have to do something to stop thinking about myself and whether I am in pain or not I have to drag myself to somebody else, to concentrate on them. And then I can forget my problems . . .

DOCTOR: What happens to you when you can't do this anymore?

PATIENT: Then I am—then I need people and then they don't come.

DOCTOR: Well, that's something, you know, where we can help.

PATIENT: Yes. But it hasn't ever happened. (Crying)

DOCTOR: But it's going to happen. That's one of the purposes.

CHAPLAIN: You mean it hasn't ever happened that they have come? When you needed them?

PATIENT: Only a tiny bit. Like when I said, when people are sick they stay away from you. You know, they think you don't want to talk, even though you can't respond, even if they just sit there, you'd know you wouldn't be alone. I mean, this would be ordinary visitors. If people would have to see this, and if it's someone who isn't screechy about praying, if they could just gently say the Lord's Prayer with you, which you haven't been able to say for days yourself because you say "Our Father" and then the rest is all confused, you know. You are again reminded of something that has a meaning. You see, if I haven't anything to give to people, they leave me. You know, if I can give to people, but there's plenty of people who don't realize how much I need.

DOCTOR: True. (Mixed conversation.)

PATIENT: And I do receive from them when I'm not critically ill. I do receive a lot but my need isn't as great then.

DOCTOR: Your need is much greater when you stop being able to give.

PATIENT: Yes, and each time I get ill, I'll worry a lot about the finances, how much it costs and another time I'll worry about if I'll have my job when I get back. And another time I'll worry if this is, you know, I'm going to be chronically ill and be always depending. Each time something different, you know, comes up so I always have some need.

DOCTOR: What happens in your outside life? I know nothing about your background or really how you live. What happens to you when you are not able to work? Then does the church support you or the place where you work now or your family? Who does?

PATIENT: Oh, sure they do. I've been hospitalized in our own hospital three times. Once during the night I had so much pain I couldn't breathe. I went down the hall and knocked on one of the nurse's door and she brought me over and gave me a hypo and then they just decided to leave me in the infirmary. This is the Sisters' infirmary. Only the Sisters can go there and it's so darn lonely in that place. You see, there's no television or radio, this isn't part of our life. Except on an educational basis at times and if people don't come in I need these things. And none of these things are presented to you and I have talked this over with my doctor so as soon as the pain has left and I can bear it, then he discharges me, knowing that psychologically I need people. And if I can go to my own room and lay down and dress four or five times a day completely and come down to meals, at least I feel a part of life. I don't feel that lonely. Even though I often have to sit in church, not being able to pray because I don't feel well, but I'm with the others. See what I mean?

DOCTOR: Yes. Why do you think loneliness is so dreadful to you?

PATIENT: I think, no, I don't think I dread loneliness because there are times when I need to be alone. I don't mean this. But unless I connect it with being abandoned in this situation, I'm not going to be able to help myself. It would be okay if I felt adequate enough, not to need people. But I, it isn't dying alone, it's the torture that pain can give you, like you just want to tear your hair out. You don't care if you don't bathe for days because it's just so much effort, like you're becoming less a human being.

CHAPLAIN: A certain sense of dignity she'd want to maintain as long as she could.

PATIENT: Yes, and I can't do this alone at times.

DOCTOR: You know, you put this so much in words what we have been doing here for this whole year and what we have attempted to do in many ways. I think you really put it in words.

PATIENT: You still want to be a person.

DOCTOR: A human being.

PATIENT: Yes. I can tell you another thing. Last year I was discharged here. I had to go home in our own hospital in a wheelchair because the leg was broken. It was a pathological fracture.

And all the kind people that pushed that wheelchair just drove me to distraction because they pushed me to where they wanted me to go, not where I wanted to go. And I couldn't always tell them where I wanted to go. I would rather have the pain in my arms, to push myself to the lavatory than to have to tell everybody where I wanted to go and then to have them wait outside and give me a time that I had to use the washroom. You see what I mean? They would call me very independent and that, and yet I wasn't. I had to maintain my dignity because they'd destroy it for me. I don't think that when I really need help I would reject it in the sense that I did. But this kind of help a lot of people give *gives me a problem.* You know? In their kindness and that I know it's goodwill, but I can't wait 'til they get out. For instance, we have one Sister that takes care of us and she offers all of these things and then she feels rejected if you don't accept it. Well, I would feel guilty. I know she has a brace on her back. They assign these to the infirmary that aren't that well, these seventy-seven-year-old Sisters. Well, I get up and crank my own bed before I'd ask one of those. But if she offers to crank it and I refuse, she feels like I'm rejecting her as a nurse. So I kind of have to grit my teeth and hope she won't come the next day and tell me how much pain she had in her back all night and couldn't sleep because I'm going to feel like I caused it.

CHAPLAIN: Hm . . . she makes you pay for it.

PATIENT: Yes.

CHAPLAIN: Can I switch. . . ?

DOCTOR: You will tell us when you are getting tired, right?

PATIENT: Yes, go ahead. I've got all day to rest.

CHAPLAIN: In terms of your own faith, what has your illness done to your faith? Has it strengthened it, weakened it, your belief in God?

PATIENT: I don't say that my illness has because I've never thought of it in those terms. I wanted to give myself to God as a nun. I wanted to be a doctor and go to the missions. Well, I haven't done any of those things. You see, I've never left the country. I've been ill many years. I know now that it was—I had decided what I wanted to do for God. I was attracted to these things and I thought they were his will. But evidently they are not. So I kind of resigned, even though if I ever get well, I still would want the same things. I still would want to go in and study for medicine. This, I think a doctor in the missions is a tremendous thing, more than a nurse even because governments put such limitations on nurses.

But, my faith, I think, received its greatest shaking here. Not through the illness, but through a man who was a patient across the hall. A Jewish man who was very kind. We met up in X-ray, in that little cubicle there. We were both waiting for an X-ray. All of a sudden I heard this voice and he said to me, "What are you so damned happy about?" And I looked at him and I said, "Well, I'm not particularly happy, but I'm not afraid of what's going to happen if that's what you mean." He had a real kind of cynical look on his face. Well, that's how we met and we found out that we were across the hall from each other more or less. And he is Jewish, and he does not practice any tradition and he has a contempt for most of the rabbis that he has met. So, he came over and he told me that there really isn't a God. That we made him up because we needed one. Now, I had never thought of that. He really believed this. I think he did because he doesn't believe in an afterworld. At the same time we had a nurse who was an agnostic and she said that sure, maybe there was a God that started the world. They talked about this to me. I think that that's what you want to talk about. They started it. And she said to me, "But he sure doesn't take care of the world since then." Well, I had never really met people like this until I came down here. You know, it was the first time I had to evaluate my faith. Meaning every time I say, "Well, sure there's a God. Look at nature and that." This is something that somebody had taught me.

CHAPLAIN: They were challenging you?

PATIENT: Yes. And also, I mean, well, the people that had taught me. Were they any more right than these people that had figured this stuff out? Meaning, I found out that I didn't have a religion. I had somebody else's religion. And this is what M. did to me. M. is the one, you know. And he'd always say something sarcastic or this nurse would say, "I don't know why I take care of the Roman Catholic Church so much when I hate it so much." I mean, this was when she'd hand me a pill. This was to get a rise out of me, a gentle one. But M. really tried to be reverent for my sake. He would say, "What do you want to talk about?" He'd say, "I want to talk about Barabbas." I'd say, "Well, M., you can't talk about Barabbas instead of Christ," and he'd say, "Well, what's the difference, really. Don't feel bad, Sister." And he would try to be reverent and respectful, but he was always challenging me. Like it was a whole hoax, you know?

DOCTOR: You like him?

PATIENT: I do. I still do.

DOCTOR: Is this happening now? Is this somebody who is here now?

PATIENT: No, this happened the second time I was hospitalized here. But we have always remained friends.

DOCTOR: Do you still have contact with him?

PATIENT: He was here the other day. Yes, he sent me a beautiful bouquet of flowers. But from him I actually got my faith. Really, it's my own faith now. And it's faith, it isn't theory of someone else, meaning I don't understand God's way and many things that happen, but I believe that God is greater than I am and when I look at the young people dying, and their parents, and everyone says what a waste and that, I can see. I say, "God is love," and I mean it now. It isn't words, I really mean it. And that he, if he is love, then he knows that this moment of this person's life is their best moment and if they had lived longer, if they had lived less, he couldn't give them as much of eternity or they would have in eternity a punishment that would be worse than it would be now. I think in his love, this is how I can accept the deaths of the young and the innocent and that.

DOCTOR: Do you mind if I ask some very personal questions?

CHAPLAIN: Just one, one fact. If I hear correctly you are saying you are stronger now in your faith and your ability to accept your illness than when you started. This has come out of it.

PATIENT: Well, no. I just mean this in terms of my faith outside my illness. But it isn't the illness, it was M. challenging my faith, without even meaning to.

DOCTOR: It's her own now and not something that somebody else taught her.

CHAPLAIN: It came from the relationship.

PATIENT: It came here. It happened here, right here in this hospital. So, I mean I worked it out these years and I've grown in it. So now I really understand what faith and trust is. Where before I was always groping to understand it more clearly. And even as I know more and that, it doesn't change the fact that there's so much more I see and like. I say to M., "If there isn't a God, I've nothing to lose, but if there is I'm worshiping him as he deserved, in the sense as much as I can now." Whereas before it was somebody else's, an automaton, the result of my education and that. I wasn't—I wasn't worshiping God. I thought I was, but believe me, if anyone had said I didn't believe in God I would have been insulted. But I see the difference now.

CHAPLAIN: You had some other questions?

DOCTOR: Yes, I have, but I think we have to finish in about five minutes. But maybe we can continue this another time.

PATIENT: I want to tell you something one patient said to me. "Don't come in and tell me this is God's will for me." Now I had never before heard anyone resent this remark. She was a twenty-seven-year-old mother who was leaving three children. "I hate it when somebody else tells me this. I know that but you're living in this pain. Nobody can put on frosting when you are hurting." It's much better at that time to say something like "You're hurting," to feel like somebody understands what you are going through than to ignore this and add something. When you are better, then it's okay. Another thing I can say, people cannot use the word cancer. It seems like this word still draws pain.

DOCTOR: There are other words like that, too.

PATIENT: But to many, much more than to me. I think that in many ways it has been a kind disease, I have gained much from it. I have met many friends, many people. I don't know if heart disease or diabetes is more acceptable. I look down the hall and I'm glad for what I've got, instead of what I haven't got. I don't begrudge other people. But when one is very sick, one doesn't think of any of these things. One just waits to see if people are going to hurt or help.

DOCTOR: What kind of a girl were you? When you were a little girl, what made you become a nun? Was this a family plan or something?

PATIENT: I was the only one in the family. We were ten children, five boys and five girls. I never remember not wanting to be a nun. But sometimes, you know, since I've studied more psychology, I wonder if it was getting me somewhere where I would stand out. Where I was so different from my sisters who were so acceptable to my family. My mother—they were good housekeepers and that, and I liked books and things like that much better. But I would say that over the years I don't believe this was true. Sometimes when I don't want to be a nun, today, because it's so darn hard, I remember that if God had wanted me to, I can accept this as being God's will. He would in some way or other have shown me a different way years before. And this too, I went on thinking—I had thought this all my life and this just was the only thing and I also can think now that I would have been a good mother and a good wife. Where at that time I thought this was the only thing that I should or could do. I mean it was not compulsion because I did it freely, but I didn't understand. I was thirteen when I went and I didn't make vows until I was twenty, meaning I had all that time and then six more years to decide that, and final vows now many years. And I say that just like in marriage, it's up to you. You either accept or you reject. You know, you can make it more full for yourself.

DOCTOR: Do you still have your mother?

PATIENT: Yes, I do.

DOCTOR: What kind of woman is she?

PATIENT: My father and mother both came as emigrants from XY. My mother learned the language on her own. She is a very

warm person. I think she did not understand my father very
well. He was an artist and he was a good salesman and she was
a very retiring, reserved person. Now I realize that she must
have had a sense of insecurity. She placed a great value on
being reserved and that and so being outgoing was kind of
looked down upon in our family. And I had a tendency for
that. Because I wanted to go and do things where my sisters
liked to stay home and embroider and my mother was real satisfied with them. I joined different clubs and that. And they
tell me now that I am an introvert. I found it hard all my life—

DOCTOR: I don't think you are an introvert.

PATIENT: Well, they just told me that about two weeks ago. I do
not often find a person who can talk to me beyond ordinary
conversation. There are so many things I am interested in. I
never had anyone to share it with. And when you find this
often in a group and you're sitting at a table with a bookkeeper
and someone, and many of our Sisters have not had the opportunity to have the education that I have, and they kind of, I
think, resent it. Meaning they think you think you are superior
to them. So right away if you meet a person like that, you shut
up, meaning you are not going to give them any ammunition
to think that. Education makes you humble, it doesn't make
you proud. And I'm not going to change my language. Meaning if I can use the word relevant, I'm not going to use something more simple. And if they think this is big talk, it's not. I
can talk as simple to a child as anybody else can, but I'm not
going to change my conversation to suit each person. But there
was a time when I wished I could. Meaning, I had to become
what everyone wanted me to be. Now I don't anymore. Now
they have to learn to accept me, too. I am kind of demanding to
them or I'm just going to kind of wait peacefully for it, it's not
going to tear me apart. People are angry at me and yet they
made themselves angry. I didn't necessarily make them angry.

DOCTOR: You are angry at people, too.

PATIENT: Yes, I am, but it even kind of made me angry for that
person to say I'm an introvert when this person hasn't cared to
discuss much that's off the beaten track. Isn't interested in

news and isn't interested in what's happening that day. I mean you could never talk about the civil rights thing . . .

DOCTOR: Who are you talking about now?

PATIENT: My own Sisters in the convent.

DOCTOR: I see. All right, I would love to go on, but I think we should finish. Do you know how long we have had the discussions?

PATIENT: No. I imagine an hour.

DOCTOR: Over an hour.

PATIENT: Yes, I suppose we have. I know counseling goes fast when you are absorbed.

CHAPLAIN: I was just wondering though—wondering if there are any questions you want to ask us.

PATIENT: Have I shocked you?

DOCTOR: No.

PATIENT: Because of my spontaneity, I might have destroyed the image of what—

DOCTOR: A nun is supposed to be like?

PATIENT: Yes, ah—

CHAPLAIN: You've impressed me, I'll say that.

PATIENT: But I would have hated to hurt someone because of my image, I know—

DOCTOR: No, you didn't.

PATIENT: I mean, I don't want you to think less of the nuns or the doctors or anything, or the nurses—

DOCTOR: I don't think I will, okay? We like to see you being you.

PATIENT: Sometimes I wonder if I'm hard for them.

DOCTOR: I'm sure you are at times.

PATIENT: I mean, being a nurse and a Sister I wonder if I'm hard for them to deal with.

DOCTOR: I'm delighted to see that you don't wear a mask of a Sister. That you remain you.

PATIENT: But this is another thing I tell you, this is another problem with me. At home I could never leave my room without my habit. Here I would find it a barrier and yet this—there's situations where I will leave my room with a dressing gown, which shocked some of the Sisters so much at home. They tried to remove me from this hospital. They thought that I was not behaving myself and that I would allow people to come in my room whenever they wanted. This was all kind of shocking to them. They would not think of giving me the same thing in my need—coming to visit me more often. And that they visit me more often when I'm here than when I'm in the infirmary. I could lie there, I did lie there for two months and very few of the Sisters ever came in to see me. But this I understand because they are working in the hospital set-up and in their free time they are getting away from it. But somehow I must convey to others that I don't need them. And even if I, you know, ask them to come again, yet they just don't seem to believe it. They believe I have a strength or something, that I do better on my own, they're not important. And yet I can't beg them for it.

CHAPLAIN: It destroys the meaning of it.

PATIENT: It isn't right. I can't beg somebody for something that I need.

CHAPLAIN: I think this—you've communicated this very well to us. Very meaningfully. The importance of one's dignity of the patient. Not having to beg or not being overwhelmed and manipulated.

DOCTOR: But I think, if I may end this with maybe a bit of advice. I don't even like the word. I think sometimes when we are in pain and agony and we look as well as you do, it is very hard perhaps for the nurse to know when you want her or when you don't want her. And I think sometimes to ask takes perhaps more and is not the same as begging. You know? It is perhaps harder to do.

PATIENT: My back is aching very much now. I will go back to that desk as I pass and ask for a pain pill. I couldn't tell when I need it but my asking for a pain pill should be enough, shouldn't it? That I have pain whether I look well or not, I have. The doctors have said that I should try and be comfortable, meaning to have the day without pain because when I go back to work I'm going to have to sweat through some classes whether I am in pain or not. Which is good, but I appreciate their understanding that you do need once in a while to be free of pain, just for somebody to relax.

This interview shows clearly the need that this patient had. She was full of anger and resentment, which seemed to originate in her early childhood. She was one of ten children and felt as an outsider within the family. While the other siblings enjoyed sitting home doing embroidery and pleasing mother, she appears to have been more like her father, reaching out, wishing to go places. This was equated as not pleasing Mama. She appeared to have compromised her needs to be different from her siblings, to have her own identity, and to be the good girl that Mama wanted by becoming a nun. It was only in her late thirties when she became ill and more demanding that it became increasingly more difficult to remain "the good girl." Part of her resentment of the nuns was a repetition of her resentment of her mother and siblings, their lack of acceptance of her, a repetition of her earlier feelings of rejection. Rather than understanding the origin of her anger and resentment, people in the environment reacted to it personally and began to reject her even more in reality. She was able to compensate for this increasing isolation only by visiting other sick people and making demands for them—thus gratifying their needs (which were really her own) and at the same time expressing her dissatisfaction and blame for the lack of care. It was this hostile demand which alienated the nursing staff, understandably, and which gave her a more acceptable rationalization for her own hostility.

In the interview, several needs were met. She was allowed to be herself, hostile and demanding without judgment and personal feelings about it. She was understood rather than judged. She was also allowed to ventilate some of her rage. Once she was able to relieve this burden, she was able to show another side of her, namely one of a warm woman, capable of love, insight, and affection. She obviously loved this Jewish man and gave him credit for finding the real meaning of her religion. He opened a door for many hours of introspection and finally made it possible for her to find an intrinsic rather than an extrinsic belief in God.

Toward the end of the interview she asked to have more opportunity to speak up like this. She paraphrased this, again angrily, in form of asking for a pain pill. We continued our visits and were surprised to hear that she had stopped visiting other dying patients and was more amenable to the staff. As she became less irritable to the nurses, they visited her more often and finally asked for a meeting with us "to understand her better." What a difference this made!

In one of my last visits to her, she looked once more at me and finally asked me something that I was never asked before, namely, to read her a chapter from the Bible. She was quite weak by then and just put her head back, telling me which pages to read, which ones to omit.

I did not enjoy this assignment as I found it somewhat peculiar and beyond the usual things I was asked to do. I would have felt much more comfortable had she asked me for a backrub, emptying a nightstool, or something like that. I also remembered, however, that I had told her we would attempt to fulfill needs, and it seemed somewhat cheap to call the hospital chaplain when her need seemed urgent at that very moment. I recall the dreaded thought that some of my colleagues might come in and laugh at my new role, and I was relieved that nobody entered her room during this "session."

I read the chapters, not really knowing what I had read. She had her eyes closed and I could not even elicit her own reactions. At the end I asked her if this was her last acting-out or if there was something else behind it that I did not understand. It was the only time that I heard a hearty laughter from her, filled with appreciation and humor. She said that it was both, but the main purpose was really a good one. It was not only her last testing of me but was at the same time her last message to me, which she hoped I would remember after she had long gone. . . .

A few days later, she visited me, fully dressed, in my office to bid farewell. She looked cheerful, almost happy. She was no longer the angry nun who alienated everybody, but a woman who had found some peace if not acceptance and who was on her way home, where she died soon thereafter.

Many of us still remember her, not for the difficulties she had caused, but for the lessons she had taught many of us. And so, in her last months of her life, she became what she wanted to be so badly, different from the others, yet still loved and accepted.

CHAPTER V

Third Stage: Bargaining

The woodcutter's axe begged for its handle from the tree.
The tree gave it.

TAGORE,
from *Stray Birds*, LXXI

The third stage, the stage of bargaining, is less well known but equally helpful to the patient, though only for brief periods of time. If we have been unable to face the sad facts in the first period and have been angry at people and God in the second phase, maybe we can succeed in entering into some sort of an agreement which may postpone the inevitable happening: "If God has decided to take us from this earth and he did not respond to my angry pleas, he may be more favorable if I ask nicely." We are all familiar with this reaction when we observe our children first demanding, then asking for a favor. They may not accept our "No" when they want to spend a night in a friend's house. They may be angry and stamp their foot. They may lock themselves in their bedroom and temporarily express their anger by rejecting us. But they will also have second thoughts. They may consider another approach. They will come out eventually, volunteer to do some tasks around the house, which under normal circumstances we never succeeded in getting them to do, and then tell us, "If I am very good all week and wash the dishes every evening, then will you let me go?" There is a slight chance naturally that we will accept the bargain and the child will get what was previously denied.

The terminally ill patient uses the same maneuvers. He knows, from past experiences, that there is a slim chance that he may be rewarded for good behavior and be granted a wish for special services. His wish is most always an extension of life, followed by the wish for a few days without pain or physical discomfort. A patient who was an opera singer, with a distorting malignancy of her jaw and face who could no longer perform on the stage, asked "to perform just one more time." When she became aware that this was impossible, she gave the most touching performance perhaps of her lifetime. She asked to come to the seminar and to speak in front of the audience, not behind a one-way mirror. She unfolded her life story, her success, and her tragedy in front of the class until a telephone call summoned her to return to her room. Doctor and dentist were ready to pull all her teeth in order to proceed with the radiation treatment. She had asked to sing once more—to us—before she had to hide her face forever.

Another patient was in utmost pain and discomfort, unable to go home because of her dependence on injections for pain relief. She had a son who proceeded with his plans to get married, as the patient had wished. She was very sad to think that she would be unable to attend this big day, for he was her oldest and favorite child. With combined efforts, we were able to teach her self-hypnosis which enabled her to be quite comfortable for several hours. She had made all sorts of promises if she could only live long enough to attend this marriage. The day preceding the wedding she left the hospital as an elegant lady. Nobody would have believed her real condition. She was "the happiest person in the whole world" and looked radiant. I wondered what her reaction would be when the time was up for which she had bargained.

I will never forget the moment when she returned to the hospital. She looked tired and somewhat exhausted and—before I could say hello—said, "Now don't forget I have another son!"

The bargaining is really an attempt to postpone; it has to include a prize offered "for good behavior," it also sets a self-imposed "deadline" (e.g., one more performance, the son's wedding), and it includes an implicit promise that the patient will not ask for more if this one postponement is granted. None of our patients have "kept their promise" ; in other words, they are like children who say, "I will never fight my sister again if you let me go." Needless to add, the little boy will fight his sister again, just as the opera singer will try to perform once more. She could not live without further performances and left the hospital before her teeth were extracted. The patient just described was unwilling to face us again unless we acknowledged the fact that she had another son whose wedding she also wanted to witness.

Most bargains are made with God and are usually kept a secret or mentioned between the lines or in a chaplain's private office. In our individual interviews without an audience we have been impressed by the number of patients who promise "a life dedicated to God" or "a life in the service of the church" in exchange for some additional time. Many of our patients also promised to give parts of or their whole body "to science" (if the doctors use their knowledge of science to extend their life).

Psychologically, promises may be associated with quiet guilt, and it would therefore be helpful if such remarks by patients were not just brushed aside by the staff. If a sensitive chaplain or physician elicits such statements, he may well wish to find out if the patient feels indeed guilty for not attending church more regularly or if there are deeper, unconscious hostile wishes which precipitated such guilt. It is for this reason that we found it so helpful to have an interdisciplinary approach in our patient care, as the chaplain often was the first one to hear about such concerns. We then pursued them until the patient was relieved of irrational fears or the wish for punishment because of excessive guilt, which was only enforced by further bargaining and more unkept promises when the "deadline" was past.

CHAPTER VI

Fourth Stage:
Depression

*The world rushes on over the strings of the lingering
heart making the music of sadness.*

TAGORE,

from *Stray Birds,* XLIV

When the terminally ill patient can no longer deny his illness,
when he is forced to undergo more surgery or hospitalization,
when he begins to have more symptoms or becomes weaker
and thinner, he cannot smile it off anymore. His numbness or
stoicism, his anger and rage will soon be replaced with a sense
of great loss. This loss may have many facets: a woman with a
breast cancer may react to the loss of her figure; a woman with
a cancer of the uterus may feel that she is no longer a woman.
Our opera singer responded to the required surgery of her
face and the removal of her teeth with shock, dismay, and the
deepest depression. But this is only one of the many losses
that such a patient has to endure.

With the extensive treatment and hospitalization, financial
burdens are added; little luxuries at first and necessities later
on may not be afforded anymore. The immense sums that

97

such treatments and hospitalizations cost in recent years have forced many patients to sell the only possessions they had; they were unable to keep a house which they built for their old age, unable to send a child through college, and unable perhaps to make many dreams come true.

There may be the added loss of a job due to many absences or the inability to function, and mothers and wives may have to become the breadwinners, thus depriving the children of the attention they previously had. When mothers are sick, the little ones may have to be boarded out, adding to the sadness and guilt of the patient.

All these reasons for depressions are well known to everybody who deals with patients. What we often tend to forget, however, is the preparatory grief that the terminally ill patient has to undergo in order to prepare himself for his final separation from this world. If I were to attempt to differentiate these two kinds of depressions, I would regard the first one a reactive depression, the second one a preparatory depression. The first one is different in nature and should be dealt with quite differently from the latter.

An understanding person will have no difficulty in eliciting the cause of the depression and in alleviating some of the unrealistic guilt or shame which often accompanies the depression. A woman who is worried about no longer being a woman can be complimented for some especially feminine feature; she can be reassured that she is still as much a woman as she was before surgery. Breast prothesis has added much to the breast cancer patient's self-esteem. Social worker, physician, or chaplain may discuss the patient's concerns with the husband in order to obtain his help in supporting the patient's self-esteem. Social workers and chaplains can be of great help during this time in assisting in the reorganization of a household, especially when children or lonely old people are involved for whom eventual placement has to be considered. We are always impressed by how quickly a patient's depression is lifted when these vital issues are taken care of. The interview of Mrs. C. in Chapter X is a good example of a woman who was deeply depressed and felt unable to deal with her own illness and impending death because so many people had to be attended to and there seemed to be no help forthcoming. She lost her ability to function in her old role but there was no one to replace her.

The second type of depression is one which does not occur as a result of a past loss but is taking into account impending losses. Our initial reaction to sad people is usually to try to cheer them up, to tell them not to look at things so grimly or so hopelessly. We encourage them to look at the bright side of life, at all the colorful, positive things around them. This is often an expression of our own needs, our own inability to tolerate a long face over any extended period of time. This can be a useful approach when dealing with the first type of depression in terminally ill patients. It will help such a mother to know that the children play quite happily in the neighbor's garden since they stay there while their father is at work. It may help a mother to know that they continue to laugh and joke, go to parties, and bring good report cards home from school—all expressions that they function in spite of mother's absence.

When the depression is a tool to prepare for the impending loss of all the love objects, in order to facilitate the state of acceptance, then encouragements and reassurances are not as meaningful. The patient should not be encouraged to look at the sunny side of things, as this would mean he should not contemplate his impending death. It would be contraindicated to tell him not to be sad, since all of us are tremendously sad when we lose one beloved person. The patient is in the process of losing everything and everybody he loves. If he is allowed to express his sorrow he will find a final acceptance much easier, and he will be grateful to those who can sit with him during this stage of depression without constantly telling him not to be sad. This second type of depression is usually a silent one in contrast to the first type, during which the patient has much to share and requires many verbal interactions and often active interventions on the part of people in many disciplines. In the preparatory grief there is no or little need for words. It is much more a feeling that can be mutually expressed and is often done better with a touch of a hand, a stroking of the hair, or just a silent sitting together. This is the time when the patient may just ask for a prayer, when he begins to occupy himself with things ahead rather than behind. It is a time when too much interference from visitors who try to cheer him up hinders his emotional preparation rather than enhances it.

The example of Mr. H. will illustrate the stage of depression which worsened because of the lack of awareness and understanding of this patient's needs on part of those in his environment, especially his immediate family. He illustrates both types of depression as he expressed many regrets for his "failures" when he was well, for lost opportunities while there was still time to be with his family, and sorrow at being unable to provide more for them. His depression paralleled his increasing weakness and inability to function as a man and provider. A chance for additional promising treatment did not cheer him up. Our interviews revealed his readiness to separate himself from this life. He was sad that he was forced to struggle for life when he was ready to prepare himself to die. It is this discrepancy between the patient's wish and readiness and the expectation of those in his environment which causes the greatest grief and turmoil in our patients.

If the members of the helping professions could be made more aware of the discrepancy or conflict between the patient and his environment, they could share their awareness with their patients' families and be of great assistance to them and to the patients. They should know that this type of depression is necessary and beneficial if the patient is to die in a stage of acceptance and peace. Only patients who have been able to work through their anguish and anxieties are able to achieve this stage. If this reassurance could be shared with their families, they too could be spared much unnecessary anguish.

Our first interview with Mr. H. follows:

PATIENT: Do I have to talk very loudly?
DOCTOR: No, that's all right. If we can't hear you then we'll say so. You speak as loud as you can as long as you are comfortable. Mr. H. said if I keep him up psychologically he will be

having a good conversation because he has been studying communication.

PATIENT: The reason for that being that I am physically very dizzy and tired.

DOCTOR: What did you mean by "psychologically keeping you up"?

PATIENT: Well, it's possible to feel physically up to par even though you don't. Providing you have a kind of psychological lift. In a way you feel extra good, you know, like if you have good news or something like that, that's all I meant.

DOCTOR: What you are really saying is to talk about good things and not about bad things.

PATIENT: You say we are?

DOCTOR: Is that what you are saying?

PATIENT: Oh, no, not at all . . .

CHAPLAIN: I think he was just saying he wants a little moral support.

DOCTOR: Yes. Well, naturally.

PATIENT: What I mean is that if I sit here more than about five minutes I'm likely to collapse from sitting here because I'm so tired and I've been up so little.

DOCTOR: Okay, so why don't we get right into the matter that we want to talk about.

PATIENT: Fine.

DOCTOR: We know practically nothing about you. What we are trying to learn from the patients is how can we talk to them as human beings without going through the whole chart and all that first. So maybe, just to start, could you give us a very brief summary of how old you are, what your profession is, and how long you have been in the hospital.

PATIENT: Been here about two weeks and, roughly, and I'm a chemical engineer, by trade. And I have a graduate degree in chemical engineering and in addition to that I took courses at the University in communications.

DOCTOR: (Not clear)

PATIENT: Well, not really, because at the time that I was doing this they had a communications course and by the time I finished with it they dropped it.

DOCTOR: I see.

CHAPLAIN: What prompted you to get interested in communications? As a chemical engineer, was this part of your job or your own interest?

PATIENT: My own interest.

DOCTOR: What brought you to the hospital this time? Is this the first time you have been in a hospital?

PATIENT: First time I've been in this hospital.

DOCTOR: What brought you here?

PATIENT: Well, the fact that I needed more work on my cancer. I had had an operation in April—

DOCTOR: April of this year?

PATIENT: —in a different hospital.

DOCTOR: Of this year? And then you were diagnosed as having cancer?

PATIENT: And then without any further diagnosis I requested admission to this hospital, and I got it.

DOCTOR: I see. How did you take it, this news? Were you told in April that you had cancer?

PATIENT: Yes.

DOCTOR: How did you take that, how was it told to you?

PATIENT: Well, naturally it was a blow.

DOCTOR: Um hm. But different people react very differently to blows.

PATIENT: Yes, well, it was more of a blow than it might be because they gave me no hope.

DOCTOR: Not a bit?

PATIENT: Not a bit. The doctor himself said that his father had had a similar operation, in the same hospital, with the same surgeon, and that he failed to recover and died within about a year and a half at the same age. And that all I could do was just to wait for the bitter end.

DOCTOR: That's pretty cruel. You know, one wonders if this doctor did that because it happened in his own family.

PATIENT: Yes, the end result was cruel but the cause was the fact that he had actually had this experience.

DOCTOR: Makes it excusable, you think. It makes it understandable.

PATIENT: Yes.

CHAPLAIN: How did you react when he did this, when he told you?

PATIENT: Well, naturally I felt quite low and stayed at home as he requested and rested up rather than doing too much. But I did do too much, I did also get around quite a bit, you know, visiting, this and that and the other thing. But after I got here and found out that there was some hope for my condition and that my condition wasn't hopeless, then I found out that I had done the wrong thing, that I had exercised too much, and that if I had only known it at that time I would be in top-notch shape right now.

DOCTOR: It means you are blaming yourself now for doing almost too much.

PATIENT: No, I'm not saying this, I didn't know. There's no blame one way or the other. I don't blame the doctor because of his own experience, and I don't blame myself because of the fact that I had no knowledge.

DOCTOR: Yes. Before you went to that hospital, did you have any hunch? What kind of symptoms did you have? Did you have pain or did you have the feeling that there was something seriously wrong?

PATIENT: Well, I had been getting lower and lower, but one day I had this very bad condition of my bowels and I had a colostomy. That was the one operation I had.

DOCTOR: Yes. What I'm really asking is how much preparation did you have for this blow. Did you somehow have a hunch?

PATIENT: None at all.

DOCTOR: Not at all. You were well, you were a healthy man until when?

PATIENT: Until I went into the hospital.

DOCTOR: And why did you go into the hospital?

PATIENT: Well, merely to have him look at it because I was having such constipation and diarrhea alternating.

DOCTOR: Um hm. What you are really saying is that you were unprepared.

PATIENT: Entirely. Not only that but they sent me over to the hospital within a couple of hours of the time I arrived in his office and within a week or so he operated.

DOCTOR: So there was a sense of urgency. And then they did the colostomy or what?

PATIENT: Yes.

DOCTOR: Yes, and that's difficult to take too, isn't it?

PATIENT: Hm?

DOCTOR: That is difficult to take.

PATIENT: Oh, no, the colostomy is easy.

DOCTOR: Is easy to take?

PATIENT: It was the idea that was only part of it; in other words the colostomy supposedly reveals all sorts of other things, but the things they revealed apparently weren't right.

DOCTOR: How everything becomes relative. Hm, I thought the colostomy caused pain to endure but when it is a question of life and death then the colostomy is the smallest of the bad things.

PATIENT: Sure, that would be nothing if the person is going to live.

DOCTOR: Yes. After you had this news you must have been thinking about how it's going to be when you die. How long are you going to live. How does a man like you deal with those questions?

PATIENT: Ah—actually I had had so many personal griefs in the meantime in my own life that it didn't seem like much. That's about it.

DOCTOR: Really?

CHAPLAIN: Personal griefs?

PATIENT: A series of them over a period of time.

CHAPLAIN: Do you feel like talking about it?

PATIENT: Oh yes, that's all right.

DOCTOR: Does that mean that you had a lot of personal losses?

PATIENT: Yes, my father and my mother died, brother died, a twenty-eight-year-old daughter died, leaving two small children which we took care of for three years, up until last December. And that was the worst blow of all because it was a constant reminder of her death.

CHAPLAIN: The children in the house. What did she die of?

PATIENT: She died of rigorous climate in Persia.

CHAPLAIN: While she was overseas?

PATIENT: A hundred and twenty degrees in the shade most of the year.

CHAPLAIN: She was away from home then.

PATIENT: She wasn't the kind that could take rigorous life.

DOCTOR: Do you have other children? Was this your only child?

PATIENT: Oh, no, we have three others.

DOCTOR: You have three others. How are they doing?

PATIENT: Fine.

DOCTOR: They are all right? You know what I don't understand? You are a man of middle-age—I don't know how old you are yet—but a middle-aged man often has lost a father and a mother. The daughter naturally is the most painful, a child is always more painful. Why do you say that because you had so many losses your own life seemed kind of insignificant?

PATIENT: I can't answer that question.

DOCTOR: It's paradoxical, isn't it? Because if your life would be insignificant it would be very easy to lose it wouldn't it? Do you see what I don't understand?

CHAPLAIN: I just was wondering if this was what he was trying to say. Is this what you were trying to communicate? I wasn't sure, what I heard you saying was that the news that you had cancer came as a different blow because of the losses you had.

PATIENT: No, oh no, I didn't mean that. I mean that in addition to the cancer I had these other blows. However, I will say, ah, I was just trying to think of a little idea I had there, that was important. You brought up the question of why I would be interested more in death than in life since I had three other children.

DOCTOR: I brought this more up to look at the sunny side too.

PATIENT: Yes, well, ah, I don't know whether you realize it but, ah, when these blows come they not only have an impact on the father but the entire family. See?

DOCTOR: Yes, that's true.

CHAPLAIN: So your wife has had a pretty hard time too?

PATIENT: My wife and all the children, all the children. And so here I was, living in a morgue you might say.

DOCTOR: For a while. Yes.

(Mixed conversation)

PATIENT: It kept on going and I look upon it as a matter of unresolved grief.

DOCTOR: Yes. What Mr. H. is really saying is there was so much grief that it is very hard to take more grief now.

PATIENT: That's right.

DOCTOR: How can we help you? Who can help you? Is there anybody that can help with this?

PATIENT: I think so.

DOCTOR: (Not clear) Has anybody helped you?

PATIENT: I've never asked anybody except you.

DOCTOR: Has anybody talked with you like we are talking now?

PATIENT: No.

CHAPLAIN: Well, how about these other losses. When your daughter died, was there anyone then that you talked with? Or that your wife talked with? Was this something that was left for the two of you to hold inside? Would you ever talk to each other?

PATIENT: Not very much.

CHAPLAIN: You had to hold it inside?

DOCTOR: Is your wife as grief-stricken now as she was then? Or has she kind of recuperated from this?

PATIENT: You can never tell.

DOCTOR: Is she a person who doesn't communicate?

PATIENT: She doesn't communicate about that. She, she's a good communicator, she's a teacher.

DOCTOR: What kind of a woman is she?

PATIENT: Well, she's a heavy-set woman, full of good spirits, the kind of person that gets a standing ovation at the beginning of every class period and gets a very valuable gift at the end.

DOCTOR: That means something, you know.

CHAPLAIN: Those are hard to come by.

PATIENT: That's right.

DOCTOR: Yes.

PATIENT: She's also a person that goes all out for me and the family.

DOCTOR: She sounds to me like a person who could talk about those things with a little additional help.

PATIENT: Yes, you would think so, wouldn't you.

DOCTOR: Are you afraid to talk about it or is she inhibited to do it?

PATIENT: Say that again.

DOCTOR: Which one of the two of you prevents such a conversation?

PATIENT: Well, we actually did have conversations. And her answer was to go overseas and raise the children. So she went over two years in a row in the summer, including this past summer. And, of course, naturally our son-in-law paid the way.

The grandchildren were with us until December and then they went back. And then Mrs. H. went over there in December for the holidays, then she went back this summer for a month. She was going to stay two months but on account of me she stayed only one month, because it was during the period of my convalescence.

CHAPLAIN: I was wondering how much conversation that you want to have about your condition with this other on your wife's mind and her concern about her responsibility for the grandchildren. Whether this had had an effect then on your ability to share or maybe your feeling that you shouldn't share and burden her with anything else. Has there been any of that feeling?

PATIENT: Well, there are other problems between her and me. Although, as I say, she is one of these very outgoing people, well, still I'm concerned, she feels that I have not done a good enough job myself.

DOCTOR: In terms of what?

PATIENT: Well, I had not earned enough money. And naturally with four children, why, she would feel that way. She feels that I ought to be like the son-in-law, you know. She also feels that I was responsible for not bringing up my youngest son well enough. Because of the fact that he has a known hereditary trait. And yet even till now she blames me.

DOCTOR: She blames you for that?

PATIENT: Blames me for that.

DOCTOR: What is he doing?

PATIENT: He was in the Marines but they discharged him.

DOCTOR: What is he doing now?

PATIENT: Well, he was supposed to be applying for a job, his old job as a stockboy.

CHAPLAIN: And your other two children?

PATIENT: Well, my second son, she blames me for him too. Because he's a little slow in school. She felt that if somebody would get in there and pitch, you know, she's just a dynamo of energy, that he would have been right on top of the heap. Of course I think that sooner or later she will realize that he wouldn't be. It's just a matter of heredity. The first son is doing fairly well because she's pushing him and he's just finishing his degree in electronics.

CHAPLAIN: Because she's pushing him?

PATIENT: Well, no, he's very brilliant, he's the only bright one, you might say, outside of the daughter.

CHAPLAIN: Well, you mentioned too the heredity. Which side do you think the weakness comes from? You gave me the impression you think it comes from your side. Or your wife suggests it's from your side.

PATIENT: Well, I don't know what she suggests on that score. I don't think she feels it's heredity. I think she feels it's just not a matter of me getting in there and doing enough work. In my spare time I should do that. I should not only be earning more money, which has been the theme of our lives. She will help me to any extent, but she will always blame me for not producing my part. I should be earning fifteen thousand a year minimum.

DOCTOR: I have a feeling what Mr. H. is really saying is that his wife is such a peppy and energetic woman she kind of wants you and her children to be the same way.

PATIENT: Exactly.

DOCTOR: And that she can't really take it well when you are not like she is—

PATIENT: Right.

DOCTOR: And that means peppy and energetic. And then she says look at my son-in-law, he makes a lot of money and he's probably very peppy and energetic.

PATIENT: Not only the son-in-law but everybody else she knows.

DOCTOR: Which would, I think, be relevant for Mr. H., the patient, because when he's sick and when he gets more weak—

PATIENT: Beg your pardon?

DOCTOR: When you are sick and you are getting weaker you will be less peppy and less energetic and make less money.

PATIENT: In fact, that's what I told her at one point. When I, when I got about forty, you know, I was slowing down a little bit and I said to myself, boy, if things are this way now imagine what it will be then because she gets peppier.

DOCTOR: It will be terrible, huh?

PATIENT: Because she gets peppier and peppier.

DOCTOR: What this means, though, for you is that this is going to be harder. Is she kind of intolerant of people who would have to sit in a wheelchair?

PATIENT: She's extremely intolerant of people who aren't brilliant enough.

DOCTOR: Well—when you are physically weak you can still be brilliant, you know—

PATIENT: Yes.

DOCTOR: But is she intolerant of people who are physically unable to do things—

PATIENT: Yes.

DOCTOR: Because you can always be brilliant.

PATIENT: Well, when we say brilliant, we mean, ah, applying brilliance in action. That's what she wants.

CHAPLAIN: I hear you saying successful.

PATIENT: Successful, that's it.

DOCTOR: Um hm.

CHAPLAIN: That they not only have the capacity but that they have done something with it. But what comes through to me here is how with this kind of thing going on it kind of pushes aside any right or opportunity you might have to actually talk about yourself and your ills.

PATIENT: That's right, and the children too.

CHAPLAIN: This is a concern that I have.

PATIENT: The children are definitely held down, I feel, by the overriding demands of their mother. She's a brilliant seamstress, for instance, in addition to being a teacher. She can tailor-make a man's suit over the weekend from the cloth. And it will be better looking than any suit you'll see, it will be like a two-hundred-and-fifty-dollar suit.

DOCTOR: But how does all that make you feel?

PATIENT: Well, it makes me feel this way, that it wouldn't make any difference to me how great she is because I admire her like—I don't know how you would say it—but like an idol, you know. It wouldn't make any difference if she didn't insist upon me being the same.

DOCTOR: Yes. How can you take your illness then?

PATIENT: This is the main thing really.

DOCTOR: That's what we are really trying to find out, how to help you—

PATIENT: This is really the main thing—Because you see if you have an illness, and you have the pain, and you have the grief that's unresolved, and you have a person that you are living with who meets every aspect on the grief business, you know, you say, well, I don't know how I'm going to live through this business of our daughter dying and that sort of thing, the answer comes right back, "Keep your chin up, positive thinking," in fact she's a fan of positive thinking.

CHAPLAIN: You keep going fast enough and you won't have to stop and think about it.

PATIENT: That's right.

DOCTOR: But he is ready to think and talk about it. You should talk about it; you have to have somebody to talk about it.

PATIENT: Your wife stops you right in the middle of a sentence. No possibility to talk to her about any of these things.

CHAPLAIN: I gather you've got a lot of faith within yourself.

PATIENT: I've done a lot of thinking within myself on how to resolve these problems. Because I'm really a very hard worker just like she would like me to be. I've always been, I've always been a very brilliant student. In the course I took at the University I got A's and B's in all the courses.

CHAPLAIN: But I hear you saying you have the capacity for it but you are aware that hard work isn't going to resolve the kind of conflicts that life has created at this point. You made a distinction between thinking of life and thinking of death, remember?

DOCTOR: Do you ever think about dying?

PATIENT: Yes. What were you going to say about it?

CHAPLAIN: I just wondered what thoughts you had about life in relationship to death and vice versa.

PATIENT: Well, ah, we'll have to admit it, I've never thought of death so much as a thing, per se, but I have thought of the worthlessness of life under such situations.

CHAPLAIN: The worthlessness?

PATIENT: That if I were to die tomorrow, my wife would go on perfectly normal.

DOCTOR: Just like nothing happened?

PATIENT: That's the way I feel. She wouldn't miss a beat.

CHAPLAIN: Just as she did with the other deaths? Or a little differently?

PATIENT: After the death of my daughter, why, she worked on her children. But if I didn't leave any children her life wouldn't change at all.

CHAPLAIN: What gives you the strength to make a comment that one of the exciting things about coming here was that they gave you a sense of hope. They said there are some things they can do for you and they are doing them. What hit you inside in your own desire to live? In spite of the worthlessness of your feelings, there is something inside you that has found satisfaction and desire to go on. Is this faith?

PATIENT: Well, it's a kind of a blind hope more than anything else, I would say, and also my church group has sustained me a great deal. I've been active in Presbyterian church work for years and years and years. The fact that I could do a little bit which my wife didn't like, of course, like sing in the choir and teaching Sunday school and things like that. Well, the fact that

I was able to do a few things like that which I felt were worth-while in the community and the work like that helped me. But every ounce of work I did along that line was considered to be worthless because of the fact that it didn't contribute to making a lot of money.

DOCTOR: But that's her concept. Your concept is still that it was worthwhile?

PATIENT: I think it's worthwhile, very worthwhile.

DOCTOR: You see, I think this is the important thing. That you still have a sense of worth. This is why I think hope is meaningful to you. You still want to live. You don't really want to die, do you? That's why you came to this hospital.

PATIENT: Right.

DOCTOR: What does death mean to you? It's a difficult question but maybe you can answer it.

PATIENT: What does death mean to me?

DOCTOR: What does death mean to you?

PATIENT: Death. It means a cessation of valuable activity. By valuable in my case I don't feel the same way as my wife. I don't mean money-making activities.

CHAPLAIN: You're talking about singing in the choir and teaching Sunday school. Being with people, this kind of thing.

DOCTOR: Yes.

PATIENT: I've always been active in community work, all sorts of different activities. That one thing that makes life worthless right now is the fact that I looked upon myself from the other doctor's point of view as not ever being able to go back to these things.

DOCTOR: And what are you doing right now in here?

PATIENT: Hm?

DOCTOR: What are you doing right now, here?

PATIENT: What I'm doing right now is exchanging views which might help.

DOCTOR: Which is a valuable activity. It may be helpful to you but it's certainly helpful to us.

CHAPLAIN: A valuable activity in his sense, not his wife's.

DOCTOR: Yes, (laughter) that's why I wanted to clarify it. What you are really saying is that life is worthwhile living as long as you can be of some value and do something worthwhile.

PATIENT: But you know, it is also a nice thing to have somebody else appreciate it. If you love them.

DOCTOR: Do you really believe that nobody else appreciates you?

PATIENT: I don't believe my wife does.

CHAPLAIN: That's what I thought he was referring to.

DOCTOR: Yes, what about your children?

PATIENT: I think they do. But the wife is the big thing you know, a man's wife. Especially if he admires her quite a bit, you know. And she's so, you might say, lovable. Because she's so full of sparkling energy and all that sort of thing.

CHAPLAIN: Has this been consistent with your marriage? Or has this been more noticeable after your periods of grief? And loss?

PATIENT: No different. Actually it's been better after the griefs and loss. Well, right now, for instance, she has been very nice to me for a while. Since I've been in the hospital, but ah, it's always been that way. When I was sick or something like that, why, she would act real nice to me for a while. But then she couldn't get rid of this fact that here was a loafer who didn't make any money.

CHAPLAIN: Well, how do you account for the things that have happened in your life? You mentioned going to church. How do you account for the things that happened to you? In terms of your attitude toward life, what some people would call your faith in life. Does God play a part of this?

PATIENT: Oh yes. Well, in the first place, as a Christian, Christ acts as an intermediator. It's very simple. When I keep the vision in view things work out pretty well. And I get relief from my—I get solutions to problems which concern people.

CHAPLAIN: The very thing he's been talking about between his wife and himself is a need for a mediator, and you mentioned Christ as a mediator in your other problems. Have you thought of this in terms of your wife and your relationship?

PATIENT: I have, but unfortunately or not, my wife is such a dynamic person.

CHAPLAIN: What I hear you saying is your wife is so dynamic and active that there is no room for an active God in her life. There would be no room for a mediator.

PATIENT: Well, that's what it amounts to in her case.

DOCTOR: Do you think she would be willing to talk to one of us?

PATIENT: I certainly would, yes.

DOCTOR: If you would ask her? Would that be okay with you?

PATIENT: My wife would never think of going to a psychiatrist, especially with me.

DOCTOR: Um hm. What's so scary about a psychiatrist?

PATIENT: The very things we have been talking about. I think she sort of covers them up.

DOCTOR: Well, let's see how that interview goes. It might be helpful. And if it's okay with you we will drop in once in a while. Okay?

PATIENT: You are going to drop in, you say?

DOCTOR: And visit you.

PATIENT: At my bed?

DOCTOR AND CHAPLAIN: Yes.

PATIENT: I'll be leaving Saturday.

DOCTOR: I see. So we don't have much time.

CHAPLAIN: Well, if you are coming back to the clinics anytime, you might be coming back to see the doctor?

PATIENT: I doubt it but might be. It's a long, long trip.

CHAPLAIN: Oh, I see.

DOCTOR: Well, if this is our last meeting, maybe you have some questions that you would like to ask.

PATIENT: Well, I think that one of the biggest advantages of what this interview is that lots of questions have been brought out that I wouldn't have thought of.

DOCTOR: It has helped us too.

PATIENT: I think that Dr. R. has made some very good suggestions and you have made good ones too. But I do know one thing, unless I make radical improvement, why, I will not be cured physically.

DOCTOR: Is this scary?

PATIENT: Scary?

DOCTOR: I don't sense any fear in you.

PATIENT: No, it wouldn't scare me, for two reasons. One, I have fairly well grounded religion which has been grounded in the fact that I have passed it on to other people.

DOCTOR: So you can say of yourself that you are a man who does not fear death and who accepts it when it comes, just like that.

PATIENT: Yes, I don't fear death but I do more or less fear the opportunity to continue my former activities. Because, you see, I didn't really like engineering as well as working with people.

CHAPLAIN: This is where your interest in communications came in.

PATIENT: Part of it, yes.

CHAPLAIN: What strikes me is not the absence of fear but also the concern, sense of regret in terms of your relationship with your wife.

PATIENT: I have regretted that all my life, that I couldn't communicate with her. You might say really, if you wanted to go down under the mat, in my study of communication was, I don't really know, but it probably might have been ninety percent trying to get together with my wife.

DOCTOR: Trying to communicate with her, no? You never got any professional help for that? You know, I have a feeling that this could be helped, it still can be helped.

CHAPLAIN: That's why tomorrow's meeting is so important.

DOCTOR: Yes, yes . . . So I don't feel really helpless, this is not irreparable, you know. You still have the time to do that.

PATIENT: Well, I would say that as long as I am actually alive there is hope for life.

DOCTOR: That's right.

PATIENT: But life isn't the whole thing in the world. The quality of life, why you live it.

CHAPLAIN: Well, I appreciate having had the chance to visit with you. I'd like to drop in on you this evening before I go home tonight.

PATIENT: Well, I would like to do that . . . Oh . . . (patient does not want to leave) . . . You were going to ask me some questions you didn't ask.

DOCTOR: I did?

PATIENT: Um hm.

DOCTOR: What did I forget?

PATIENT: I understood from what you said that she was in charge not only of this seminar but—Well, what are you in charge of, let's put it that way. Somebody was interested in the relationship between religion and psychiatry.

DOCTOR: Yes, I'm beginning to understand. You see, a lot of people have different concepts of what we are doing here. What I am most interested in is to talk with sick people or dying patients. To get to understand them a little bit more. To teach the hospital personnel how we can help them better, and the only way we can teach it is to have the patient be our teacher, you know.

CHAPLAIN: Were there questions you had about relationships of religion—

PATIENT: Yes, I had some. For instance, one of the things was that the average patient is only going to call a chaplain, he's not going to call the psychiatrist if he happens to feel bad.

DOCTOR: That's right.

PATIENT: All right. Then the question was asked me before by you or someone, ah, how do I feel about the service of the chaplains. And I would say that I was dumbfounded to find that I requested a chaplain in the middle of the night and there was no night chaplain. I mean this is just unbelievable to me, unbelievable. Because when does a man need a chaplain? Only at night, believe me. That's the time when you get down with those boxing gloves and have it out with yourself. That's the time when you need a chaplain. I would say mostly between twelve and so on—

DOCTOR: The early morning hours.

PATIENT: And if you were to show a chart it would probably have a peak at about three o'clock. And it should be just like that. You call the buzzer, the nurse comes, "I'd like to have a chaplain," within five minutes the chaplain shows up and you are on the road to, ah—

DOCTOR: To really communicate.

PATIENT: Yes.

DOCTOR: This is the question you wanted me to ask, how you are satisfied with the services of the chaplain. I see, I asked this question perhaps indirectly when I asked you who helped you, was there anybody who was helpful to you. You didn't mention the chaplain at that time—

PATIENT: That's the trouble with the church itself. When does a man need a minister.

DOCTOR: Yes.

PATIENT: He needs him about three o'clock ordinarily.

DOCTOR: Well, Chaplain N. can answer this because he was up all night last night seeing patients.

CHAPLAIN: I don't feel as guilty as I would have, I only had two hours sleep last night. I can appreciate this though, I think there is a lot more being said that is felt.

PATIENT: And I don't think that anything else should take precedence over that.

CHAPLAIN: The genuine concern of somebody reaching out for help.

PATIENT: Sure, the minister, the Presbyterian minister that married my father and mother, was that kind of a man. It didn't hurt him at all. I met him at ninety-five, his hearing was just as good as ever, his seeing was just as good as ever, his handshake was like a man of twenty-five.

CHAPLAIN: This again symbolizes some of the disappointments that you've experienced.

DOCTOR: This is part of the seminar, to find out those things, so we may become more effective.

PATIENT: That's right. And in the case of ministers I would imagine you'd have less chance of consultation when you needed it than you would in the case of a psychiatrist—this is a peculiar thing—because a minister is supposed to be non-moneymaking, and a psychiatrist is supposed to be out for a minimum amount of money. So, here you have a fellow making money, he could make money in the daytime, at night or anytime he wants to, but yet you could make an arrangement with a therapist to come at night, but try and get a minister out of bed at night.

CHAPLAIN: Seems like you have had some experiences with clergy.

PATIENT: My own clergyman right now is very good but the trouble with it is he is settled with a whole flock of children. At least four. Well, when is he gonna get out? Then they tell me about how they, ah, have young fellows in the seminary and things like that. Not a lot of them, fact we even had trouble getting some for Christian Education work. But I think if they had a going church they wouldn't have any trouble getting the young people.

CHAPLAIN: I think we've got some things to talk about that aren't part of the seminar. He and I will get together sometime and we'll revise the church. I'm in agreement with a part of what he says.

DOCTOR: Yes, but I'm glad he brought this up here. This is an important part. How was the nursing service?

PATIENT: Here?

DOCTOR: Yes.

PATIENT: Well, practically every night that I needed a chaplain, it was because that I had to deal with a wrong kind of a nurse, during the daytime. There are some nurses here that are efficient but they rub the patient the wrong way. Fact, my roommate said, you get better twice as fast if you didn't have that nurse. She fights every minute, you know what I mean? You come in and you say, well, would you give me a little help and start on eating because I have an ulcer and liver trouble and this and that and the other thing. She says, well, we are very busy, it's up to you to do that. If you want to eat you can eat, if you don't want to, you don't have to. Then there is another nurse who is pretty nice and in the way she helps you, but she never smiles one bit. And for a person like me who ordinarily, you know, smiles and takes on the badge of goodwill, why, it seems sad to look at her. Every night she comes in and not a trace of a smile.

DOCTOR: How is your roommate?

PATIENT: Well, I haven't been able to talk to him since he started these breathing treatments, but otherwise I imagine he would get along pretty well because he doesn't have so many different ailments as I have.

DOCTOR: You know originally you planned only about five or ten minutes and then you said you would get very, very tired. Can you still sit comfortably?

PATIENT: Well, it so happens that I'm all right.

DOCTOR: Do you know for how long we talked? One hour.

PATIENT: I never would have imagined I could have lasted an hour.

CHAPLAIN: We are getting very conscious of it in not wanting to tire you here.

DOCTOR: Yes, I really think we should stop it now.

PATIENT: I think we have talked about most of the things.

CHAPLAIN: I'll drop by around dinnertime before I go home, to see you again.

PATIENT: Ah, six o'clock?

CHAPLAIN: Five thirty to six, somewhere along there.

PATIENT: That's very good. You can help me eat because I have a bad nurse.

CHAPLAIN: Okay.

DOCTOR: Thank you for coming. I appreciate it.

Mr. H.'s interview is a good example of what we called the "door-opening interview."

He was regarded as a grim, noncommunicating man by the hospital staff, and their prediction was that he would not agree to talking with us. At the beginning of the session, he warned us that he was likely to collapse if he sat for more than five minutes—yet, after a full hour of conversation he had difficulty leaving and felt perfectly all right physically as well as emotionally. He was preoccupied with many personal losses, the most serious one the death of a daughter far away. What grieved him most, however, was the loss of hope. It was related at first as the doctor's presentation of his illness: ". . . they gave me no hope. The doctor himself said that his father had had a similar operation, in the same hospital, with the same surgeon, and that he failed to recover and died within about a year and a half at the same age. And that all I could do was just to wait for the bitter end . . ."

Mr. H. did not give up and admitted himself to another hospital, where hope was offered.

Later in the interview he expresses another sense of hopelessness, namely, his inability to have his wife share some of his interests and values in life. She often made him feel like a failure, he was blamed for the children's lack of achievements, he did not bring enough money home, and he was fully aware that it was too late to satisfy her demands and ever meet her expectations. As he felt weaker and unable to work, looking back at his life, he became even more aware of the discrepancy between her values and his own. The gap seemed to be so great that communication became almost impossible. All this happened to this man during the mourning process for his daughter and reawakened the sadness he experienced after his parents' deaths. As he describes it, we had the feeling that he had so much grief, he was unable to add more sorrow to it—thus leaving the most vital dialogue unspoken, which would have, we hope, given him a sense of peace. In all this depression there was a sense of pride, a feeling of worth in spite of his family's lack of appreciation. So we could not help but wish to be instrumental in a final communication between the patient and his wife.

We finally understood why the hospital staff was unable to tell how much Mr. H. was aware of his illness. He was not thinking of his cancer as much as he was reviewing the meaning of his life and searching for ways to share this with the most significant person—his wife. He was deeply depressed not because of his terminal illness but because he had not finished his own mourning for the dead parents and child. When there is so much pain already, some added pain is not experienced as much as when it hits a healthy pain-free body. Yet we felt that this pain could be eliminated if we could find means to communicate all this to Mrs. H.

The following morning we met with her, a strong, powerful, healthy woman, energetic as he had described. She confirmed almost verbatim what he had said the day before: "Life will go on much the same when he has ceased to be." He was weak, he could not even cut the lawn or else he might faint. Men on the farm were different kind of people, they had muscles and were strong. They worked from sunrise to sundown and he was not much interested in making money either . . . Yes, she knew he had not long to live, but she was unable to take him home. She had made plans to bring him to a nursing home and she would visit him there . . . Mrs. H. said this all in a tone of a busy woman who had a lot of other things to attend to and could not be bothered. Maybe at that time I felt impatient or had a sense of Mr. H.'s hopelessness, but I repeated in my own words once more the essence of her communications. I summarized briefly that Mr. H. had not fulfilled her expectations, he was not very good in many things really, and would not be mourned when he ceased to be. Looking back at his life, one might wonder if there was anything memorable in it. . . .

Mrs. H. suddenly looked at me, and with feeling in her voice she almost yelled: "What do you mean, he was the most honest and the most faithful man in the world. . . ."

We sat for another few minutes during which time I shared with her some of the things that we had heard in the interview. Mrs. H. admitted that she had never thought of him in these terms and was quite willing to give him credit for these assets. We returned to the patient's room together and Mrs. H. repeated on her own what we exchanged in our office. I shall not forget the patient's pale face deep in his pillows, the expectant look on his face, the wonderment in his expression at whether we were able to communicate. And then his eyes lit up when he heard his own wife say, ". . . and I told her that you were the most honest and most faithful man in the world, and that's hard to find these days. And on the way home we would pass by the church and pick up some of your church work that was so meaningful to you. It will keep you busy for the next few days. . . ."

There was some genuine warmth in her voice when she talked with him and prepared him to leave the hospital. "I shall never forget you as long as I live," he said when I left the room—both of us knowing that this would not be long, but it mattered little at this point.

CHAPTER VII

Fifth Stage: Acceptance

I have got my leave. Bid me farewell, my brothers!
I bow to you all and take my departure.
Here I give back the keys of my door—and I give up
all claims to my house. I only ask for last kind words
from you.
We were neighbours for long, but I received more
than I could give. Now the day has dawned and the
lamp that lit my dark corner is out. A summons has
come and I am ready for my journey.

TAGORE,
from *Gitanjali*, XCIII

If a patient has had enough time (i.e., not a sudden, unexpected death) and has been given some help in working through the previously described stages, he will reach a stage during which he is neither depressed nor angry about his "fate." He will have been able to express his previous feelings, his envy for the living and the healthy, his anger at those who do not have to face their end so soon. He will have mourned the impending loss of so many meaningful people and places

123

and he will contemplate his coming end with a certain degree of quiet expectation. He will be tired and, in most cases, quite weak. He will also have a need to doze off or to sleep often and in brief intervals, which is different from the need to sleep during the times of depression. This is not a sleep of avoidance or a period of rest to get relief from pain, discomfort, or itching. It is a gradually increasing need to extend the hours of sleep very similar to that of the newborn child but in reverse order. It is not a resigned and hopeless "giving up," a sense of "what's the use" or "I just cannot fight it any longer," though we hear such statements too. (They also indicate the beginning of the end of the struggle, but the latter are not indications of acceptance.)

Acceptance should not be mistaken for a happy stage. It is almost void of feelings. It is as if the pain had gone, the struggle is over, and there comes a time for "the final rest before the long journey" as one patient phrased it. This is also the time during which the family needs usually more help, understanding, and support than the patient himself. While the dying patient has found some peace and acceptance, his circle of interest diminishes. He wishes to be left alone or at least not stirred up by news and problems of the outside world. Visitors are often not desired and if they come, the patient is no longer in a talkative mood. He often requests limitation on the number of people and prefers short visits. This is the time when the television is off. Our communications then become more nonverbal than verbal. The patient may just make a gesture of the hand to invite us to sit down for a while. He may just hold our hand and ask us to sit in silence. Such moments of silence may be the most meaningful communications for people who are not uncomfortable in the presence of a dying person. We may together listen to the song of a bird from the outside. Our presence may just confirm that we are going to be around until the end. We may just let him know that it is all right to say nothing when the important things are taken care of and it is only a question of time until he can close his eyes forever. It may reassure him that he is not left alone when he is no longer talking and a pressure of the hand, a look, a leaning back in the pillows may say more than many "noisy" words.

A visit in the evening may lend itself best to such an encounter as it is the end of the day both for the visitor and the patient. It is the time when the hospital's page system does not interrupt such a moment, when the nurse does not come in to take the temperature, and the cleaning woman is not mopping the floor—it is this little private moment that can complete the day at the end of the rounds for the physician, when he is not interrupted by anyone. It takes just a little time but it is comforting for the patient to know that he is not forgotten when nothing else can be done for him. It is gratifying for the visitor as well, as it will show him that dying is not such a frightening, horrible thing that so many want to avoid.

There are a few patients who fight to the end, who struggle and keep a hope that makes it almost impossible to reach this stage of acceptance. They are the ones who will say one day, "I just cannot make it anymore," the day they stop fighting, the fight is over. In other words, the harder they struggle to avoid the inevitable death, the more they try to deny it, the more difficult it will be for them to reach this final stage of acceptance with peace and dignity. The family and staff may consider these patients tough and strong, they may encourage the fight for life to the end, and they may implicitly communicate that accepting one's end is regarded as a cowardly giving up, as a deceit or, worse yet, a rejection of the family.

How, then, do we know when a patient is giving up "too early" when we feel that a little fight on his part combined with the help of the medical profession could give him a chance to live longer? How can we differentiate this from the stage of acceptance, when our wish to prolong his life often contradicts his wish to rest and die in peace? If we are unable to differentiate these two stages we do more harm than good to our patients, we will be frustrated in our efforts, and will make his dying a painful last experience. The following case of Mrs. W. is a brief summary of such an event, where this differentiation was not made.

Mrs. W., a married fifty-eight-year-old woman, was hospitalized with a malignancy in her abdomen which gave her much pain and discomfort. She had been able to face her serious illness with courage and dignity. She complained very rarely and attempted to do as many things as possible by herself. She rejected any offer of help as long as she was able to do it herself and impressed the staff and her family by her cheerfulness and ability to face her impending death with equanimity.

Briefly after her last admission to the hospital she became suddenly depressed. The staff was puzzled about this change and asked for a psychiatric consultation. She was not in her room when we looked for her and a second visit a few hours later found her still absent. We finally found her in the hallway outside of the X-ray room where she lay uncomfortably and obviously in pain on a stretcher. A brief interview revealed that she had undergone two rather lengthy X-ray procedures and had to wait for other pictures to be taken. She was in great discomfort because of a sore on her back, had not had any food or drink for the past several hours, and most uncomfortable of all, needed to go to the bathroom urgently. She related all this in a whispering voice, describing herself as being "just numb from pain." I offered to carry her to the adjacent bathroom. She looked at me—for the first time smiling faintly—and said, "No, I am barefoot, I'd rather wait until I am back in my room. I can go there myself."

This brief remark showed us one of the patient's needs: to care for herself as long as possible, to keep her dignity and independence as long as it was possible. She was enraged that her endurance was tested to the point where she was ready to scream in public, where she was ready to let go of her bowel movements in a hallway, where she was on the verge of crying in front of strangers "who only did their duty."

When we talked with her a few days later under more favorable circumstances, it was obvious that she was increasingly tired and ready to die. She talked about her children briefly, about her husband who would be able to carry on without her. She felt strongly that her life, especially her marriage, had been a good and meaningful one and that there was little left that she could do. She asked to be allowed to die in peace, wished to be left alone—even asked for less involvement on the part of her husband. She said that the only reason that kept her still alive was her husband's inability to accept the fact that she had to die. She was angry at him for not facing it and for so desperately clinging on to something that she was willing and ready to give up. I translated to her that she wished to detach herself from this world and she nodded gratefully as I left her alone.

In the meantime, unbeknown to the patient and myself, the medical-surgical staff had a meeting which included the husband. While the surgeons believed that another surgical procedure could possibly prolong her life, the husband pleaded with them to do everything in their power to "turn the clock back." It was unacceptable to him to lose his wife. He could not comprehend that she did not have the need to be with him any longer. Her need to detach herself, to make dying easier, was interpreted by him as a rejection which was beyond his comprehension. There was no one there to explain to him that this was a natural process, a progress indeed, a sign perhaps that a dying person has found his peace and is preparing himself to face it alone.

The team decided to operate on the patient the following week. As soon as she was informed of the plans she weakened rapidly. Almost overnight she required double the dose of medication for her pains. She often asked for drugs the moment she was given an injection. She became restless and anxious, often calling for help. She was hardly the patient of a few days before; the dignified lady who could not go to the bathroom because she was not wearing slippers!

Such behavioral changes should make us alert. They are communications of our patients who try to tell us something. It is not always possible for a patient to openly reject a life-prolonging operation, in the face of a pleading, desperate husband and children who hope to have mother home once more. Last but not least, we should not underestimate the patient's own glimpse of hope for a cure in the face of impending death. As outlined earlier, it is not in human nature to accept the finality of death without leaving a door open for some hope. It is therefore not enough to listen only to the overt verbal communications of our patients.

Mrs. W. had clearly indicated that she wished to be left in peace. She was in much more pain and discomfort after the announcement of the planned surgery. Her anxiety increased as the day of the operation approached. It was not in our authority to cancel the operation. We merely communicated our strong reservations and felt sure that the patient would not tolerate the operation.

Mrs. W. did not have the strength to refuse the operation nor did she die before or during the procedure. She became grossly psychotic in the operating room, expressed ideas of persecution, screamed and carried on until she was returned to her room minutes before the planned surgery was to take place.

She was clearly delusional, had visual hallucinations and paranoid ideas. She looked frightened and bewildered and made no sense in her communications to the staff. Yet, in all this psychotic behavior, there was a degree of awareness and logic that remained impressive. As she was returned to her room, she asked to see me. When I entered the room the following day, she looked at her bewildered husband and then said, "Talk to this man and make him understand." She then turned her back to us, clearly indicating her need to be left alone. I had my first meeting with her husband, who was at a loss for words. He could not understand the "crazy" behavior of his wife who had always been such a dignified lady. It was hard for him to cope with her rapidly deteriorating physical illness, but incomprehensible what our "crazy dialogue" was all about.

Her husband said with tears in his eyes that he was totally puzzled by this unexpected change. He described his marriage as an extremely happy one and his wife's terminal illness as totally unacceptable. He had hopes that the operation would allow them once more to be "as close together as they had been" for the many happy years of their marriage. He was disturbed by his wife's detachment and even more so by her psychotic behavior.

When I asked him about the patient's needs, rather than his own, he sat in silence. He slowly began to realize that he never listened to her needs but took it for granted that they were the same. He could not comprehend that a patient reaches a point when death comes as a great relief, and that patients die easier if they are allowed and helped to detach themselves slowly from all the meaningful relationships in their life.

We had a long session together. As we talked, things slowly began to clear and came into focus. He gave much anecdotal material to confirm that she had tried to communicate her needs to him, but that he could not hear it because they were opposing his needs. Mr. W. felt obviously relieved when he left and rejected an offer to return with him to the patient's room. He felt more capable of talking with his wife frankly about the outcome of her illness and was almost glad that the operation had to be canceled because of her "resistance" as he called it. His reaction to her psychosis was, "My God, maybe she is stronger than all of us. She sure fooled us. She made it clear she did not want the operation. Maybe the psychosis was the only way out of it without dying before she was ready."

Mrs. W. confirmed a few days later that she was not able to die until she knew that her husband was willing to let go. She wanted him to share some of her feelings rather than "always pretend that I am going to be all right." Her husband did make an attempt to let her talk about it, though it came hard and he "regressed" many times. Once he clung to the hope for radiation, at another time he tried to put pressure on her to come home, promising to hire a private nurse for her care.

During the following two weeks he often came to talk about his wife and his hopes but also about her eventual death. Finally he came to accept the fact that she would become weaker and less able to share the many things that had been so meaningful in their life.

She recovered from her psychotic episode as soon as the operation was permanently canceled and her husband acknowledged the impending death and shared this with her. She had less pain and resumed her role of the dignified lady who continued to do as many things as her physical condition allowed. The medical staff became increasingly sensitive to the subtle expressions to which they responded tactfully, always keeping in mind her most important need: to live to the end with dignity.

Mrs. W. was representative of most of our dying patients, though she was the only one I have seen to resort to such an acute psychotic episode. I am sure that this was a defense, a desperate attempt to prevent a life-prolonging intervention which came too late.

As stated earlier, we have found that those patients do best who have been encouraged to express their rage, to cry in preparatory grief, and to express their fears and fantasies to someone who can quietly sit and listen. We should be aware of the monumental task which is required to achieve this stage of acceptance, leading towards a gradual separation (decathexis) where there is no longer a two-way communication.

We have found two ways of achieving this goal more easily. One kind of patient will achieve it with little if any help from the environment—except a silent understanding and no interference. This is the older patient who feels at the end of his life, who has worked and suffered, raised his children and completed his tasks. He will have found meaning in his life and has a sense of contentment when he looks back at his years of work.

Others, less fortunate ones, may reach a similar state of body and mind when they are given enough time to prepare for their death. They will need more help and understanding from the environment as they struggle through all the previously described stages. We have seen the majority of our patients die in the stage of acceptance, an existence without fear and despair. It is perhaps best compared with what Bettelheim describes about early infancy: "Indeed it was an age when nothing was asked of us and all that we wanted was given. Psychoanalysis views earliest infancy as a time of passivity, an age of primary narcissism when we experience the self as being all."

And so, maybe at the end of our days, when we have worked and given, enjoyed ourselves and suffered, we are going back to the stage that we started out with and the circle of life is closed.

*   *   *

The following two interviews are examples of husband and wife attempting to reach the stage of acceptance.

Dr. G., a dentist and father of a twenty-four-year-old son, was a deeply religious man. We have used his example in Chapter IV on anger, when the question is raised, "Why me?" and he remembered old George and wondered why that man's life could not be taken instead of his. In spite of the picture of acceptance that he presented during the interview, he also demonstrates the aspect of hope. He was intellectually quite aware of the state of his malignancy and as a professional man realized the slim chances of continuing to work. Yet he was unwilling or unable to consider the closing of his office until briefly before this interview. He maintained an office girl to accept his calls and sustained the hope that the Lord might repeat an incident that happened to him during the war years when he was shot at at a close distance and missed "being shot from twenty feet away and the person misses you, you know that there is some other power than the fact that you are a god dodger or whatever."

DOCTOR: Can you tell us how long you have been in the hospital and what reasons brought you here?

PATIENT: Yes. I am a dentist as you probably know and have been practicing for quite a number of years. In the last part of June, I experienced this sudden pain that I realized was unusual and I had X-rays immediately and the 7th of July of this year I was operated on for the first time.

DOCTOR: In 1966?

PATIENT: In 1966, yes. And I realized that there was ninety percent chance that it was malignant but this was a slight consideration on my part since this was my first episode and my first feeling of any kind of pain. I came through the operation in very good shape, recovered remarkably and then had a subsequent bowel blockage and had to go back in for further surgery on the 14th of September. And from the 27th of October I was not happy with my progress. My wife got in touch with a doctor here and we came here. So I have been constantly in treatment since the 27th of October. This covers my hospitalization about as well as I can summarize it.

DOCTOR: At what time of this illness did you know what you actually had?

PATIENT: I actually knew that it was very possibly a malignancy immediately after seeing the X-rays because a growth in this particular area is ninety percent malignant. But as I said, it didn't occur to me that it would be very serious and I was getting on so well. Now the doctor did not tell me, but they did tell the family the seriousness of the condition as soon as they were out of surgery. And it was a short time later I was riding to a town nearby with my son. We have always been a closely knit family and we'd got to talking about my general condition and he said, "Has Mom ever told you what you really have?" I said no, she hasn't. And so I know it wrenched him deeply but he told me that when they did their first surgery it was not only malignant but it was metastatic and it covered all the organs of the body with the exception of the liver and the spleen, which was fortunate. It was inoperable and I had begun to suspect this. My boy came to know the Lord when he was ten years old and through the years we had wanted to share some of his experience of the Lord, as he matured and went away to college. This experience had matured him tremendously.

DOCTOR: How old is he now?

PATIENT: He will be twenty-four Sunday. I realized the depth of his maturity after our conversation.

DOCTOR: How did you react to your son telling you that?

PATIENT: Well, to be very frank, I had more or less suspected this, due to several things that I had noticed. I am not completely without knowledge myself; I have been associated with a hospital for twenty years, been on the hospital staff that long, and I understand these things. At that time he also told me that the assisting surgeon told my wife that I had from four to fourteen months to live. I had felt nothing. I've been at complete peace with my soul since I found this out. I've had no period of depression. I suppose most anybody in my position would look at somebody else and say, well, why couldn't it have been him. And this has crossed my mind several times. But it is only a fleeting passage. I remember once we went down to the office to pick up the mail and an old man came down the street who I have known ever since I was a little kid. He is eighty-two years old, and he is of no earthly use as far as we mortals can tell. He's rheumatic, he's a cripple, he's dirty, just not the type of a person you would like to be. And the thought hit very strongly, now why couldn't it have been old George instead of me. But this hasn't been a major consideration. This has possibly been the only thing that I have thought of. I do look forward to meeting the Lord, but at the same time I would like to stay around on earth as long as possible. The thing that I feel the most deeply is the parting of the family.

DOCTOR: How many children do you have?

PATIENT: Just the one.

DOCTOR: One son.

PATIENT: As I say, we have been a very closely knit family.

DOCTOR: Being so close, and you being a dentist knowing almost for sure that this was a cancer when you saw the X-rays, how come you never talked with your wife or your son about this?

PATIENT: Well, I don't know for sure. Now I know that my wife and son fully expected it to be a major surgery and with a short duration of discomfort we expected a successful outcome. I didn't care to upset them further. I understand that my wife did go right to pieces when she was told the truth. My son, this is where his maturity came in, was a bulwark of strength in that period. But my wife and I have talked about it since very frankly, and we are seeking treatment because I feel that the Lord can heal. He is able, and through whatever method he is able to heal that I will accept it. We don't know what medicine will do, we don't know where the medical discoveries come from. How can a man dig a root from the ground and say I think this might be useful in treating such and such and yet it has happened. And in all our hospital laboratories you'll find the little things growing profusely now because they feel that it has a direct relationship to cancer research. How would you arrive at that conclusion? This is mysterious and it's miraculous as far as I'm concerned and I think this comes from the Lord.

CHAPLAIN: Your faith has been a lot to you, I gather, not only during this illness but before.

PATIENT: Yes it has been. I achieved a saving knowledge of the Lord Jesus Christ about ten years ago. I came to this position through a study of the Scriptures which I did not complete. The thing that finally settled as far as I was concerned was the realization that I was a sinner. This I had not realized, because I'm a good boy, always been a good boy.

DOCTOR: What got you started on this ten years ago?

PATIENT: It has gone back further than that. Overseas I had contact with a chaplain who talked to me considerably concerning things such as this. And I don't think anybody can be shot at more than once and be missed and not realize that there is something besides you standing there, especially when the man is standing within twenty feet of you. As I say, I had always been a good boy, I didn't swear, I didn't use vile language, I didn't drink, I didn't smoke, I didn't particularly care for them. I didn't chase women, very much, that is, and I was always a pretty good boy. And so I didn't realize I was a sinner until this particular moment at a meeting he was holding. There were about three thousand people there. And at the conclusion of his service, I don't remember what he preached on now, he asked for people to come forward to dedicate themselves to the Lord. I don't know why I went forward but I had a compulsion to. Afterwards I questioned my decision, I was sort of like I was when I was six years old. I thought when I was going to be six years old, this world was going to blossom out beautifully and everything would be changed. Mother came downstairs that morning. I was standing in front of a mirror about ten feet square that we had in our living room, and she said, "Happy birthday, Bobby." She said, "What are you doing?" I said I was looking at myself. She said, "What do you see?" "Well," I said, "I'm six years old but I look the same, I feel the same, and by God I am the same." But I found out as my experience went deeper, that I wasn't the same, that I couldn't tolerate things that I had tolerated before.

DOCTOR: Like what?

PATIENT: Well, as you know, as you associate with people you meet—this is something that business people meet rather regularly—is the realization all of a sudden that they are making many contacts in bars. Before a professional meeting most of the men will retire to the bar of the motel or hotel and sit there and drink and have fellowship together. This didn't bother me particularly. I didn't drink but it didn't bother me, but it began to bother me later because I didn't believe in this. And I couldn't quite accept it. I didn't do things I did before and this is where I achieved the realization that I was different.

DOCTOR: Has all this helped you now that you have to deal with your own dying and your terminal illness?

PATIENT: Yes, very much so. As I said, I have been at complete peace with myself since I first came out of anesthesia after surgery. I was just as peaceful as I could be.

DOCTOR: You have no fears?

PATIENT: I cannot honestly say that I have feared.

DOCTOR: You are an unusual man, Dr. G., you know. Because we very rarely see men who face their own death without any fear.

PATIENT: Well, it is because I expect to be at home with the Lord when I die.

DOCTOR: On the other hand you still have some hope for a cure or for a medical discovery, right?

PATIENT: Yes.

DOCTOR: I think this is what you were saying before.

PATIENT: The Scripture promises a healing if we call upon the Lord. I have called upon the Lord and claimed this promise. But on the other hand I want his will to be done. And this above all, beyond my personal considerations.

DOCTOR: What have you changed in your day-to-day life since you have been aware of your cancer? Has anything changed in your life?

PATIENT: Meaning in activity? I will be out of the hospital in just a couple of weeks and I don't know what will take place. I have just been living, more or less, from day to day in the hospital. Because you know hospital routine, you know what goes on.

CHAPLAIN: If I hear you correctly in what you said earlier, it struck me as familiar. What you are saying is what Jesus said before he faced the cross, "Not my will but thine be done."

PATIENT: I hadn't thought about that.

CHAPLAIN: It is the meaning of what you said. You have wished for hope if possible that it not be your time, but you override that wish with a deeper wish that thy will be done.

PATIENT: I know that I have a very short period to live, maybe a few years with the treatment I'm taking now and it may be a few months. Of course, none of us have any guarantee that we are going to get back to our homes tonight.

DOCTOR: Do you have any concrete picture of how it is going to be?

PATIENT: No. I know that it has been provided, the Scriptures tell us so and on this I lay my hope.

CHAPLAIN: I don't think we should continue. Dr. G. hasn't been able to be up until just recently, maybe a couple of more minutes.

PATIENT: Well, I feel very well.

CHAPLAIN: Do you? I told the doctor you wouldn't be kept very long.

DOCTOR: We'll leave it up to you to say if you get just slightly tired. This talking together very frankly about such dreaded topic, how does this make you feel, Dr. G.?

PATIENT: Well, I don't find that a dreaded topic at all. After Rev. I. and Rev. N. left the room this morning, I had some time to think and it didn't affect me in any way particularly other than I hope that I might be of value to somebody else who is facing this if he doesn't have the faith that I have.

DOCTOR: What do you think we can learn from our interviewing dying patients and very sick patients that would help us to be more effective in helping them face it, especially those who are not in a way as lucky as you are? Because you have this faith and it's apparent that it really helps you.

PATIENT: This is something I have explored quite a bit since I have been sick. I am of the temperament that I want to know the complete prognosis, whereas there are some people who when they find out they have a terminal illness they almost all go completely to pieces. Now this is something that I feel only experience can tell, what you can do as you approach a patient. DOCTOR: This is one of the reasons why we interview patients here with nursing staff and other hospital personnel able to see this. To see patient after patient, to elicit which ones really want to talk about it and which ones prefer not to mention it. PATIENT: Your first visits, I think, should be of a neutral nature, until you find out how deeply the patient felt about himself and his experience and his religion and faith. CHAPLAIN: I think that Dr. R. referred to Dr. G. as being lucky, but I think here you are saying meaningful things come out of this experience such as your relationship with your son which is at a different level and your appreciation of his growth came out of this. PATIENT: Yes, I thought we were lucky too. I was going to comment on this because I don't feel that this particular area is a thing of luck. This thing of knowing the Lord your Saviour is something that is not luck; it is a very deep and wonderful experience and I think it prepares one for the vicissitudes of life as it were, the trials that we face. We all have to face trials, or face illnesses. But this does prepare you to accept them, because you know that as I said a little bit ago being shot from twenty feet away and the person misses you, you know that there is some other power than the fact that you are a good dodger or whatever. But we have heard it said that there are no atheists in the foxholes, which is true. You hear men become very close to the Lord in a foxhole, or when their life is in danger, not a foxhole but even coming into a serious accident and realizing suddenly that they are in it and they automatically call on the name of the Lord. It is not a case of luck. It is a case of seeking and finding that which the Lord has for us. DOCTOR: I didn't mean lucky in a casual way, just as a chance happening, more like a happy, fortunate thing. PATIENT: I understand, yes. Yes, it is a happy experience. It is amazing how you can feel this experience during a period of illnesses like this when you have others praying for you, and realize that others are praying for you. It is a tremendous help to me. It has been.

CHAPLAIN: It's interesting I did mention to Dr. R. just as we came to the seminar—not only have you experienced people remembering you but your wife was also able to give some strength to people who had relatives dying here and offer a prayer to them.

PATIENT: This is another thing that I was going to mention. My wife has changed quite a bit in this period. She has become much stronger. She was quite dependent on me. I am, you probably already imagine, a very independent individual and I believe in taking my responsibilities as they come. Therefore she hasn't had the opportunity, as it were, to do many of the things that some women do such as taking care of the business of the family and so on, and it has made her quite dependent. But she has changed quite a bit. She is now much deeper and much stronger.

DOCTOR: Do you think it would help if we would talk with her a little bit about it, or would it be too much for her?

PATIENT: Oh, I don't think it would hurt a bit. She is a Christian, she knows the Lord is her Saviour and has ever since she was a child. In fact she had a healing, as a child, of an eye. The specialists were ready to send her to the hospital in St. Louis to have an eye removed because of an ulcer on the eye. She received a miraculous cure and in this cure she brought other individuals, one a physician, to a knowledge of the Lord. She is a strong Methodist woman anyway, but this was the solidifying element. She was about ten years old, but the experience itself with this physician was the solidifying element in her life.

DOCTOR: Before you had this illness, in your younger days, did you have any big stress or something very sad happen to you? So that you could compare how you took it then compared to how you take this now.

PATIENT: No, I have often looked at myself and wondered how I've been able to do this. I know it has only been through the support of the Lord. Because I've never had any deep stress other than danger that affected me at all. And of course I was a combat man during World War II. This was my first stress and the first time in my life that I actually faced, knew that I was facing death if I did such and such a thing.

DOCTOR: I think we have to finish, maybe we can drop in once in a while.

PATIENT: I appreciate it.

DOCTOR: Thank you very much for coming.

PATIENT: I've enjoyed coming.

Mrs. G., Dr. G.'s wife, came visiting as we were taking the patient down the hall for the interview. The chaplain, who knew her from previous visits, explained to her briefly what we were in the process of doing. She expressed interest in it and we invited her to join us later on. While the interview with her husband was in progress, she waited in the adjoining room and was asked to come in as her husband was returned to his room. She thus had little time for reflection or second thoughts. (We usually attempt to allow enough time between request and actual interview in order to give the interviewee a truly free choice.)

DOCTOR: This takes you kind of by surprise to come and visit your husband and then come to an interview like this. Have you spoken with the chaplain of what this is all about?

MRS. G: Sort of.

DOCTOR: How did you deal with the awareness of your husband's quite unexpected and serious illness?

MRS. G: Well, I might say I was shook up at first.

DOCTOR: He was a healthy man until that summer?

MRS. G: Yes, that's right.

DOCTOR: Never very ill or complaining, nothing?

MRS. G: Yes. Just complaining of a few pains.

DOCTOR: And then?

MRS. G: We doctored and someone suggested X-rays. And then we had the surgery done. And really it wasn't until then that I was real aware of the fact that it was real serious.

DOCTOR: Who told you and how did they tell you?

MRS. G: Our physician is a very close friend of ours. Well, before he entered into surgery he called me and told me, now this possibly could be a malignancy. And I said, "Oh, no." He said, "Yes, so I'm just warning you." So I was a little prepared but to the extent when I was told that it was more serious this just didn't click with me that we had bad news. "We didn't get it all," the doctor said. That was the first thing I remember. Well, I was really shook up because I thought, well now, it couldn't have been going on very long. One of the physicians said that he had only about three to four months and, how soon can you catch these things? So, the first thing I did is I prayed about it. While he was in surgery I prayed. I prayed a very selfish prayer, that this would not be malignant. Of course, the way the human being is this way. You want it to be your way. Until I put it in God's will I didn't have the peace that I really should. Of course the day of the surgery was bad anyhow, and that long night was terrible. In the night I really found a peace that really gave me courage. I found many passages in the Bible that gave me strength. We have a family altar in our home. I might say, just before this happened we memorized a Scripture and we repeat it and repeat it. It's found in Isaiah 33:3 and it says, "Call unto me, I will answer thee and show thee great and mighty things that thou knowest not," and we all memorized that.

DOCTOR: That was before the awareness of this illness?

MRS. G: Just about two weeks before. And you know that came right to me and I kept repeating that. And then I had so many things in the book of John that came to me. If you ask *anything* in my name I will do it. And I wanted God's will, but it was only through this that I found myself. I could go on because we have been very devoted and we just had the one boy. My boy had been away to college. College kids are occupied with so many things, but he came in, he came right along with me and we literally searched the Scriptures for help. He made such nice prayers along with me, and then the people of our church were very, very nice. They would come in and have different passages in the Bible to read. I've read them many many times but they never meant what they did to me now.

CHAPLAIN: At this point they seemed to pick up and almost verbalize your feelings.

MRS. G: Every time I opened the Bible there would be something just standing there, just like it was speaking forth to me. I got to the point where I just thought, well, now maybe there will be some good out of this. That's just the way I would take it and I found daily strength to meet it. My husband had a great faith and when he was told all about his condition he said to me, "What would you do if this were told to you, that you had four to fourteen months to live?" I'd just put it all in God's hands and trust in him. Of course, in the medical field I wanted everything possible that could be done for him. And our doctors told us there wasn't anything else and I even suggested cobalt, or even some type of X-ray or radiation, you know. They didn't suggest it, they said it was a fatal case. And my husband just isn't the type to give up either. So then when I talked it over with him, and I said, you know God, the only way God can work is through man and he inspires doctors. And, I said, we saw this little article, a neighbor brought over a magazine and we read it. I didn't even consult my husband. I just contacted the doctor here at the hospital.

DOCTOR: There was an article?

MRS. G: Yes, in a magazine. I thought, well now, they are having so much success. I know there isn't a cure, but they are having success. I'll just contact him. I wrote a letter and sent it special delivery and he received it at his desk on Saturday morning. His secretary wasn't in so he called me. He said, "I was very interested in your letter, it was very explanatory but I need a microspic report. You could get it from your doctor and send it just like you did my letter. You mailed it yesterday and I got it this morning." So that's what I did. I sent it. He called and he said, "Just as soon as I get a bed, they are remodeling this section, I'll call you." He says now, "I can't make you too many promises, but I certainly don't believe in this fatalistic approach." So, that really sounded wonderful to me. There was something else that we could do rather than just sit and wait like our doctors had told us.

Then it seemed like everything went so fast. We came by ambulance. And I might say that the night they examined him, they couldn't give us very much hope. We were almost tempted to turn around and go home. And again I prayed about this. I left the hospital that night to go and stay with relatives. I didn't know what I would find the next morning. They left it so we could think about it, whether to go on with this treatment. Again I went and prayed about it and just said we'll try everything possible. I thought this is my husband's decision, not mine. That morning when I came in to the hospital, he had already made up his mind, "I'm going ahead with it." They said he would lose forty to sixty pounds and he had already lost so much through both surgeries. I really didn't know what to do. I just wasn't too surprised because I felt this was the way it would be going. And then, after they started the treatment, he was very, very ill. But like I said, they didn't make us any promises so we just had this one ray of hope that the treatment would possibly help to decrease the tumor and that the bowel would open up. We had a partial bowel obstruction and this was a chance. All the way through I had my moments of discouragement, but I would talk to different patients, here in the hospital, that had been very ill people. And I think, well, here I am encouraging them and look how black things look on our side a lot of times. But, I just kept staying right in there. I still have that approach. I know that research is going on in this field and I know that again the Scripture says that nothing is impossible with God.

DOCTOR: Though you accept the fate, you also have some hope that something might still happen.

MRS. G: That's right.

DOCTOR: You also talk in terms of *we*, we had surgery, we decided to go ahead. It's really like you and he are really in tune to do things together.

MRS. G: I really think if it isn't meant for him to get well, if this is his time, I believe it's in God's will.

DOCTOR: How old is your husband?

MRS. G: He was fifty the day we came in here.

DOCTOR: The day he came to the hospital.

CHAPLAIN: Would you say that this experience has brought your family closer together?

MRS. G: Oh, my, it has brought us closer. If nothing else, it has been a dependency on God. We are pretty self-sufficient, we think, but in times like these you find that you are not very much. I have learned to depend and live one day at a time and quit planning. We have today but we may not have tomorrow. And I say if this is fatal for my husband, I feel like it must be in God's hands, and maybe through our experience maybe somebody can have an added hope or strength in God.

CHAPLAIN: Have you had a good relationship with the staff? I know you have a pleasant relationship with other patients because we've talked together in trying to bring some help to relatives of other patients. I sat there and listened to some of this. I was reminded of what you said a while ago. You found yourself talking to other people with optimism. What's it been like here for someone from out of town? What kind of support have you received from staff? What does a family member experience at this point in terms of someone as close to death as your husband?

MRS. G: Well, since I am a nurse, I have talked with nurses quite a bit. I find there are some very devout Christian nurses who say that faith in God has a lot to do, that fighting, that not giving up has a lot to do with it. As a whole I think I have been able to talk with them. They have been so frank and so open, that's what I like about it. And I believe that members of the family are less in confusion if they're explained and told the facts even though hope is dim. I think people accept it. And I really think a lot of the hospital, I really think that they make a mighty fine team.

CHAPLAIN: Would you say this was true not only for yourself but from what you have experienced with other families that have been here?

MRS. G: Yes.

CHAPLAIN: They want to know?

MRS. G: Yes. So many families will say, oh, they are just wonderful here and if they don't know, nobody else does. That's the attitude I find, people just going out on the sun porches and talking with different visitors. They are saying this is a wonderful place. They are right on the ball.

DOCTOR: Is there anything we could improve?

MRS. G: I suppose we all could improve. I do realize there is a shortage of nursing care. I think sometimes the bells are being unanswered when they really should be, but as a whole I think this is pretty general everywhere. It's just a shortage, comparing back thirty years, when I nursed, it has changed a lot. But I do think that the critically ill people are given a lot of attention without special nurses.

DOCTOR: Do you have any questions? Mrs. G., who told your husband how ill he was?

MRS. G: I told him first.

DOCTOR: How did you tell him that and when?

MRS. G: Three days after the first surgery in the hospital I told him. He said on the way to the hospital, "Now, if this is malignant don't flip your lid." That's the term he used. I said, "I won't, but it won't be." But the third day our physician friend went on vacation. This was in July, and I told him. He just kind of looked at me and I said, "I suppose you want to know what they have done." "Oh," he says, "nobody has told me." I said, "Well, they took eighteen inches of your lower colon." He said, "Eighteen inches?!" He said, "Well good, then they hooked on to healthy tissue." I didn't go on with the rest of it until we got home. And then I would judge about three weeks after the surgery, we were sitting in our family room, just the two of us, and I told him. He said, "Well, we just have to make the best of what is left." That's just his attitude. So then for two months he went back to the office and worked. We took a vacation. My son had a break in college and we went out to Estes Park. We really had a nice time. He even played some golf.

DOCTOR: In Colorado?

MRS. G: Yes. My son was born in Colorado. We were stationed there when my husband was in the service. We love it there and we vacation there almost every year. And I was so thankful that we had that time together because we really did enjoy it. It was just about a week after that he went back to the office and then started with this bowel obstruction. And the tumor where they had operated had grown again.

DOCTOR: Did he close his office up completely?

MRS. G: He closed it five weeks only. Then he went back after his first surgery. And he opened up after we took our vacation. He was just there about a week, sixteen days he has worked since his surgery on July the 7th.

DOCTOR: What is happening now with the office?

MRS. G: The office is just still closed up. The office girl takes calls. Everyone wants to know when he is coming back. So we, I have advertised for sale, and we would like to sell it. It's kind of a bad time of the year too. I have a man coming this month to look at it. And my husband has just been so ill and they put him on the critical list. I just couldn't leave but there are so many things I have to attend to back home. But my son has been coming back and forth.

DOCTOR: What is he studying?

MRS. G: Now he's finished. He started out in predental but then he switched and right now he has just been tending to things at home. Like I say, he has been in school steady and after his father went on critical his draft board gave him a deferment for a few months. So he is just kind of at a decision of what to do.

DOCTOR: I think we should finish. Do you have any questions, Mrs. G.?

MRS. G: You are doing all this to see if you can improve things?

DOCTOR: Well, it has a multitude of reasons. The main reason is to understand from the very sick patient what they are going through. What kind of fears and fantasies or loneliness they experience and how we can understand and help them. Each patient we interview in here has different kinds of problems and conflicts. Once in a while we also like to see the family, how they are dealing with the situation and how the staff can be of assistance.

MRS. G: I've had people say to me, "I don't know how you can do it." Why, I know just how much a piece of God is in a person's life and I've always felt that way. I went through nurses' training and I was always fortunate to meet good Christian people. I've heard and read different things, even about movie stars. If they have a faith and believe in God, it seems like it's just something to stand on. That's what I really think and I think a happy marriage is based on that.

Dr. G.'s wife gives a good description of the reaction of a close family member to such unexpected news of a malignancy. Her first reaction, shock, followed by a brief denial, "No, it cannot be true." She then attempts to find some meaning in this turmoil and finds solace in the Scriptures, which have always been a source of inspiration for this family. In spite of her apparent acceptance, she too maintains the hope "research is going on" and prays for a miracle. While this change in her family has deepened their religious experiences, it has also allowed her time to become more self-sufficient and independent.

The outstanding feature of this double interview is perhaps again the two different stories we hear about how the patient was told. This is quite typical and has to be understood if we are not to take things at face value.

Dr. G. explains how his son had matured and finally faced up to the responsibility by sharing the bad news with him. He is obviously proud of his son, sees him as a mature, grown-up man, who can take on the responsibilities when he has to leave his rather dependent wife. Mrs. G., on the other hand, insists that it was she who had the courage and strength to tell her husband about the outcome of the operation, not giving her son credit for this difficult task. She contradicted herself later on several occasions so that it seems unlikely that her version was the reality. Nevertheless her wish to have told her husband also says something about her needs. She wishes to be strong, to be able to face it, and to talk about it. She wants to be the one who shares good and bad with her husband and who seeks solace and strength in the Scriptures to accept whatever may come.

A family like this can best be helped by a reassuring physician who communicates that everything will be done that is possible and by an available pastor who visits the patient and his family as often as possible, making use of the resources the family has used in the past.

CHAPTER VIII

————— ◆ —————

Hope

*In desperate hope I go and search for her in all the
corners of my room; I find her not.*
   *My house is small and what once has gone from it
can never be regained.*
   *But infinite is thy mansion, my lord, and seeking her
I have come to thy door.*
   *I stand under the golden canopy of thine evening sky
and I lift my eager eyes to thy face.*
   *I have come to the brink of eternity from which
nothing can vanish—no hope, no happiness, no vision
of a face seen through tears.*
   *Oh, dip my emptied life into that ocean, plunge it
into the deepest fullness. Let me for once feel that lost
sweet touch in the allness of the universe.*

TAGORE,
from *Gitanjali*, LXXXVII

We have discussed so far the different stages that people go
through when they are faced with tragic news—defense
mechanisms in psychiatric terms, coping mechanisms to deal
with extremely difficult situations. These means will last for
different periods of time and will replace each other or exist at

times side by side. The one thing that usually persists through all these stages is hope. Just as children in Barracks L 318 and L 417 in the concentration camp of Terezin maintained their hope years ago, although out of a total of about 15,000 children under fifteen years of age only around 100 came out of it alive.

The sun has made a veil of gold
So lovely that my body aches
Above, the heavens shriek with blue
Convinced I've smiled by some mistake.
The world's abloom and seems to smile.
I want to fly but where, how high?
If in barbed wire, things can bloom
Why couldn't I? I will not die!

1944, ANONYMOUS
"On a Sunny Evening"

In listening to our terminally ill patients we were always impressed that even the most accepting, the most realistic patients left the possibility open for some cure, for the discovery of a new drug or the "last-minute success in a research project," as Mr. J. expressed it (his interview follows in this chapter). It is this glimpse of hope which maintains them through days, weeks, or months of suffering. It is the feeling that all this must have some meaning, will pay off eventually if they can only endure it for a little while longer. It is the hope that occasionally sneaks in, that all this is just like a nightmare and not true; that they will wake up one morning to be told that the doctors are ready to try out a new drug which seems promising, that they will use it on him and that he may be the chosen, special patient, just as the first heart transplant patient must have felt that he was chosen to play a very special role in life. It gives the terminally ill a sense of a special mission in life which helps them maintain their spirits, will enable them to endure more tests when everything becomes such a strain—in a sense it is a rationalization for their suffering at times; for others it remains a form of temporary but needed denial.

No matter what we call it, we found that all our patients main-

tained a little bit of it and were nourished by it in especially difficult times. They showed the greatest confidence in the doctors who
allowed for such hope—realistic or not—and appreciated it when
hope was offered in spite of bad news. This does not mean that doctors have to tell them a lie; it merely means that we share with them
the hope that something unforeseen may happen, that they may
have a remission, that they will live longer than is expected. If a
patient stops expressing hope, it is usually a sign of imminent
death. They may say, "Doctor, I think I have had it," or "I guess this
is it," or they may put it like the patient who always believed in a
miracle, who one day greeted us with the words, "I think this is the
miracle—I am ready now and not even afraid any more." All
these patients died within twenty-four hours. While we maintained
hope with them, we did not reinforce hope when they finally
gave it up, not with despair but in a stage of final acceptance.

The conflicts we have seen in regard to hope arose from two
main sources. The first and most painful one was the conveyance
of hopelessness either on part of the staff or family when the
patient still needed hope. The second source of anguish came
from the family's inability to accept a patient's final stage; they
desperately clung to hope when the patient himself was ready to
die and sensed the family's inability to accept this fact (as illus-
trated in the cases of Mrs. W. and Mr. H.).

What happens with the "pseudo-terminal syndrome" patient
who has been given up by his physician and then—after being
given adequate treatment—makes a comeback? Implicitly or
explicitly these patients have been "written off." They may have
been told that "there is nothing else we can do for you" or they
may just have been sent home in unexpressed anticipation of
their imminent death. When these patients are treated with all
available therapy, they will be able to regard their comeback as "a
miracle," "a new lease on life," or "some extra time I did not ask
for," depending on previous management and communications.

The relevant message that Dr. Bell* communicates is to give
each patient a chance for the most effective possible treatment

*See Bibliography.

and not to regard each seriously ill patient as terminal, thus giving up on them. I would add that we should not "give up" on any patient, terminal or not terminal. It is the one who is beyond medical help who needs as much if not more care than the one who can look forward to another discharge. If we give up on such a patient, he may give up himself and further medical help may be forthcoming too late because he lacks the readiness and spirit to "make it once more." It is far more important to say, "To my knowledge I have done everything I can to help you. I will continue, however, to keep you as comfortable as possible." Such a patient will keep his glimpse of hope and continue to regard his physician as a friend who will stick it out to the end. He will not feel deserted or abandoned the moment the doctor regards him as beyond the possibility of a cure.

The majority of our patients made a comeback, in some way or another. Many of them had given up hope of ever relating their concerns to anyone. Many of them felt isolated and deserted, more of them felt cheated out of the opportunity of being considered in important decisions. Approximately half of our patients were discharged to go home or to a nursing home, to be readmitted later on. They all expressed their appreciation of sharing with us their concern about the seriousness of their illness and their hopes. They did not regard their discussions of death and dying as either premature or contraindicated in view of their "comeback." Many of our patients related the ease and comfort of their return home, after having settled their concerns prior to their discharge. Several of them asked to meet with their families in our presence before going home, in order to drop the façade and to enjoy the last few weeks together fully.

It might be helpful if more people would talk about death and dying as an intrinsic part of life just as they do not hesitate to mention when someone is expecting a new baby. If this were done more often, we would not have to ask ourselves if we ought to bring this topic up with a patient, or if we should wait for the last admission. Since we are not infallible and can never be sure which is the last admission, it may just be another rationalization which allows us to avoid the issue.

We have seen several patients who were depressed and morbidly uncommunicative until we spoke with them about the terminal stage of their illness. Their spirits were lightened, they began to eat again, and a few of them were discharged once more, much to the surprise of their families and the medical staff. I am convinced that we do more harm by avoiding the issue than by using time and timing to sit, listen, and share.

I mention timing because patients are no different from the rest of us in that we have our moments when we feel like talking about what burdens us and times when we wish to think about more cheerful things, no matter how real or unrealistic they are. As long as the patient knows that we will take the extra time when *he* feels like talking, when we are able to perceive his cues, we will witness that the majority of patients wish to share their concerns with another human being and react with relief and more hope to such dialogues.

If this book serves no other purpose but to sensitize family members of terminally ill patients and hospital personnel to the implicit communications of dying patients, then it has fulfilled its task. If we, as members of the helping professions, can help the patient and his family to get "in tune" to each other's needs and come to an acceptance of an unavoidable reality together, we can help to avoid much unnecessary agony and suffering on the part of the dying and even more so on the part of the family that is left behind.

The following interview with Mr. J. represents an example of the stage of anger and demonstrates—at times in a disguised way—the phenomenon of ever-present hope.

Mr. J. was a fifty-three-year-old Negro man who was hospitalized with mycosis fungoides, a malignant skin disorder which he describes in detail in the following interview. This illness necessitated his resorting to disability insurance and is characterized by states of relapses and remissions.

When I visited him the day before our seminar session, the patient felt lonely and in a talkative mood. He related very quickly in a dramatic and colorful fashion the many aspects of this unpleasant illness. He made it difficult for me to leave and held me back on several occasions. Much in contrast to that unplanned meeting, he expressed more annoyance, at times even anger, during the session behind the one-way mirror. The day before the seminar session he had initiated the discussion of death and dying, whereas during the session he said, "I don't think about dying, I think about living."

I mention this since it is relevant to our care of terminally ill patients, that they have days, hours, or minutes when they wish to talk about such matters. They may, like Mr. J. the day before, volunteer their philosophy of life and death and we may consider them ideal patients for such a teaching session. We tend to ignore the fact that the same patient may wish to talk only about the pleasant aspects of life the next day; we should respect his wishes. We did not do this during the interview, as we attempted to regain some of the meaningful material he presented the day before.

I should say that this is a danger mainly when an interview is part of a teaching program. Forcing questions and answers for the benefit of students should never occur during such an interview. The person should always come first and the patient's wishes should always be respected even if it means having a classroom of fifty students and no patient to interview.

DOCTOR: Mr. J., just for the introduction, how long have you been in the hospital?

PATIENT: This time I've been in since April the 4th of this year.

DOCTOR: How old are you?

PATIENT: I'm fifty-three years old.

DOCTOR: You have heard what we are doing in this seminar?

PATIENT: I have. Will you lead me with questions?

DOCTOR: Yes.

PATIENT: All right, you just go right ahead, whenever you are ready.

DOCTOR: I'd be curious to get a better picture of you because I know very little about you.

PATIENT: I see.

DOCTOR: You have been a healthy man, married, working, ah—

PATIENT: That's right, three children.

DOCTOR: Three children. When did you get sick?

PATIENT: Well, I went on disability in 1963. I think I first came in contact with this disease around 1948. I first started out with small rashes on my left chest, and under my right shoulder blade. And first it was no more than what anybody gets in the course of a lifetime. And I used the usual ointments, calamine lotion, vaseline, and different things that you buy in the drug store. Didn't bother me too much. But gradually by, I'd say by 1955, the lower part of my body was involved, not to any great extent. There was a dryness, a scalyness had settled in, and I'd use a lot of greasy ointments and things like that to keep myself moist and as comfortable as possible. I still kept on working. In fact, certain periods through there I had two jobs because my daughter was going to college and I wanted to make sure that she finished. So I'd say by 1957 it had reached a point where I had started going to different doctors. I went to Dr. X for a period of about three months and he didn't make any improvement. The visits were cheap enough, but the prescriptions were about fifteen to eighteen dollars a week. When you are raising a family of three children on a workman's salary, even if you are working two jobs, you can't handle a situation like that. And I did go through the clinic and they made a casual examination which didn't satisfy me. I didn't bother to go back to them. And I just knocked around, feeling, I guess, more and more miserable all the time until in 1962 Dr. Y had me admitted to the P. Hospital. I was in there about five weeks and really nothing happened and I came out of there and finally went back to the first clinic. Finally in March of 1963 they admitted me to this hospital. I was in such bad shape by then that I went on disability.

DOCTOR: This was in '63?

PATIENT: In '63.

DOCTOR: Did you have any idea what kind of illness you had by then?

PATIENT: I knew it was mycosis fungoides and everybody else knew it.

DOCTOR: So, how long did you know the name of your illness?

PATIENT: Well, I was suspicious of it for some time, but then it was confirmed by a biopsy.

DOCTOR: A long time ago?

PATIENT: Not a long time ago, just a few months before the actual diagnosis was made. But you get one of these conditions and you read everything you can get your hands on. You listen to everything, and you learn the names of the different diseases. And from what I read, mycosis fungoides fit right into the picture and finally it was confirmed, and by then I was just about shot. My ankles had started to swell up on me, I was in a constant state of perspiration, and I was thoroughly miserable.

DOCTOR: Is that what you mean by "by then I was thoroughly shot?" That you felt so miserable? Is that what you mean?

PATIENT: Sure. I was just miserable—itching, scaling, perspiring, ankle hurting, just a completely, thoroughly, utterly miserable human being. Now, of course, these kind of times you get a little resentful. I guess you wonder, why does this happen to me. And then you come to your senses, and you say, "Well, you are no better than anybody else, why not you?" That way you can sort of reconcile yourself because then everybody you see you start looking at their skin. You look if they have any blemishes, any signs of dermatitis since your whole sole interest in life is to see if they have any blemishes and who else is suffering from something similar, you know. And I guess, too, people are looking at you because you're much different-looking from them—

DOCTOR: Because this is a visible kind of illness.

PATIENT: It is a visible kind of an ailment.

DOCTOR: What does this illness mean to you? What is this mycosis fungoides to you?

PATIENT: It means to me that up to now they haven't cured anybody. They have had remissions for certain periods of time, they have had remissions for indefinite periods of time. It means to me that somewhere, someone is going to do research. There are a lot of good brains working on this condition. They might discover a cure while in the process of working on something else. And it means to me that I grit my teeth and go on from day to day and hope that some morning I'll sit up on the side of the bed and the doctor will be there and he will say, "I want to give you this shot," and it will be something like a vaccine or something, and in a few days it will clear up.

DOCTOR: Something that works!

PATIENT: I will be able to go back to work. I like my job because I did work myself into a supervisory capacity.

DOCTOR: What did you do?

PATIENT: Actually, I was active general foreman in the main post office down here. I had worked myself to the point where I was in charge of the foremen. I had seven or eight foremen who accounted to me every night. Rather then dealing with just the help, I dealt with more or less operations. I had good prospects for advancement because I knew and enjoyed my work. I didn't begrudge any time that I spent on the job. I was always helping my wife when the kids were getting up. We hoped they would be out of the way and maybe we could enjoy some of the things that we had read about and heard about.

DOCTOR: Like what?

PATIENT: Traveling a little, I mean we never had a vacation. Our first child was a premature baby and it was touch and go for a long time. She was sixty-one days old before she came home. I still have a sack of receipts from the hospital at home now. I paid her bill out at two dollars a week and in those days I was only making about seventeen dollars a week. I used to get off the train and rush two bottles of my wife's breast milk to the hospital, pick up two empty bottles, come back to the station, and go on to my job in the city. I would then work all day and bring those two empty bottles home at night. And she had enough milk for, I guess, for all the premature kids in the nursery over there. We kept them pretty well supplied and this meant to me that we got over the hump with everything. I would soon be in a salary bracket where you don't have to pinch every nickel. It just meant for me that we would maybe sometime look forward to a planned vacation instead of, well, we can't go anywhere, this kid has to have some dental work, or something like that. That's all it meant to me. It meant a few good years of more or less relaxed living.

DOCTOR: After a long, hard life of trouble.

PATIENT: Well, most people put in a longer and harder struggle than I do. I never considered it much of a struggle. I worked in that foundry and we did piece work. I could work like a demon. I had fellows that came to my house and told my wife that I worked too hard. Well, she jumped all over me about that, and I would tell her it was a matter of jealousy when you work around men with muscle, they don't want you to have more muscle than they have and I definitely did, because wherever I went to work, I worked. And whenever there was any advancement, I made it, whatever advancement there was to be made. In fact, they called me into the office over where I was working and they told me when we make a colored foreman, you will be it. I was elated for a moment but when I went out—they said *when*—that could be anywhere from now to the year two thousand. So it deflated me to an extent that I had to work under those conditions. But still nothing was hard for me in those days. I had plenty of strength, I had my youth, and I just believed I could do anything.

DOCTOR: Tell me, Mr. J., now that you are not that young anymore, and maybe you can't do all those things anymore, how do you take it? Presumably there is no doctor who stands there with an injection, a medical cure.

PATIENT: That's right. You learn how to take these things. You first get that realization that maybe you won't ever get well.

DOCTOR: What does that do to you?

PATIENT: It shakes you up, you try not to think about things like that.

DOCTOR: Do you ever think about it?

PATIENT: Sure, there are a lot of nights I don't sleep very well. I think about a million things during the night. But you don't dwell on those things. I had a good life as a child and my mother is still living. She comes out here quite often to see me. I can always run back over my mind and go over some incident that happened. We used to take the jalopy and travel within our area. We did quite a bit of traveling in those days when they had very few paved roads and the other roads were muddy. You'd get somewhere, stuck on a muddy road up to the hubcaps, and you might have to push or pull or something like that. And so I guess I had a pretty nice childhood, my parents were very nice. There was no harshness or ill temper in our house. It made for a pleasant life. I think in terms of those things and I realize I'm pretty well blessed because there has been a rare man put in this world who has nothing but misery. I look around and find that I have had what I call a few bonus days.

DOCTOR: You have had a fulfilled life is really what you are saying. But does it make dying any easier?

PATIENT: I don't think about dying. I think about living. I think, you know I used to tell the kids, they were coming up, I would tell them now, do your best under all circumstances, and I said lots of times you are still gonna lose. I said, now you remember in this life you have to be lucky. That was an expression I used. And I always considered myself lucky. I look back and I think of all the boys who came along with me and are in jail and various prisons and places like that. And I had as good a chance as they had but I didn't make it. I always pulled away when they were about to get started into something that wasn't right. I had a lot of fights on account of that, they think you are afraid. But it is better to be leery of those things and fight for what you believe in, than it is to kick in and say, well, I'll go along. Because invariably sooner or later you are involved in something that can start you off on a life that you can't reverse. Oh, they say you can pull yourself up by your boot straps and all that but you get yourself some kind of a record and the first thing that happens in your neighborhood, and I don't care how old you get to be, they pick you up and want to know where were you such and such a night. I was fortunate enough to steer clear of all of that. So when I look it all over I have to say that I've been lucky and I project that a little further. I still have a little luck left. I mean, I have had some rough luck you might call it, so sooner or later this thing has to even out and that's going to be the day that I walk out of here and people won't even recognize me.

DOCTOR: Is this what kept you from ever getting desperate?

PATIENT: Nothing keeps you from ever getting desperate. I don't care how well adjusted you are, you will get desperate. But I will say this has kept me from the breaking point. You get desperate. You get to a place where you can't sleep and after a while you are fighting it. The harder you fight it, the harder it is on you, because it can actually get to be a physical battle. You will break out into a sweat just as though you are exerting yourself physically but it's all mental.

DOCTOR: How do you fight it? Does religion help you? Or certain people help you?

PATIENT: I don't call myself a particularly religious man.

DOCTOR: What gives you the strength to do this for twenty years? It's just about twenty years isn't it?

PATIENT: Well, yes, I guess your sources of strength come from so many different angles it would be pretty hard to say. My mother has a deep abiding faith. Any effort that I give this thing less than my full effort, I would feel that I am letting her down. So I say with the help of my mother. My wife has a deep abiding faith, so it is also with the help of my wife. My sisters, it always seems to be the females in the family who have the deeper religion, and they are the ones who are, I guess, the most sincere in their prayers. To me, the average person praying is begging for something. Always had too much pride to actually beg. I think maybe that's why I can't put all the full feeling into what I say here. I can't give vent to all my feelings along those lines, I guess.

DOCTOR: What did you have as a religious background, Catholic or Protestant. . . ?

PATIENT: I'm a Catholic now, I was converted Catholic. One of my parents was Baptist and one was Methodist. They made it fine.

DOCTOR: How did you become a Catholic?

PATIENT: It seemed to fit into my idea of what a religion should be.

DOCTOR: When did you make that change?

PATIENT: When the kids were small. They went to Catholic schools. In the early '50's I figure.

DOCTOR: Was this in any way connected with your illness?

PATIENT: No, because at the time the skin didn't bother me too much and I just thought that as soon as I get a chance to settle down and go to a doctor this will be cleared up, you know?

DOCTOR: Ah—

PATIENT: But it never happened like that.

DOCTOR: Is your wife Catholic?

PATIENT: Yes, she is. She was converted at the time I was.

DOCTOR: Yesterday you told me something. I don't know if you want to bring it up again. I think it would be helpful. When I asked you how you take all this, you gave me the whole scale of possibilities of how a man can become—ending it all and thinking about suicide, and why this is not possible for you. You mentioned also a fatalistic approach, can you repeat that again?

PATIENT: Well, I said that I had a doctor once who told me, "I couldn't, I don't know how you take it. I'd kill myself."

DOCTOR: That was a doctor who said that?

PATIENT: Yes. So then I said, killing myself is out because I'm too yellow to kill myself. That eliminates one possibility that I don't have to think about. I finally rid my mind of encumbrances as I go on, so that I have less and less and less to think about. So I eliminated the idea of killing myself by the process of eliminating death. Then I reached the conclusion that, well, you're here now. Now you can either turn your face to the wall or you can cry. Or you can try to get whatever little fun and pleasure out of life you can, considering your condition. And certain things happen. You may watch a good TV program or listen to interesting conversation and after a few minutes you are not aware of the itching and the uncomfortable feeling. All these little things I call bonuses and I figure that if I can have enough bonuses together one of these days everything will be a bonus and it will stretch out to infinity and every day will be a good day. So I don't worry too much. When I have my miserable feelings I just more or less distract myself or try to sleep. Because after all, sleep is the best medicine that has ever been invented. Sometimes I don't even sleep, and I just lie there quietly. You learn how to take these things, what else can you do? You jump up and scream and holler and you can beat your head against the wall, but when you do all that you're still itching, you're still miserable.

DOCTOR: It's the itching that seems to be the worst part of your illness. Do you have any pain?

PATIENT: So far the itching has been the worst, but right along the bottom of my feet it is so sore that it's like torture to put any weight on them. So I'd say up to now the itching, and the dryness and the scaliness has been my biggest problem. I have a personal warfare on these scales. It gets to be a funny thing. You get your bed full of scales and you make a brush like that, and ordinarily any kind of debris just sails right off. The scales jump up and down in one place like they have claws and it gets to be a frantic effort.

DOCTOR: To get rid of them?

PATIENT: To get rid of them, because they will fight you to a standstill. You'll be exhausted and you'll look and they are still there. So I even thought about a small vacuum cleaner, to keep myself clean. Staying clean gets to be an obsession with you because by the time you take a bath and put all this goo on you, you don't feel clean anyway. So right away you feel like you need another bath. You could spend your life going in and out of the bath.

DOCTOR: Who is most helpful in this trouble? As long as you are in the hospital, Mr. J?

PATIENT: Who is the most helpful? I'd say you couldn't meet anybody around here, everybody, they anticipate my needs and help. They do a lot of things I don't even think about. One of the girls noticed that my fingers were sore and I was having trouble lighting a cigarette. I heard her tell the rest of the girls, "When you come through here you check with him and see if he wants a cigarette." Why, you can't beat that.

DOCTOR: They really care.

PATIENT: You know, it's a wonderful feeling, but everywhere I have been and all through my life, people have liked me. I am profoundly thankful for that. I am humbly thankful. I have never gone out of my way, I don't think, to be a do-gooder. But I can find any number of people in this city who could point out times on various jobs that I helped them out. I don't even know why, it was just a part of me to put a person mentally at ease. I would go to the effort to help this person adjust himself. And I can find so many people and they tell other people how I helped them. But by the same token everybody I have ever known has helped me. I don't believe I have an enemy in the world. I don't believe I know a person in the world who wishes me any kind of harm. My roommate from college was here a couple of years ago. We talked about the days we were in school together. We remembered the dormitory when at any hour of the day someone would make a suggestion, let's go down and turn out so-and-so's room. And they would come down and throw you out bodily, out of your own room. Good clean horseplay, rough, but good fun. And he was telling his son how we used to stand them off and stack them up like cord wood. We were both strong, we were both the tough type. And we would actually stack them up in that hall, they never turned our room out. We had one roommate in there with us and he was on the track team and he ran the hundred-yard dash. Before five guys came in the door he could get out of that door and down that hall, was about seventy yards long. Nobody could have had him once he got started. So way late he would come back, we would have order restored and the room cleaned up and everything, and we'd all go to bed.

DOCTOR: Is this one of the bonuses you think about?

PATIENT: I look back on it and I think of the foolish things we did. Some guys came up one night and the room was cold. We wondered who could stand the most cold and naturally each one of us knew we could stand the most cold. So we decided to raise the window. No heat coming up or anything and it was seventeen below zero outside. I remember I had one of those woolen skullcaps on and two pair of pajamas and a robe and two pair of socks. I guess everybody else did the same thing. But when we awakened in the morning everything, every glass, and everything else in that room was frozen solid. And any wall you touched you were just liable to stick to it, it was just frozen solid. It took us four days to thaw out that bedroom and warm it up. I mean that's the kind of foolish thing you would do, you know. And sometimes somebody looks at me and sees a smile across my face, and thinks the guy is nuts, he is finally cracking. But it's just some incident that I think about that I get a kick out of. Now yesterday, you asked me what is the main thing that the doctors and nurses could do to help a patient. It depends a lot on the patient. It depends a lot on how sick the patient is. If you are really sick, you don't want to be bothered at all. You would just like to lay there and you don't want anybody fumbling over you or taking your blood pressure or your temperature. I mean, it seems that every time you relax someone has to do something with you. I think the doctors and the nurses should disturb you as little as possible. Because the minute you feel better, you are going to raise your head and be interested in things. And that's the time for them to come in and start gradually cheering you up and coaxing you.

DOCTOR: But Mr. J., when the very sick people are left alone, aren't they more miserable and more scared?

PATIENT: I don't think so. It's not a matter of leaving them alone, I don't mean to isolate these people or anything like that. I mean you are there in the room and you are resting nicely and there's someone plumping your pillows, you don't want your pillows plumped. Your head is resting nicely. They all mean well, so you go along with them. Then someone else comes along and "Do you want a glass of water?" Why, really if you wanted a glass of water you could ask for it, but they will pour you a glass of water. They are doing this out of sheer kindness of heart, trying to make you more comfortable. Whereas under certain conditions if everybody would just ignore you—just for the time being, you feel much better.

DOCTOR: Would you like to be left alone now, too?

PATIENT: Not, not too much, last week I had—

DOCTOR: I mean now, now during this interview. Is this making you tired, too?

PATIENT: Oh, I say tired, I mean I've got nothing to do but go down there and rest anyway. But ah, I don't see much point in this thing too much longer because after a while you get repetitious.

DOCTOR: You had some concern about that yesterday.

PATIENT: Yes, well, I had reason to be concerned because a week ago, had you seen me, you would not have even considered me for an interview because I was speaking in half sentences, I was speaking in half thoughts. I would not have known my name. But ah, I've come a long way since then.

CHAPLAIN: How do you feel about what has happened in this past week? Is this another stroke of your bonus?

PATIENT: Well, I look forward to having it happen like this, this thing travels in cycles, you know like a big wheel. It goes around and with the new medicine they tried on me, I look for some extenuation of these different feelings. I either expect to feel real well or feel real bad at first. I went through the bad spell and now I will have a good spell and I will feel pretty good because it happens like that. Even if I don't take any kind of medicine, if I just let things go.

DOCTOR: So you are entering your good cycle, now, right?

PATIENT: I think so.

DOCTOR: I think we will take you back to your room now.

PATIENT: Appreciate it.

DOCTOR: Thank you, Mr. J, for coming.

PATIENT: You are quite welcome.

Mr. J., whose twenty years of illness and suffering had made him somewhat of a philosopher, shows many signs of disguised anger. What he is really saying in this interview is. "I have been so good, why me?" He describes how tough and strong he was in his younger years, how he endured cold and hardship; how he cared for his children and family, how hard he worked and never allowed the bad guys to tempt him. After all this struggle, his children are grown up and he hoped for a few good years, to travel, to take a vacation, to enjoy the fruits of his labor. He knows on some level that these hopes are in vain. It takes all his energy now to stay sane, to fight the itching, the discomfort, the pain, which he so adequately describes.

He looks back at this fight, and eliminates step by step considerations which pass his mind. Suicide is "out," an enjoyable retirement is out of the question as well. His field of possibilities shrinks as the illness progresses. His expectations and requirements become smaller and he has finally accepted the fact that he has to live from one remission to the next. When he feels very bad he wants to be left alone to withdraw and attempt to sleep. When he feels better he will let the people know that he is ready to communicate again and becomes more sociable. "You have got to be lucky" means that he maintains the hope that there will be another remission. He also maintains the hope that some cure may be found, some new drug developed in time to relieve him of the suffering.

He maintained this hope to the very last day.

CHAPTER IX

The Patient's Family

The father came back from the funeral rites.
His boy of seven stood at the window, with eyes wide open and a golden amulet hanging from his neck, full of thoughts too difficult for his age.
His father took him in his arms and the boy asked him, "Where is mother?"
"In heaven," answered his father, pointing to the sky.

The boy raised his eyes to the sky and long gazed in silence. His bewildered mind sent abroad into the night the question, "Where is heaven?"
No answer came: and the stars seemed like the burning tears of that ignorant darkness.

TAGORE,
from *The Fugitive*, Part II, XXI

CHANGES IN THE HOUSEHOLD AND EFFECTS ON THE FAMILY

We cannot help the terminally ill patient in a really meaningful way if we do not include his family. They play a significant role during the time of illness and their reactions will contribute a lot to the patient's response to his illness. Serious illness and hospitalization of a husband, for example, may bring about relevant changes in the household which the wife has to get accustomed to. She may feel threatened by the loss of security and the end of her dependence on her husband. She will have to take on many chores previously done by him and will have to adjust her own schedule to the new, strange, and increased demands. She may suddenly have to get involved in business matters and their financial affairs, which she previously avoided doing.

If hospital visits are involved, arrangements may have to be made for transportation and for babysitters during her absence. There may be subtle or dramatic changes in the household and in the atmosphere at home, to which the children will also react, thus adding to the burden and increased responsibility of the mother. She will suddenly be faced with the fact that she is—at least temporarily—a lone parent.

With the worries and concerns about her husband, added work and responsibility also comes increased loneliness and—often—resentment. The expected assistance from relatives and friends may not be forthcoming or may take on forms which are both bewildering and unacceptable to the wife. Neighborly advice may be rejected as it may add to rather than decrease the burden. On the other hand, an understanding neighbor who does not come to "hear the latest" but who comes to relieve the mother of some of her tasks, cook an occasional meal, or take the children to a play, can be greatly appreciated. An example of this is given in the interview of Mrs. S.

A husband's sense of loss may be even greater, since he may be less flexible or at least less used to concerning himself with matters of children, school, after-school activities, meals, and clothing. This sense of loss may appear as soon as the wife is bedridden or limited in her functioning. There may be a reversal of roles which is more difficult to accept for a man than it is for a woman. Instead of being served, he may be expected to serve. Instead of getting some rest after a long day's work, he may watch his wife sit on his couch watching television. Consciously or unconsciously he may resent these changes, no matter how much he understands the rationale behind it. "Why did she have to get sick on me, when I just started this new project?" one man said. His reaction is a frequent and understandable one, when we look at it from the point of view of our unconscious. He reacts to his wife as the child responds to mother's desertion. We often tend to ignore how much of a child is still in all of us. Such husbands can be helped greatly by giving them an opportunity to ventilate their feelings, e.g., by finding a helping hand for one evening a week during which time he can go bowling perhaps, enjoying himself without feelings of guilt and by letting off some steam which he can hardly do in the house of a very sick person.

I think it is cruel to expect the constant presence of any one family member. Just as we have to breathe in and breathe out, people have to "recharge their batteries" outside the sickroom at times, live a normal life from time to time; we cannot function efficiently in the constant awareness of the illness. I have heard many relatives complain that members of the family went on pleasure trips over weekends or continued to go to a theater or movie. They blamed them for enjoying things while someone at home was terminally ill. I think it is more meaningful for the patient and his family to see that the illness does not totally disrupt a household or completely deprive all members of any pleasurable activities; rather, the illness may allow for a gradual adjustment and change toward the kind of home it is going to be when the patient is no longer around. Just as the terminally ill patient cannot face death all the time, the family member cannot and should not exclude all other interactions for the sake of being with the patient exclusively. He too has a need to deny or avoid the sad realities at times in order to face them better when his presence is really needed.

The family's needs will change from the onset of the illness and continue in many forms until long after death has occurred. It is for this reason that family members should handle their energies economically and not exert themselves to a point that they collapse when they are most needed. An understanding helper can contribute a lot in helping them to maintain a sound balance between serving the patient and respecting their own needs.

PROBLEMS OF COMMUNICATION

It is often the wife or the husband who is told about the seriousness of an illness. The decision is often left to them whether to share it with the patient or how much to convey to him or other members of the family. It is often left to them when and how to inform children, which is perhaps the most difficult task, especially if the children are young.

During these crucial days or weeks it depends a great deal on the structure and unity of a given family, on their ability to communicate, and on the availability of meaningful friends. A neutral outsider, who is himself not emotionally overinvolved, can be of great assistance in listening to the family's concerns, their wishes, and needs. He or she can give counsel in legal matters, help prepare the last will, and arrange for the care—temporary or permanent—of children left without a parent. Aside from these practical matters, the family often needs a mediator as demonstrated in the interview of Mr. H. (in Chapter VI).

The dying patient's problems come to an end, but the family's problems go on. Many of these problems can be decreased by discussing them before the death of a family member. The tendency is, unfortunately, to hide the feelings from the patient, to attempt to keep a smiling face and a front of make-believe cheerfulness which has to break down sooner or later. We have interviewed a terminally ill husband who said, "I know I have only a short time to live, but don't tell my wife, she could not take it." When we spoke to the visiting wife in a casual encounter, she volunteered almost the same words. She knew and he knew, but neither had the courage to share it with the other—and this after thirty years of marriage! It was the young chaplain who was able to encourage them to share their awareness, while he remained in the room at the patient's request. Both were greatly relieved that they no longer had to play a deceitful game and proceeded to make arrangements which either one alone was unable to do. Later they were able to smile about their "childish game," as they themselves called it, and were wondering who knew it first and how long it would have taken them without help from outside.

I think the dying person can be of great help to his relatives in helping them meet his death. He can do this in different ways. One of the ways is naturally to share some of his thoughts and feelings with the members of the family in order to help them do the same. If he is able to work through his own grief and show his family by his example how one can die with equanimity, they will remember his strength and bear their own sorrow with more dignity.

Guilt is perhaps the most painful companion of death. When an illness is diagnosed as a potentially fatal one, the family members often ask themselves if they are to be blamed for it. "If I had only sent him to a doctor earlier" or "I should have noticed the change earlier and encouraged him to seek help" are frequent statements made by wives of terminally ill patients. Needless to say, a friend of the family, a family physician, or chaplain can be of great help to such a woman by relieving her of her unrealistic reproach and by assuring her that she probably did everything possible to obtain help. I do not feel, however, that it is enough to say, "Don't feel guilty, because you are not guilty." By listening to such wives carefully and attentively, we can often elicit the more realistic reason for their guilt. Relatives are often guilt-ridden because of very real angry wishes toward the dead person. And who, in anger, has not at times wished someone would disappear, go away, or even dared to say, "Drop dead"? The man in our interview in Chapter XII is a good example of this. He had good reasons to be angry at his wife, who deserted him to live instead with her brother, whom he regarded as a Nazi. She walked out on our Jewish patient and raised his only son as a Christian. She died while he was absent and the patient blamed her for this too. Unfortunately there was no chance ever to express all this unresolved anger and the man was grief-stricken and guilty to the extent that he himself became quite sick.

A high percentage of widowers and widows seen in clinics and by private physicians present themselves with somatic symptoms as a result of the failure to work through their grief and guilt. If they had been helped before the death of their partner to bridge the gulf between themselves and the dying one, half of the battle would have been won. It is understandable that people are reluctant to talk freely about death and dying, especially if death suddenly becomes a personal thing which affects us, has somehow come close to our own doorstep. The few people who have experienced the crisis of impending death have found that communication is only difficult the first time and becomes simpler with gained experience. Instead of increasing alienation and isolation the couple find themselves communicating in more meaningful and deeper senses and may find a closeness and understanding that only suffering can bring.

Another example of lack of communication between the dying and the family is the example of Mrs. F.

> Mrs. F. was a terminally ill and severely debilitated Negro woman who lay in her bed for weeks, motionless. Looking at her dark-skinned body in those white bed sheets reminded me in a gruesome way of tree roots. Due to her crippling disease, it was hard to define the outline of her body or her features. Her daughter, who had been living with her all her life, sat equally motionless and speechless next to her mother. It was the nursing staff who asked us for help, not for the patient but for the daughter, for whom they were rightfully concerned. They watched how she spent more hours every week at her mother's bedside. She had stopped working and finally spent practically day and night silently with her dying mother. The nurses might have worried less had they not sensed the peculiar dichotomy between the ever increasing presence and the complete lack of communication. The patient had had a stroke recently and was unable to speak; she was also unable to move any limbs, and it was presumed that her mind was no longer functioning. The daughter just sat there in silence, never said a word to the mother, never gave her a verbal or nonverbal gesture of care or affection—except for her mute presence.
>
> We entered the room to ask the daughter, who was in her late thirties and single, to come and join us for a brief discussion. What we hoped to achieve was some understanding of her

increasing presence, which also meant an increasing detachment from the outside world. The nurses were concerned about her reaction after her mother's death but found her as uncommunicative as her mother, though for different reasons. I don't know what made me turn to the mother before I left the room with the daughter. Maybe I felt I was depriving her of a visitor; maybe it was just an old habit of mine to keep my patients informed of what was going on. I told her that I was taking her daughter away for a while because we were concerned about her well-being once she was alone. The patient looked at me and I understood two things: First, she was fully aware what was going on in her environment, in spite of her apparent inability to communicate; the second, and unforgettable lesson, was never to classify anybody as a so-called vegetable even if they appear to be nonreactive to many stimuli.

We had a long talk with the daughter, who had given up her job, her few acquaintances, and almost her apartment in order to spend as much time as possible with her dying mother. She had not given any thought to what would happen if she died. She felt obliged to stay in the hospital room almost day and night and actually had had only about three hours of sleep a night during the preceding couple of weeks. She began to wonder whether she made herself so tired to prevent her from thinking. She dreaded the idea of leaving the room out of fear that her mother might die. She had never talked with her mother about those things, though the mother had been ill for a long time and able to talk until recently. At the end of the interview the daughter was able to express some feelings of guilt, ambivalence, and resentment—both for having lived such an isolated life and more perhaps for being deserted. We encouraged her to express her feelings more often, to return to a part-time job in order to have some ties and occupations outside the sickroom, and made ourselves available if she needed someone to talk to.

Returning with her to the sickroom, I again informed the patient of our discussion. I asked her for her approval to have her daughter only come part of the day to visit her. She looked us fully in our eyes, and, with a sigh of relief, closed her eyes again.

A nurse who witnessed this encounter expressed her surprise at so much reaction. She was grateful to have observed this because the nursing staff had become quite attached to the patient and felt some discomfort themselves with the daughter's quiet agony and inability to express herself. The daughter found a part-time job and—to the pleasure of the staff—shared this news with her mother. Her visits were now filled with less ambivalence, less feelings of obligation and resentment, and thus more meaningful. The daughter also resumed communication with other people in and outside the hospital walls and made a few new acquaintances before her mother's death, which came peacefully a few days later.

Mr. Y. was another man we will always remember, for he presented to us the agony, despair, and loneliness of the old man who is in the process of losing his wife after many decades of happy marriage.

Mr. Y. was an old, somewhat haggard, "weatherproof" farmer who had never set foot in a big city. He had plowed his land, delivered many calves, and raised children who were all living in different corners of the country. He and his wife had been alone for the past many years and had, as he said, "grown accustomed to each other." Neither one could ever imagine living without the other.

In the fall of 1967 his wife became seriously ill and the doctor advised the old man to seek help in the big city. Mr. Y. struggled for a while, but as his wife grew weaker and thinner, he took her to the "big hospital," where she was taken to the intensive treatment unit. Whoever has seen such a unit will appreciate the difference of life there compared to an improvised sickroom in a farmhouse. Every bed is occupied by critically ill patients, from newborn babies to old dying men. Every bed is surrounded by the most modern equipment this farmer had ever seen. Bottles hang from poles on the bedside, suction machines are going, a monitor ticks away, and staff members are forever busy keeping the equipment going and watching for critical signals. There is a lot of noisy business, an air of urgency and critical decisions,

people coming and going, and no room for an old farmer who
has never seen a big city.

Mr. Y. insisted on being with his wife, but he was firmly told
that he was allowed to see her only five minutes every hour. And
so he stood there for five minutes every hour, just looking at her
white face, trying to hold her hand, mumbling a few desperate
words—to be told firmly and consistently to "please leave, your
time is up."

Mr. Y. was spotted by one of our students, who felt that he
looked awfully desperate as he walked up and down the hallway,
a lost soul in a big hospital. He brought him to our seminar
where he shared some of his agony, being relieved to have someone to talk to. He had rented a room at the International House,
a house mainly filled with students, many of them just returning
for the new quarter. He was told that he had to leave soon to
make room for the arriving students. The place was not far away
from the hospital, but the old man walked the distance dozens of
times. There was no place for him, no human being to talk to,
not even the assurance of a room available in case his wife lived
longer than a few days. Then there was the nagging awareness
that he might actually lose her, that he might have to return
without her.

As we listened to him, he became increasingly angry at the
hospital—angry at the nurses for being so cruel as to allow him
only five minutes every hour. He felt that he was in their way
even during those all too brief moments. Was that the way he
was to say good-bye to his wife of almost fifty years? How do
you explain to an old man that an intensive treatment unit is run
this way, that there are administrative rules and laws that regu-
late visiting hours and that too many visitors in such a unit
would be intolerable—if not for the patients, maybe for the sensitive equipment? It would certainly not have helped him to say,
"Well, you loved your wife and you lived on the farm for so
many years, why could you not let her die there?" He would
have answered perhaps that he and his wife were one, like a tree
and its roots, and one could not live without the other. The big
hospital bore the promise of extending her life and he, the old

man from the farm, was willing to venture into such a place for the glimpse of hope that it had offered.

There was little we could do for him except help him find more secure living quarters within his financial means, to inform his sons of his loneliness and the need for their presence. We also talked to the nursing staff. We did not succeed in getting longer visiting rights but did at least in making him feel more welcome during the short periods he was allowed to stay with his wife.

Needless to say, such incidents happen every day in every big hospital. Arrangements should be made increasingly to facilitate accommodations for members of the family of patients in such treatment units. There should be adjacent rooms where relatives can sit, rest, and eat, where they could share their loneliness and perhaps console each other during the endless periods of waiting. Social workers or chaplains should be available to relatives, with sufficient time for each one of them, and physicians and nurses should be frequent visitors in such rooms in order to be available for questions and concerns. As things stand now, the relatives are often left completely alone. They spend their hours waiting in hallways, cafeterias, or around the hospital, walking aimlessly back and forth. They may make some meager attempts to see the physician or talk to a nurse, often to be told that the doctor is busy in the operating room or somewhere else. Since there is an increasing number of staff responsible for the welfare of each patient, no one knows the patient very well nor does the patient know the name of his doctor. It happens frequently that the relatives are sent from one person to the other and finally end up in the chaplain's office, not expecting many answers in regard to the patient but hoping to find some solace and understanding for their own agony.

Some relatives would be of greater service to the patient and the staff if they would visit less often and less long. I am reminded of a mother who would not allow anybody to care for her twenty-two-year-old son whom she treated like a baby. Though the young man was quite capable of taking care of his own needs, she washed him, insisted on brushing his teeth, and even cleaned him after a bowel movement. The patient was irritable and angry whenever she was around. The nurses were appalled by her and disliked her increasingly. The social worker tried in vain to talk with the mother, only to be brushed away with some rather unkind remarks.

What makes a mother become so oversolicitous in such a hostile way? We tried to understand her and to find means and ways to cut down on her attendance, which was both annoying and belittling to the patient and the nursing staff. After a discussion of the problem with the staff, we realized that we may have been projecting our own wishes to the patient, and that,—on second thought—he was actually contributing to if not inviting his mother's behavior. He was expected to be in the hospital for a few weeks of radiation treatment; he would leave the hospital to return home for a few weeks, probably to be readmitted again. Did we do him a service by interfering with his relationship with his mother, no matter how unhealthy it appeared to us? Did we not mainly act out of our own anger at this oversolicitous mother who made the nurses feel like "no-good mothers" and thus provoked our rescue fantasy? After we were able to acknowledge this, we reacted with less resentment to the mother but also treated the young man more like an adult, communicating to him that it was up to him to set limits if his mother's behavior became too belittling to him.

I do not know if this had any effect as he left shortly afterwards. I think, however, that this is an example worth mentioning since it points out the need not to be carried away by one's own feelings of what is good and right for a given person. It may be that this man could only tolerate his illness by temporarily regressing to the level of a small child and that the mother gained some consolation out of the fact that she could gratify those needs. I do not believe that this was entirely true in this case, as the patient was obviously angry and resentful when his mother was present, but he also made few if any attempts to stop her, though he was quite able to set limits with other members of the family and the hospital personnel.

COPING WITH THE REALITY OF TERMINAL ILLNESS
IN THE FAMILY

Family members undergo different stages of adjustment similar to the ones described for our patients. At first many of them cannot believe that it is true. They may deny the fact that there is such an illness in the family or "shop around" from doctor to doctor in the vain hope of hearing that this was the wrong diagnosis. They may seek help and reassurance (that it is all not true) from fortune-tellers and faith healers. They may arrange for expensive trips to famous clinics and physicians and only gradually face up to the reality which may change their life so drastically. Greatly dependent on the patient's attitude, awareness, and ability to communicate, the family then undergoes certain changes. If they are able to share their common concerns, they can take care of important matters early and under less pressure of time and emotions. If each one tries to keep a secret from the other, they will keep an artificial barrier between them which will make it difficult for any preparatory grief for the patient or his family. The end result will be much more dramatic than for those who can talk and cry together at times.

Just as the patient goes through a stage of anger, the immediate family will experience the same emotional reaction. They will be angry alternately with the doctor who examined the patient first and did not come forth with the diagnosis and the doctor who confronted them with the sad reality. They may project their rage to the hospital personnel who never care enough, no matter how efficient the care is in reality. There is a great deal of envy in this reaction, as family members often feel cheated at not being able or allowed to be with the patient and to care for him. There is also much guilt and a wish to make up for missed past opportunities. The more we can help the relative to express these emotions before the death of a loved one, the more comfortable the family member will be.

When anger, resentment, and guilt can be worked through, the family will then go through a phase of preparatory grief, just as the dying person does. The more this grief can be expressed before death, the less unbearable it becomes afterward. We often hear relatives say proudly of themselves that they always tried to keep a smiling face when confronted with the patient, until one day they just could not keep that façade any longer. Little do they realize that genuine emotions on the part of a member of the family are much easier to take than a make-believe mask which the patient can see through anyway and which means to him a disguise rather than a sharing of a sad situation.

If members of a family can share these emotions together, they will gradually face the reality of impending separation and come to an acceptance of it together. The most heartbreaking time, perhaps, for the family is the final phase, when the patient is slowly detaching himself from his world including his family. They do not understand that a dying man who has found peace and acceptance in his death will have to separate himself, step by step, from his environment, including his most loved ones. How could he ever be ready to die if he continued to hold onto the meaningful relationships of which a man has so many? When the patient asks to be visited only by a few more friends, then by his children and finally only by his wife, it should be understood that that is the way of separating himself gradually. It is often misinterpreted by the immediate family as a rejection, and we have met several husbands and wives who have reacted dramatically to this normal and healthy detachment. I think we can be of greatest service to them if we help them understand that only patients who have worked through their dying are able to detach themselves slowly and peacefully in this manner. It should be a source of comfort and solace to them and not one of grief and resentment. It is during this time that the family needs the most support, the patient perhaps the least. I do not mean to imply by this that the patient should then be left alone. We should always be available, but a patient who has reached this stage of acceptance and decathexis usually requires little in terms of interpersonal relationship. If the meaning of this detachment is not explained to the family, problems can arise as described in the case of Mrs. W. (Chapter VII).

The most tragic death is perhaps—aside from the very young—the death of the very old when we look at it from point of view of the family. Whether the generations have lived together or separately, each generation has a need and a right to live their own lives, to have their own privacy, their own needs fulfilled appropriate to their generation. The old folks have outlived their usefulness in terms of our economic system and have earned, on the other hand, a right to live out their lives in dignity and peace. As long as they are healthy in body and mind and self-supporting, this may all be quite possible. We have seen many old men and women, however, who have become disabled physically or emotionally and who require a tremendous sum of money for a dignified maintenance at a level their family desires for them. The family is then often confronted with a difficult decision, namely, to mobilize all available money, including loans and savings for their own retirement, in order to afford such final care. The tragedy of these old people is perhaps that the amount of money and often financial sacrifice does not involve any improvement of the condition but is a mere maintenance at a minimal level of existence. If medical complications occur, the expenses are manifold and the family often wishes for a quick and painless death, but rarely expresses that wish openly. That such wishes bring about feelings of guilt is obvious.

I am reminded of an old woman who had been hospitalized for several weeks and required extensive and expensive nursing care in a private hospital. Everybody expected her to die soon, but day after day she remained in an unchanged condition. Her daughter was torn between sending her to a nursing home or keeping her in the hospital, where she apparently wanted to stay. Her son-in-law was angry at her for having used up their life savings and had innumerable arguments with his wife, who felt too guilty to take her out of the hospital. When I visited the old woman she looked frightened and weary. I asked her simply what she was so afraid of. She looked at me and finally expressed what she had been unable to communicate before, because she herself realized how unrealistic her fears were. She was afraid of "being eaten up alive by the worms." While I was catching my breath and tried to understand the real meaning of this statement, her daughter blurted out, "If that's what's keeping you from dying, we can burn you," by which she naturally meant that a cremation would prevent her from having any contact with earthworms. All her suppressed anger was in this statement. I sat with the old woman alone for a while. We talked calmly about her life-long phobias and her fear of death which was presented in this fear of worms, as if she would be aware of them after her death. She felt greatly relieved for having expressed it and had nothing but understanding for her daughter's anger. I encouraged her to share some of these feelings with her daughter, so that the latter might not have to feel so bad about her outburst.

When I met the daughter outside the room I told her of her mother's understanding, and they finally got together to talk about their concerns, ending up by making arrangements for the funeral, a cremation. Instead of sitting silently in anger, they communicated and consoled each other. The mother died the next day. If I had not see the peaceful look on her face during her last day, I might have worried that this outburst of anger might have killed her.

Another aspect that is often not taken into account is what kind of a fatal illness the patient has. There are certain expectations of cancer, just as there are certain pictures associated with heart disease. The former is often viewed as a lingering, pain-producing illness while the latter can strike suddenly, painless but final. I think there is a great deal of difference if a loved one dies slowly with much time available for preparatory grief on both sides, compared to the feared phone call, "It happened, it's all over." It is easier to talk with a cancer patient about death and dying than it is with a cardiac patient, who arouses concerns in us that we might frighten him and thus provoke a coronary, i.e., his death. The relatives of a cancer patient are therefore more amenable to discussing the expected end than the family of someone with heart disease, when the end can come any moment and a discussion may provoke it, at least in the opinion of many members of families whom we have spoken with.

I remember a mother of a young man in Colorado who did not allow her son to take any exercise, not even the most minimal kind, in spite of the contrary advice on part of his doctors. In conversations this mother would often make statements like "if he does too much he will drop dead on me," as if she expected a hostile act on the part of her son to be committed against her. She was totally unaware of her own hostility even after sharing with us some of her resentment for having "such a weak son," whom she very often associated with her ineffective and unsuccessful husband. It took months of careful, patient listening to this mother before she was able to express some of her own destructive wishes toward her child. She rationalized these by the fact that he was the cause of her limited social and professional life, thus rendering her as ineffective as she regarded her husband to be. These are complicated family situations, in which a sick member of the family is rendered more incapable of functioning because of the relative's conflicts. If we can learn to respond to such family members with compassion and understanding rather than judgement and criticism, we also help the patient bear his handicap with more ease and dignity.

The following example of Mr. P. demonstrates the difficulties that can occur for the patient when he is ready to separate himself but the family is unable to accept the reality, thus contributing to the patient's conflicts. Our goal should always be to help the patient and his family face the crisis together in order to achieve acceptance of this final reality simultaneously.

Mr. P. was a man in his mid-fifties who looked about fifteen years older than his age. The doctors felt that he had only a poor chance to respond to treatment, partially because of his advanced cancer and marasmus, but mainly because of his lack of "fighting spirit." Mr. P. had his stomach removed because of cancer five years prior to this hospitalization. At first he accepted his illness quite well and was full of hope. As he grew weaker and thinner, he became increasingly depressed until the time of his readmission, when a chest X-ray revealed metastatic tumors in his lungs. The patient had not been informed of the biopsy result when I saw him. The question was raised as to the advisability of possible radiation or surgery for a man in his weak condition. Our interview proceeded in two sessions. The first visit served the purpose of introducing myself and of telling him that I was available should he wish to talk about the seriousness of his illness and the problems that this might cause. A telephone interrupted us and I left the room, asking him to think about it. I also informed him about the time of my next visit.

When I saw him the next day, Mr. P. put his arm out in welcome and signaled to the chair as an invitation to sit down. In spite of many interruptions by a change of infusion bottles, distribution of medication, and routine pulse and blood pressure measurements, we sat for over an hour. Mr. P. had sensed that he would be allowed to "open his shades" as he called it. There was no defensiveness, no evasiveness in his accounts. He was a man whose hours seemed to count, who had no precious time to lose, and who seemed to be eager to share his concerns and regrets with someone who could listen.

The day before, he made the statement, "I want to sleep, sleep, sleep and not wake up." Today he repeated the same thing, but added the word "but." I looked at him questioningly and he proceeded to tell me with a weak soft voice that his wife had come to visit him. She was convinced that he would make it. She expected him home to take care of the garden and the flowers. She also reminded him of his promise to retire soon, to move to Arizona perhaps, to have a few more good years. . . .

He talked with much warmth and affection about his daughter, twenty-one years old, who came to visit him on a leave from college, and who was shocked to see him in this condition. He mentioned all these things, as if he was to be blamed for disappointing his family, for not living up to their expectations.

I mentioned that to him and he nodded. He talked about all the regrets he had. He spent the first years of his marriage accumulating material goods for his family, trying to "make them a good home," and by doing so spent most of his time away from home and family. After the occurrence of cancer he spared every moment to be with them, but by then, it seemed to be too late. His daughter was away at school and had her own friends. When she was small and needed and wanted him, he was too busy making money.

Talking about his present condition he said, "Sleep is the only relief. Every moment of awakening is anguish, pure anguish. There is no relief. I am thinking in envy of two men I saw executed. I sat right in front of the first man. I felt nothing. Now, I think, he was a lucky guy. He deserved to die. He had no anguish, it was fast and painless. Here I lie in bed, every hour, every day is agony."

Mr. P. was not so much concerned about pain and physical discomfort as he was tortured by regrets for not being able to fulfill his family's expectations, for being "a failure." He was tortured by his tremendous need to "let go and sleep, sleep, sleep" and the continuous flow of expectations from his environment. "The nurses come in and say I have to eat or I get too weak, the doctors come in and tell me about the new treatment they started, and expect me to be happy about it; my wife comes and tells me about the work I am supposed to do when I get out of here, and my daughter just looks at me and says 'You have to get well'—how can a man die in peace this way?"

For a brief moment he smiled and said, "I will take this treatment and go home once more. I will return to work the next day and make a bit more money. My insurance will pay for my daughter's education anyway, but she still needs a father for a while. But you know and I know, I just cannot do it. Maybe they have to learn to face it. It would make dying so much easier!"

Mr. P. showed as well as Mrs. W. (in Chapter VII) how difficult it is for patients to face impending and anticipated death when the family is not ready to "let go" and implicitly or explicitly prevents them from separating themselves from the involvements here on earth. Mrs. W.'s husband just stood at her bedside, reminding her of their happy marriage which should not end and pleading with the doctors to do everything humanly possible to prevent her from dying. Mr. P.'s wife reminded him of unfulfilled promises and undone tasks, thus communicating the same needs to him, namely, to have him around for many more years to come. I cannot say that both these partners used denial. Both of them knew the reality of the condition of their spouses. Yet both, because of their own needs, looked away from this reality. They faced it when talking with other people but denied it in front of the patients. And it was the patients who needed to hear that they too were aware of the seriousness of their condition and were able to accept this reality. Without this knowledge "every moment of awakening is pure anguish," in Mr. P.'s words. Our interview ended with the expression of hope that the important people in his environment would learn to face the reality of his dying rather than expressing hope for a prolonging of his life.

This man was ready to separate himself from this world. He was ready to enter the final stage when the end is more promising or there is not enough strength left to live. One might argue whether an all-out medical effort is appropriate in such circumstances. With enough infusions and transfusions, vitamins, energizers, and antidepressant medication, with psychotherapy and symptomatic treatment, many such patients may be given an additional "lease on life." I have heard more curses than words of appreciation for the gained time, and I repeat my conviction that a patient has a right to die in peace and dignity. He should not be used to fulfill our own needs when his own wishes are in opposition to ours. I am referring to patients who have a physical illness but who are sane and capable enough to make decisions for themselves. Their wishes and opinions should be respected, they should be listened to and consulted. If the patient's wishes are contrary to our beliefs or convictions, we should express this conflict openly and leave the decisions up to the patient in respect to further interventions or treatments. In the many terminally ill patients I have so far interviewed, I have not seen any irrational behavior or unacceptable requests, and this includes the two psychotic women earlier described, who followed through with their treatment, one of them in spite of her otherwise almost complete denial of her illness.

THE FAMILY AFTER DEATH HAS OCCURRED

Once the patient dies, I find it cruel and inappropriate to speak of the love of God. When we lose someone, especially when we have had little if any time to prepare ourselves, we are enraged, angry, in despair; we should be allowed to express these feelings. The family members are often left alone as soon as they have given their consent for autopsy. Bitter, angry, or just numb, they walk through the corridors of the hospital, unable often to face the brutal reality. The first few days may be filled with busywork, with arrangements and visiting relatives. The void and emptiness is felt after the funeral, after the departure of the relatives. It is at this time that family members feel most grateful to have someone to talk to, especially if it is someone who had recent contact with the deceased and who can share anecdotes of some good moments towards the end of the deceased's life. This helps the relative over the shock and the initial grief and prepares him for a gradual acceptance.

Many relatives are preoccupied by memories and ruminate in fantasies, often even talk to the deceased as if he was still alive. They not only isolate themselves from the living but make it harder for themselves to face the reality of the person's death. For some, however, this is the only way they can cope with the loss, and it would be cruel indeed to ridicule them or to confront them daily with the unacceptable reality. It would be more helpful to understand this need and to help them separate themselves by taking them out of their isolation gradually. I have seen this behavior mainly in young widows who had lost their husbands at an early age and were rather unprepared. It may be more frequently encountered in the days of war where death of a young person occurs elsewhere, though I believe a war always makes relatives more aware of the possibility of no return. They are therefore more prepared for that death than, for example, for the unexpected death of a young man through a rapidly progressing illness.

A last word should be mentioned about the children. They are often the forgotten ones. Not so much that nobody cares; the opposite is often true. But few people feel comfortable talking to a child about death. Young children have different concepts of death, and they have to be taken into consideration in order to talk to them and to understand their communications. Up to the age of three a child is concerned only about separation, later followed by the fear of mutilation. It is at this age that the small child begins to mobilize, to take his first trips out "into the world," the sidewalk trips by tricycle. It is in this environment that he may see the first beloved pet run over by a car or a beautiful bird torn apart by a cat. This is what mutilation means to him, since it is the age when he is concerned about the integrity of his body and is threatened by anything that can destroy it.

Also, death, as outlined in Chapter I, is not a permanent fact for the three-to-five-year-old. It is as temporary as burying a flower bulb into the soil in the fall to have it come up again the following spring.

After the age of five death is often regarded as a man, a bogeyman who comes to take people away; it is still attributed to an outward intervention.

Around the ages of nine to ten the realistic conception begins to show, namely, death as a permanent biological process.

Children will react differently to the death of a parent, from a silent withdrawal and isolation to a wild loud mourning which attracts attention and thus a replacement of a loved and needed object. Since children cannot yet differentiate between the wish and the deed (as outlined in Chapter I), they may feel a great deal of remorse and guilt. They will feel responsible for having killed the parents and thus fear a gruesome punishment in retribution. They may, on the other hand, take the separation relatively calmly and utter such statements as "She will come back for the spring vacation" or secretly put an apple out for her—in order to assure that she has enough to eat for the temporary trip. If adults, who are upset already during this period, do not understand such children and reprimand or correct them, the children may hold inside their own way of grieving—which is often a root for later emotional disturbance.

With an adolescent, however, things are not much different than with an adult. Naturally adolescence is in itself a difficult time and added loss of a parent is often too much for such a youngster to endure. They should be listened to and allowed to ventilate their feelings, whether they be guilt, anger or plain sadness.

RESOLUTION OF GRIEF AND ANGER

What I am saying again here is, let the relative talk, cry, or scream if necessary. Let them share and ventilate, but be available. The relative has a long time of mourning ahead of him, when the problems for the dead are solved. He needs help and assistance from the confirmation of a so-called bad diagnosis until months after the death of a member of the family.

By help I naturally do not assume that this has to be professional counseling of any form; most people neither need nor can afford this. But they need a human being, a friend, doctor, nurse, or chaplain—it matters little. The social worker may be the most meaningful one, if she has helped with arrangements for a nursing home and if the family wishes to talk more about their mother in that particular set-up, which may have been a source of guilt feelings for not having kept her at home. Such families have at times visited other old folks in the same nursing home and continued their task of caring for someone, perhaps as a partial denial, perhaps just to do good for all the missed opportunities with Grandma. No matter what the underlying reason we should try to understand their needs and to help relatives direct these needs constructively to diminish guilt, shame, or fear of retribution. The most meaningful help that we can give any relative, child or adult, is to share his feelings before the event of death and to allow him to work through his feelings, whether they are rational or irrational.

If we tolerate their anger, whether it is directed at us, at the deceased, or at God, we are helping them take a great step towards acceptance without guilt. If we blame them for daring to ventilate such socially poorly tolerated thoughts, we are blameworthy for prolonging their grief, shame, and guilt which often results in physical and emotional ill health.

CHAPTER X

Some Interviews
with Terminally Ill Patients

*Death, thy servant, is at my door. He has crossed the
unknown sea and brought thy call to my home.*
   *The night is dark and my heart is fearful—yet I will
take up the lamp, open my gates and bow to him my
welcome. It is thy messenger who stands at my door.*
   *I will worship him with folded hands, and with
tears. I will worship him placing at his feet the
treasure of my heart.*
   *He will go back with his errand done, leaving a
dark shadow on my morning; and in my desolate home
only my forlorn self will remain as my last offering to
thee.*

TAGORE,
from *Gitanjali*, LXXXVI

In previous chapters we have tried to outline the reasons for
the increasing difficulties patients have in communicating
their needs at the time of serious or perhaps fatal illness. We
have summarized some of our findings and attempted to
describe the methods used to elicit the patient's awareness,

problems, concerns, and wishes. It seems helpful to include more random examples of such interviews as they give a better picture of the variety of responses and reactions demonstrated by both the patient and the interviewer. It should be remembered that the patient rarely knew the interviewer; both had met only for a few minutes in order to arrange for the interview.

I have selected one interview of a patient whose mother was visiting at the same time and who volunteered to meet with us in order to share her responses. I think they demonstrate well how different members of a family cope with terminal illness and how, at times, both members have completely different recollections of the same event. Each interview is followed by a brief summary relating the material to statements made in earlier chapters. These original interviews will speak for themselves. They were purposely left unedited and unabbreviated and demonstrate moments when we were perceptive of a patient's implicit or explicit communications and times when we did not react in the most responsive manner. The part that cannot be shared with the reader is the experience that one has during such a dialogue: the many nonverbal communications that go on constantly between patient and physician, physician and chaplain, or patient and chaplain; the sighs, wet eyes, the smiles, gestures with the hands, the empty look, the astonished glance, or the outstretched hands—all communications of significance which often go beyond words.

Though the following interviews were, with a few exceptions, the first meetings we had with these patients, they were in most cases not the only ones. All patients were seen as often as indicated until they died. Many of our patients were able to be discharged home once more, either to die there or to be readmitted to the hospital later on. They asked to be called once in a while when at home, or they called one of the interviewers "to keep in touch." It happened occasionally that a relative would drop in at our office for an informal visit either to gain some insight into a patient's behavior and ask for help and understanding, or to share some memories with us later after the patient's death. We tried to remain as available to them as we were to the patient during hospitalization and thereafter.

*   *   *

The following interviews may be studied in regard to the role the relatives played during these difficult times.

Mrs. S. had been deserted by her husband, who was only indirectly informed by their two small boys of her fatal illness. It was a neighbor and friend who played the most significant role during her terminal illness though she expected her estranged husband and his second wife to take care of her children after her death.

The seventeen-year-old girl demonstrates the courage of a young person in facing such a crisis. Her interview is followed by one with her mother; both of them speak for themselves.

Mrs. C. felt unable to face her own death because of the many family obligations she had to fulfill. Here again is a good example of the importance of family counseling when sick, dependent, or old people have to be taken care of by the patient.

Mrs. L., who had been the eyes for her visually handicapped husband, uses this role to prove that she can still function, and both husband and wife use partial denial in the time of their crisis.

Mrs. S. was a forty-eight-year old, Protestant woman, mother of two young boys whom she raised alone. She had expressed a wish to talk to someone and we invited her to come to our seminar. She was reluctant and somewhat anxious about coming, but felt greatly relieved after the seminar. On the way to the interviewing room she talked casually about her two boys, and it seemed obvious that they were her biggest concern during this hospitalization.

DOCTOR: Mrs. S., we really know nothing about you except for the minute, you know, we talked with you before. How old are you?

PATIENT: Let's see. Sunday I'll be forty-eight.

DOCTOR: This coming? I'll have to think of it. This is the second time you have been in the hospital? When did you come in the first time?

PATIENT: In April.

DOCTOR: What did you come in for?

PATIENT: This tumor, on my chest.

DOCTOR: What kind of a tumor?

PATIENT: Well, now that I really can't tell you. You see, I don't know enough about this disease to know one kind from another.

DOCTOR: What do you think it is? How were you told what you have?

PATIENT: Well, you see when I went to the hospital they took a biopsy, and then about two days later my family doctor came in and said that the results came back and that it was malignant. But actually the name of what kind it was I don't—

DOCTOR: But they told you it was malignant.

PATIENT: Yes.

DOCTOR: When was that?

PATIENT: That was in, oh, that must have been in the last part of March.

DOCTOR: Of this year? So until this year you were healthy?

PATIENT: No, no. You see, I have an arrested case of TB, so I have spent months in the sanitarium, at one time or another.

DOCTOR: I see. Where, in Colorado? Where did you go to the sanitarium?

PATIENT: In Illinois.

DOCTOR: So, you have had a lot of illness in your life.

PATIENT: Yes.

DOCTOR: Are you kind of almost used to hospitals?

PATIENT: No. I don't think you ever get used to them.

DOCTOR: And then, how did this illness start? What brought you to the hospital? Can you tell us about the beginning of this illness?

PATIENT: I had this little lump. It was like, oh, like maybe a blackhead or something, you know. Right here. And it kept getting larger, and painful and, ah, I don't think I'm any different than anyone else, I didn't want to go to a doctor and kept putting it off, until finally I realized it was getting worse and worse and I had to go and see someone. Well, a few months before that my family doctor that I've had for years passed away. And I didn't know who to go to. Naturally, I mean, I don't have a husband, I was married for twenty-two years and my husband decided there was someone else he wanted. So it was just the boys and I, and I felt that they needed me. I think probably that's one reason why I thought that if there was something very serious the matter, why, well, I kept saying it just couldn't be. I have to be home with the boys. That was the main reason that I put it off. Well, and then when I did go it was getting very large and so painful I couldn't stand it, stand the pain any longer. And when I went to the family doctor, why, he just said that he couldn't do anything there in the office. I would have to go to the hospital. And so, I went. I think four or five days later I was admitted to the hospital and—I also had a tumor on one ovary.

DOCTOR: At the same time? This was found?

PATIENT: Yes. And I think he intended to do something about that also while I was there, and then when he took the biopsy of this and he came back, it was a malignant one and naturally he wouldn't do anything else. And so he said he could do nothing more for me there, I would have to make up my mind where I wanted to go.

DOCTOR: Meaning to which hospital?

PATIENT: Yes.

DOCTOR: And then you picked this hospital?

PATIENT: Yes.

DOCTOR: How come you picked this hospital?

PATIENT: Well, we have a friend who was a patient here at one time. I know him through my insurance, and he couldn't speak high enough of it and the doctors and the nurses. He said the doctors are specialists and you'll get wonderful care.

DOCTOR: Are you?

PATIENT: Yes.

DOCTOR: I'd be curious how you took this, when it was told to you that you had a malignancy. How did you take it after postponing, postponing to hear the truth. Or to hear the fact, you know, out of your needs to be home and take care of your children. How did you take it when it finally had to be said?

PATIENT: When I first heard it I went all to pieces.

DOCTOR: How?

PATIENT: Emotionally.

DOCTOR: Depressed, crying?

PATIENT: Ah ha. I always thought that I couldn't have anything like that. Then when I realized how serious it was I thought it's something I have to accept, going all to pieces will solve nothing, and I suppose the sooner I can go to someone who can help me the better it will be.

DOCTOR: Did you share this with your children?

PATIENT: Yes. I told them both. I mean, ah, I don't know really how much they really do understand. I mean they know it's something that's very serious but as far as how much they understand I don't know.

CHAPLAIN: How about the rest of your family. Did you share this with any others? Do you have any others?

PATIENT: I have a fellow, a friend that I've been going with for about five years. He's a very nice person and he has been very good to me. And he's been good to the boys, I mean, since I've had to be away from the boys he has been overseeing them, seeing that someone was there with them to get their meals at night, to be with them. I mean that they aren't entirely alone, you know, entirely on their own. Of course, the older boy, probably he would be responsible enough but he is still a minor, I feel, until he is twenty-one.

CHAPLAIN: You feel more comfortable with somebody there.

PATIENT: Yes. And then I have a neighbor there. It's more like a duplex, she lives in the other half of the house. And she's in and out every day. And she's been helping me with my housework at home, between those two months that I was home. She took care of me, you know, she'd give me my baths and see that I had a meal to eat. She's a very wonderful person. She's a very religious person, you know, in her own faith, and she has done just an awful lot for me.

DOCTOR: What faith does she have?

PATIENT: I don't know whether I really know what church she does go to.

CHAPLAIN: Protestant?

PATIENT: Yes.

CHAPLAIN: Do you have other family or is this—

PATIENT: I have a brother who lives here.

CHAPLAIN: But he's not as close as—

PATIENT: We haven't been too close, no. I feel that in the short time that I've known her, she's really the closest one I have. I mean, I can talk to her and she talks to me, which makes me feel better.

DOCTOR: Um hm. You are lucky.

PATIENT: She's wonderful. I've just never known anyone like her. Nearly every day I get a card or a few lines in the mail from her. It might be silly, it might be serious, but, I mean, I even look forward to just hearing from her.

DOCTOR: Just that somebody cares.

PATIENT: Yes.

DOCTOR: How long ago did your husband leave you?

PATIENT: In September of '59.

DOCTOR: '59. Then did you have tuberculosis?

PATIENT: The first time was in 1946. I lost my little girl. She was two and a half years old. And at that time my husband was in the service. She got very sick and we took her to a specialist in the hospital. And, ah, the hardest thing was that I couldn't see her while she was there. And she went into a coma and she never did come out of it. They asked if it would be all right to perform an autopsy, and I said yes, perhaps it might help someone else someday. So they performed an autopsy, and she had what they call miliary TB. That was in the bloodstream. And when my husband went in the service, my father came to live with me. And so afterward we all had checkups and my father had quite a large cavity in one lung, and I had just a small amount of trouble. So he and I both went into the sanitarium at that time. And I was there about three months, the only medication I had to have was bedrest and shots. I didn't have to have any surgery. And then, well, on through the years, I was there before and after each one of the boys was born. And I haven't been there now as a patient since after the youngest boy was born in '53.

DOCTOR: Your girl was your first child?

PATIENT: Yes.

DOCTOR: And the only girl you had. That must have been quite something. How did you recover from that?

PATIENT: Well, it was very hard.

DOCTOR: What gave you strength?

PATIENT: Prayer, probably, more than anything. She and I were, I mean, she was all I had for all that time. She was three months old when my husband left. She was just, well, I really lived for her, you know. And I didn't think I could accept but I did.

DOCTOR: And now since your husband left it's the boys that you live for.

PATIENT: Yes.

DOCTOR: That must make it very hard. And now does your religion or prayers or what help you to take care of all the times when you have the blues or you feel depressed about your illness?

PATIENT: Prayers I think are the main thing.

DOCTOR: Do you ever think or talk with anybody in terms of how it's going to be if you would die of this disease or—You don't think about these things?

PATIENT: Well, ah, I haven't too much, no. Other than this lady friend of mine, she will talk with me you know about how serious it is and things that, ah, other than her I haven't talked with anyone.

CHAPLAIN: Does your priest come to see you or do you attend church?

PATIENT: Well, I did go to church before. You know, I hadn't been feeling well for months, even before I came in here. And I hadn't been too good at going to church. But—

CHAPLAIN: Does the priest come to see you?

PATIENT: The priest came to see me when I was in the hospital there at home before I came here. And he was coming down to see me again before I came in, and I guess I just all of a sudden decided to come here, so he didn't get to see me before I came. And then after I was here for about two or three weeks, Father D. came to see me.

CHAPLAIN: Primarily, though, your faith has been nourished by your own private resources at home. Where you haven't had an outlet talking to anyone at church.

PATIENT: No.

CHAPLAIN: But your friend has played this role.

DOCTOR: You sounded like this friend was a relatively new friend. Did you just move into this duplex or did she just move in?

PATIENT: I've known her for about, oh, maybe a year and a half.

DOCTOR: Is that all? Isn't that wonderful. How did you click in such a short time?

PATIENT: Well, I don't know. It's really rather hard to explain. I mean she said all her life she always wanted a sister and in talking I said why I always wanted a sister too. I said there were just the two of us, my brother and I, and she said, well, I think we've found each other and I think you have a sister now and so do I. Just to have her walk in the room, she makes you feel, oh, you just feel good like it's home.

DOCTOR: Did you ever have a sister?

PATIENT: No. Just my brother and I.

DOCTOR: You had just one brother. What kind of parents did you have?

PATIENT: Well, my father and mother were divorced when we were very small.

DOCTOR: How small?

PATIENT: I was two and a half and my brother was about three and a half. And we were raised by an aunt and uncle.

DOCTOR: How were they?

PATIENT: They were very wonderful to us.

DOCTOR: Who are your real parents?

PATIENT: My mother is still living. She lives here and my father passed away not too long after he had been sick and been in the sanitorium.

DOCTOR: Your father died of his tuberculosis?

PATIENT: Yes.

DOCTOR: I see. Whom did you feel closer to?

PATIENT: Well, I mean, like my aunt and uncle, they were really my father and mother. I mean, we were with them from the time we were little. And, I mean, they never, they told us they were an aunt and uncle, but I mean they were like parents to us.

DOCTOR: There's nothing phony about it. They were honest about it.

PATIENT: Yes, yes.

CHAPLAIN: Are they living?

PATIENT: No. My uncle has been dead for several years. My aunt is still living. She is eighty-five years old.

CHAPLAIN: Does she know about your illness?

PATIENT: Yes.

CHAPLAIN: Do you have much contact with her?

PATIENT: Well, yes I do. I mean she doesn't get out too much, she's not too well. Last year she had arthritis of the spine and she was in the hospital for quite some time. I didn't know whether she would be able to live through that illness or not. She did, and she is doing quite well now. She has her own little place, she lives by herself, takes care of herself which I think is wonderful.

DOCTOR: Eighty-four?

PATIENT: Eighty-five.

DOCTOR: How do you make your living? Were you working?

PATIENT: I worked part-time up until the time I came in here.

DOCTOR: In April?

PATIENT: Yes. But my husband gives us so much a week support.

DOCTOR: I see. So you are not dependent on working?

PATIENT: No.

DOCTOR: Your husband has still some contact with you?

PATIENT: Well, he, he sees the boys whenever he wants to and that's always—I always felt whenever he wanted to see them that it was up to him. He lives in the same town as I do.

DOCTOR: Um hm. Is he married again?

PATIENT: Yes, he's married. He was remarried, oh, perhaps a year or so after he left.

DOCTOR: Does he know about your illness?

PATIENT: Yes.

DOCTOR: How much does he know?

PATIENT: Ah, I don't know really, I mean, nothing but perhaps what the boys have told him.

DOCTOR: You don't verbally communicate with him.

PATIENT: No.

DOCTOR: I see. You haven't seen him then personally?

PATIENT: Not to talk to him. I don't—no.

DOCTOR: What kind of parts of your body are involved now with this malignancy?

PATIENT: Well, it's this tumor here and this spot on the liver. And then I had this large tumor on my leg that had eaten most of the bone away and so they inserted that pin in my leg.

DOCTOR: That was in the spring or summer?

PATIENT: In July. And then I also have that tumor on my ovary which is questionable—though you see they have as yet to find out where it started.

DOCTOR: Yes. They know it's in different places now but they don't know where the original came from. Yes. What's the worse part about having such a malignancy for you? How much does it interfere with your normal life and activities? You can't walk, for example, can you?

PATIENT: No. Only with crutches.

DOCTOR: You can walk around in the house with crutches?

PATIENT: Yes. But as far as doing, say your cooking and your housework, you are very limited.

DOCTOR: What else does it do to you?

PATIENT: Well, I really don't know.

DOCTOR: I thought you said upstairs that you had lots of pain.

PATIENT: I do.

DOCTOR: Yes. Do you still have that?

PATIENT: Um hm. I think after so many months you rather learn to live with it, I mean, when it gets so bad you can't stand it and you ask for something. But I never was one that cared to take any medicine.

DOCTOR: Mrs. S. impresses me as one who will take a lot of pain, until she says something. Like she waits a long time and sees the tumor grow before she sees the doctor.

PATIENT: That's always been my biggest trouble.

DOCTOR: Are you difficult for the nurses? Do you tell them when you need something? What kind of a patient are you, do you know?

PATIENT: I think you had better ask the nurses that. (Jokingly)

CHAPLAIN: Oh, that's easy, but we are interested in how you feel.

PATIENT: Oh, I don't know. I, I think I can get along with anyone.

DOCTOR: Ah ha. I think so. But maybe you don't ask enough.

PATIENT: I don't ask any more than I have to.

DOCTOR: How come?

PATIENT: I really don't know. I mean, different people are different. You see, I always was happy when I could take care of myself, do my own housework, and do things for the boys. That is what bothers me the most. That I feel that someone else has to take care of me now. That is very hard for me to accept.

DOCTOR: Is getting more sick the worst part of it? Would be not being able to give to others?

PATIENT: Yes.

DOCTOR: How else could you give to others without being physically active?

PATIENT: Well, you can remember them in your prayers.

DOCTOR: Or what you are doing here right now?

PATIENT: Yes.

DOCTOR: Do you think that's going to help some other patient?

PATIENT: Yes. I think it does. I hope it does.

DOCTOR: How else do you think we can be of help? How is dying for you? What does it mean to you?

PATIENT: I'm not afraid to die.

DOCTOR: No?

PATIENT: No.

DOCTOR: It has no bad connotations?

PATIENT: I don't mean that. Naturally everyone wants to live as long as they can.

DOCTOR: Naturally.

PATIENT: But I wouldn't be afraid of dying.

DOCTOR: How do you conceive of it?

CHAPLAIN: This is what I wondered, not that we are communicating anything to you except that people do have problems. Do you think of what will happen if this leads to death? Have you thought about this? You mentioned talking to your friend.

PATIENT: Yes. We have talked about it.

CHAPLAIN: Could you share some of your feelings about this?

PATIENT: It's sort of hard for me to, you know, talk . . .

CHAPLAIN: It's more comfortable to talk with her about it than with someone else.

PATIENT: To someone else you know.

CHAPLAIN: Could I ask you a related question, in terms of how has your illness, and this is the second illness for you, you've had tuberculosis, and you've lost your daughter—how have these experiences affected your attitude toward life, your religious thoughts?

PATIENT: I guess it has brought me closer to God.

CHAPLAIN: In what way? In feeling that he could be of help, or—

PATIENT: Yes. I just feel that I have put myself in his hands. It would be up to him if I could get well again—lead a normal life.

CHAPLAIN: You mentioned difficulty in being dependent on other people, and yet you are able to find a good deal of help from this friend of yours. Is it difficult to depend on God?

PATIENT: No.

CHAPLAIN: He's more like this friend, eh?

PATIENT: Yes.

DOCTOR: But if I understood right, your friend has the same needs that you have. She also needs a sister, so it's a give and take, it's not just a taking.

PATIENT: She's had sorrow and difficulties in her life, perhaps that has brought her closer to me.

DOCTOR: Is she a lonely woman?

PATIENT: She can understand. She's a married woman, she never had any children, she loves children, she has never had any of her own. But she loves everyone else's. She and her husband have work there at the children's home, they've been house parents. Oh, they always have children around them all the time, and they have been very nice to my boys too.

DOCTOR: Who takes care of both of them if you should be in a hospital for a long time, or if you should die?

PATIENT: Well, ah, I think it would be natural if anything happened to me that their father would. It would just be his place to—

DOCTOR: How do you feel about that?

PATIENT: I think that would be the best thing.

DOCTOR: For the boys.

PATIENT: I don't know if it would be the best thing for the boys, but—

DOCTOR: How do they get along with his second wife? Who would really be their substitute mother?

PATIENT: Well, they really have no use for her.

DOCTOR: In what way?

PATIENT: Well, I don't know whether she resents the boys, or I don't know. But I do think, in his heart, that their father loves the boys, I think he always has. If it came down to it I don't know if there is anything he wouldn't do for them.

CHAPLAIN: Your boys are pretty far along. The younger one is thirteen?

PATIENT: Thirteen. He is in the eighth grade this year.

DOCTOR: Thirteen and eighteen, eh?

PATIENT: The oldest boy graduated from high school last year. He was just eighteen in September. So he had to sign up for the draft, which doesn't make him too happy, which doesn't make me happy either. I don't think about that. I try not to but then I do.

DOCTOR: Especially at times like this I think it is very difficult to think about. Has the hospital as a whole, and individuals on your floor been helpful in every way they could or do you have any suggestions how things could be improved for patients like you, who have, I'm sure, a lot of problems and conflicts and worries, and very hardly talk about it, like you.

PATIENT: Oh, I think, I feel that, I wish that my doctors could explain a little more to me. I realize, I mean I still feel like I'm in the dark, as far as really knowing about. Well, now maybe there are some people who want to know how sick they are and some people that don't. Well, if I thought that I just had a short time to live I would want to know that.

DOCTOR: Did you ask him?

PATIENT: No. But the doctors are always in a hurry—

DOCTOR: Will you please grab him the next time and ask him?

PATIENT: I feel that their time is valuable. I mean I don't—

CHAPLAIN: This isn't too different than what she said about her other relationships. She doesn't impose on anybody and to take somebody's time is sort of an imposition unless she is going to feel comfortable with them.

DOCTOR: Unless the tumor gets so big, and the pain so unbearable that you can't take it anymore—right? Who is the doctor you would like to hear from? Do you have several doctors? With whom do you feel more comfortable?

PATIENT: I have so much confidence in Dr. Q., it seems like when he walks in the room, I just, I feel that anything he tells me is, well, it's all right.

DOCTOR: Maybe he waits for an opening to be asked?

PATIENT: I've always felt that way toward him.

DOCTOR: Do you think it's possible that he waits for an opening to be asked from you?

PATIENT: Well, I don't know, I don't—He probably tells me what he thinks is necessary.

DOCTOR: But it's not enough for you.

CHAPLAIN: Well, she states this in terms of wanting to be told more. The examples she gives was, well, if I'm going to have a short time to live, which raised the question in my mind as to whether this is something that you are concerned about? Is this the way you are phrasing it in you own mind?

DOCTOR: What is a short time to live, Mrs. S.? That's terribly relative.

PATIENT: Oh, I don't know. I would say six months or a year.

CHAPLAIN: Did you feel as strongly about knowing if it weren't that kind of condition? I mean that's the illustration you used.

PATIENT: Whatever I have I have, and I would still want to know. I mean, there are some people I think you could tell and there are other people that you couldn't.

DOCTOR: What would change?

PATIENT: Oh, I don't know. Maybe I'd just try to enjoy each day a little bit more if I—

DOCTOR: You know no doctor can tell you the time. You know, he doesn't know—But some doctors mean well and give an approximate estimation, and some patients get terribly depressed and don't enjoy a single day after that. What do you say to that?

PATIENT: It wouldn't bother me.

DOCTOR: But you understand why some doctors are very leery.

PATIENT: Yes. I'm sure there are people who'd go and jump out a window or—do something drastic.

DOCTOR: Some people are like this, yes. But you have apparently thought about this for a long time, because you know where you stand. I think you should talk to the doctor, you should tell him. Just open the door and see how far you can get.

PATIENT: Maybe he doesn't think I should know just what I have, I mean that's—

CHAPLAIN: You'd find out.

DOCTOR: You always have to ask and then you get the answer.

PATIENT: My first doctor that I knew when I came in here, you know the first time when I came in to the clinic for my first checkup, I just had so much confidence in him, from the first day that I saw him.

CHAPLAIN: That's, I think, a justified confidence.

DOCTOR: That's very important.

PATIENT: I mean, I get home, you have your family doctor, you feel you are quite close to him.

DOCTOR: And then you lost him too.

PATIENT: And that was very hard because he was such a wonderful man. He had so much to live for. He was just, he was in his late fifties. And of course, as you know, a doctor's life isn't an easy life. And I think that he probably just didn't take care of himself like he should have. His patients came first.

DOCTOR: Like you! Your boys came first—

PATIENT: They always did.

DOCTOR: Was this so difficult now? You know, you came here kind of leery. Here to the conference.

PATIENT: Well, I didn't really feel too enthusiastic about coming.

DOCTOR: I know.

PATIENT: But then I thought, well, I just made up my mind I would.

CHAPLAIN: How do you feel about it now?

PATIENT: I'm glad I came.

DOCTOR: It wasn't so terrible, was it? You know you said you are not a good speaker. I think you did a very good job.

CHAPLAIN: Yes, I amen that. I was wondering, though, if you had any questions to ask us—catching the cue earlier that doctors don't slow down long enough to get the patient to ask a question. We are slowing down enough to where if you have any questions to ask us about the session, anything—

PATIENT: Oh, I mean, I, when you came and when you mentioned that, I just didn't quite understand what it would solve or what it would—what was the main idea, you know.

CHAPLAIN: Has this been answered in part, by the conference?

PATIENT: Partially, yes.

DOCTOR: You see, what we are trying to do is to learn from the patient really, how we can talk to complete strangers we haven't met before, and we haven't known each other at all, how can we get to know a patient, fairly well and pick up what kind of needs and wants he has. Then go about it to serve this, like I learned a lot from you now, that you know fairly well what your illness is, you know it's serious, you know it's in different places. I don't think anybody can tell you how long this is going to be going on. They tried a new diet, which I think they haven't given to many patients, but they have a lot of hopes with this. This I know is an unbearable kind of diet for you. I think everybody tries their best to make it, you know—

PATIENT: If that's what they think will help me then I want to try it.

DOCTOR: They do. That's why they give it to you. But what you are saying, I think, is that you would like to have some time to sit with the doctor and talk about it. Even if he can't give you all the answers all clear and pat; I think nobody can. But just to talk about it. The kind of things you do with your family doctor, the kind of things we are trying to do here.

PATIENT: I don't feel as nervous as I thought I would. I mean I feel quite at ease.

CHAPLAIN: I thought you were very relaxed sitting here.

PATIENT: When I first came in here I was just a little bit jumpy.
CHAPLAIN: You made that comment.
DOCTOR: I think we will take you back then. We'll drop in once in a while. Okay?
PATIENT: Sure.
DOCTOR: Thank you for coming.

In summary, then, we have here a typical example of a patient who has had many losses in her life, who needed to share her concerns with someone, and who felt relieved to ventilate some of her feelings with someone who cared.

Mrs. S. was two and a half when her parents divorced and she was raised by relatives. Her only daughter died at age two and a half from tuberculosis while her husband was in the service and she had no one else as close as this little girl. Soon afterward she lost her father in the sanatorium and had to be hospitalized herself with tuberculosis. After twenty-two years of marriage her husband left her with two small boys for another woman. A family doctor in whom she had great confidence and trust died when she needed him the most, namely, when she noticed a suspicious lump which later proved to be malignant. Raising the boys alone, she postponed treatment until the pain became unbearable and her malignancy was spread. In all her misery and loneliness she always found some meaningful friends, however, with whom she was able to share her concerns. They too were substitutes—just like her aunt and uncle were substitutes for her real parents; the boy friend replaced the husband, the neighbor substituted for a sister she never had. The latter was the most meaningful relationship as she became a substitute mother for the patient and her children as her illness progressed. This service fulfilled a need of her own and was done in an unintrusive, sensitive manner.

The social worker played a crucial role in the later management of this patient as well as her doctor, who was informed of her wish to share more personal matters with him.

The following is an interview of a seventeen-year-old girl with aplastic anemia, who asked to be seen in the presence of the students. An interview with her mother took place immediately afterwards, followed by a discussion among the medical students, attending physician, and nursing staff of her ward.

DOCTOR: I think I'll make it a little easy on you, okay, and let us know please if you get too tired or are in pain. Do you want to tell the group how long you have been ill and when it all started?

PATIENT: Well, it just came on me.

DOCTOR: And how did it come on?

PATIENT: Well, we were at a church rally in X, a small town from where we live, and I had gone to all the meetings. We had gone over to the school to have dinner and I got my plate and sat down. I got real cold, got the chills and started shaking and got a real sharp pain in my left side. So they took me to the minister's home and put me to bed. The pain kept getting worse and I just kept getting colder and colder. So this minister called his family doctor and he came over and said that I had an appendicitis attack. They took me to the hospital and it seemed like the pain kind of went away; it just kind of disappeared by itself. They took a lot of tests and found that it wasn't my appendix so they sent me home with the rest of the people. Everything was okay for a couple of weeks and I went back to school.

STUDENT: What did you think you had?

PATIENT: Well, I did not know. I went to school for a couple of weeks and then I got real sick one day and fell down the stairs and felt real weak and was blacking out. They called my home doctor and he came and told me that I was anemic. He put me in the hospital and gave me three pints of blood. Then I started getting these pains in here. They were bad and they thought maybe it was my spleen. They were going to take it out. They took a whole bunch of X-rays and everything. I kept having a lot of trouble and they didn't know what to do. Dr. Y. was consulted and I came up here for a checkup and they put me in the hospital for ten days. They ran a whole bunch of tests and that's when they found out that I was aplastic.

STUDENT: When was this?

PATIENT: That was about the middle of May.

DOCTOR: What did this mean to you?

PATIENT: Well, I wanted to be sure it was too, because I was missing so much school. The pain hurt quite a bit and then, you know, just to find out what it was. So I stayed in the hospital for ten days and they ran all kinds of tests and then they told me what I had. They said it was not terrible. They didn't have any idea what had caused it.

DOCTOR: They told you that it was not terrible?

PATIENT: Well, they told my parents. My parents asked me if I wanted to know everything, and I told them yes, I wanted to know everything. So they told me.

STUDENT: How did you take that?

PATIENT: Well, at first I didn't know and then I kind of figured that it was God's purpose that I got sick because it had happened all at once and I had never been sick before. And I figured that it was God's purpose that I got sick and that I was in his care and he would take care of me so I didn't have to worry. And I've just gone on like that ever since and I think that's what kept me alive, knowing that.

STUDENT: Ever get depressed about it?

PATIENT: No.

STUDENT: Do you think others might?

PATIENT: Oh, someone might get real, real sick. I feel that, you know, there's no reassuring thing, but I think everybody who gets sick feels that way once in a while.

STUDENT: Do you wish at times that it was not your parents that had told you about the condition—you wish maybe the doctors had told you about it, had come to you?

PATIENT: No, I like my parents to tell me better. Oh, I guess it was all right that they had told me, but I would have kind of enjoyed that so much . . . if the doctor had shared it with me.*

STUDENT: The people that have been working around you, the

*Here she expresses her ambivalence about being told by her parents instead of the doctor.

doctors, and nurses, do you think they have been avoiding the issue?

PATIENT: They never tell me anything, you know, just mostly my parents. They have to tell me.

STUDENT: Do you think you've changed your feelings about the outcome of this disease since the first time you heard about it?

PATIENT: No, I still feel the same.

STUDENT: Have you thought about it long?

PATIENT: Uh huh.

STUDENT: And this hasn't changed your feelings?

PATIENT: No, I went through the trouble, they can't find veins on me now. They give me so many other things like that with all these other problems, but we just have to keep our faith now.

STUDENT: Do you think you've got more faith during this time.

PATIENT: Uh huh. I really do.

STUDENT: Do you think this would be one way that you've changed? Your faith is the most important thing then that will pull you through?

PATIENT: Well, I don't know. They say that I might not pull through, but if he wants me to be well, I've got to get well.

STUDENT: Has your personality changed, have you noticed any changes each day?

PATIENT: Yes, because I get along with more people. I usually do, though. I go around and visit a few of the patients and help them. I get along with the other roommates, so I get someone else to talk to. You know, when you feel depressed it helps to talk to someone else.

DOCTOR: Do you get depressed often? Two of you were in this room before, now you are all alone?

PATIENT: I think it was because I was worn out. I haven't been outdoors for a week now.

DOCTOR: Are you getting tired now? Tell me when you get too tired, then we will finish this session.

PATIENT: No, not at all.

STUDENT: Have you noticed any change in your family or friends, in their attitude toward you?

PATIENT: I've been a lot closer to my family. We get along well, my brother and I were always close when we were small. You know he's eighteen and I'm seventeen, just fourteen months apart. And my sister and I were always real close. So now they and my parents are a lot closer. You know, I can talk to them more and they, oh, I don't know, it's just a feeling of more closeness.

STUDENT: It's deepened, enriched your relationship with your parents?

PATIENT: Uh huh, and with other kids, too.

STUDENT: Is this a sense of support for you during this illness?

PATIENT: Yes, I don't think I could go through it now without my family and all the friends.

STUDENT: They want to help you in every way possible. How about you, do you help them, too, in some way?

PATIENT: Well, I try to . . . whenever they come I try to make them feel at home and make them go home feeling better and things like that.

STUDENT: Do you feel very depressed when you're alone?

PATIENT: Yes, I kind of panic because I like people and I like to be around people and being with someone . . . I don't know, when I'm alone all the problems come up. Sometimes you do feel more depressed when there's nobody there to talk to.

STUDENT: Is there anything in particular that you feel when you're alone, anything that sort of scares you about being alone?

PATIENT: No, I just get to feeling that there's nobody there and nobody to talk to.

DOCTOR: Before you were sick, what kind of girl were you? Were you very outgoing or did you like to be alone?

PATIENT: Well, I was pretty outgoing. I liked to do sporty things, go places, go to games and to a lot of meetings.

DOCTOR: Have you ever been alone for any length of time before you were sick?

PATIENT: No.

STUDENT: If you had to do it over again, would you rather your parents had waited before telling you?

PATIENT: No, I'm glad I knew right from the start. I mean I'd rather know right at the beginning and know that I have to die and they can face me.

STUDENT: What is it that you do have to face, what's your vision of what death is like?

PATIENT: Well, I think it's wonderful because you go to your home, your other one, near to God, and I'm not afraid to die.

DOCTOR: Do you have a visual picture of this "other home," realizing, you know, all of us have some fantasies about it though we never talk about it. Do you mind talking about it?

PATIENT: Well, I just kind of think it's like a reunion where everybody is there and it is real nice and where there's someone else there—special, you know. Kind of makes the whole thing different.

DOCTOR: Is there anything else you can say about it, how it feels?

PATIENT: Oh, you would say you have a wonderful feeling, no more needs and just being there and never again alone.

DOCTOR: Everything just right?

PATIENT: Just right, uh huh.

DOCTOR: No need for food to stay strong?

PATIENT: No, I don't think so. You'll have a strength within you.

DOCTOR: You don't need all these earthly things?

PATIENT: No.

DOCTOR: I see. Well, how did you get this strength, all this courage to face it right from the beginning? You know many people have a religion, but very few at the time will just face it like you. Have you always been that way?

PATIENT: Uh huh.

DOCTOR: You never had any real deep hostile—

PATIENT: No.

DOCTOR: Or got angry at people who weren't sick.

PATIENT: No, I think I got along with my parents because they were missionaries for two years in S.

DOCTOR: I see.

PATIENT: And they've both been wonderful workers of the church. They just brought us all up in a Christian home and that has helped a great deal.

DOCTOR: Do you think we, as physicians, should speak to people who face a fatal illness about their future? Can you tell us what you would teach us if your mission was to teach us what we should do for other people?

PATIENT: Well, a doctor will just come in and look you over and tell you "How are you today" or something like that, a real phoney. It just kind of makes you resent being sick because they never speak to you. Or they come in like they are a different kind of people. Most of the ones I know do that. Well, they come down and talk with me for a little while and ask me how I feel and visit with me. They say things about my hair and that I'm looking better. They just talk to you and then they'll ask you how you feel and some get into explaining things as much as they can. It's kind of hard for them because I'm underage and they aren't supposed to tell me anything, because they are supposed to tell my parents. I think that's so important to talk to a patient because if there's a cold feeling between the doctors you kind of dread to have them come in if he's going to be cold and businesslike. When he comes in and is warm and human that means a great deal.

DOCTOR: Did you have a feeling of discomfort or unpleasantness about coming here and talking about it to us?

PATIENT: No, I don't mind talking about it.

STUDENT: How have the nurses handled this problem?

PATIENT: Most of them have been real wonderful and talk a great deal and I know most of them pretty well.

DOCTOR: You have the feeling that the nurses are able to handle it better than the physicians in a way?

PATIENT: Well, yes, because they are there more and they do more than the doctors.

DOCTOR: Uh huh, they just may be less uncomfortable.

PATIENT: I'm sure of that.

STUDENT: May I ask, has anybody in your family ever died since you grew up?

PATIENT: Yes, my dad's brother, my uncle died. I went to his funeral.

STUDENT: How did you feel?

PATIENT: Well, I don't know. He looked kind of funny, he looked different. But, you know that's the first person that I'd ever seen dead.

DOCTOR: How old were you?

PATIENT: I'd say about twelve or thirteen.

DOCTOR: You said "he looked funny" and you smiled.

PATIENT: Well, he did look different, you know, his hands didn't have any color and they did look so still. And then my grandmother died but I wasn't there. My grandfather died on my mother's side, but I wasn't there either, I just went on, you know. Oh, then my aunt died and I couldn't go to the funeral because it was not too long ago and I was sick and we didn't go.

DOCTOR: It comes in different forms and ways, doesn't it?

PATIENT: Yes, he was my favorite uncle. You don't really have to cry when somebody dies because you know they're going to heaven and it's kind of a happy feeling for them, to know that they're going to be in paradise.

DOCTOR: Did any of them talk about it to you at all?

PATIENT: A real, real close friend of mine just died, over a month ago and his wife and I went to his funeral. That meant a lot to me because he had been so wonderful and had done so much for me when I got sick. He left you feeling so comfortable and everything.

DOCTOR: So what you say is to be a little more understanding and take a little time and talk with the patients.

The interview with this young girl's mother follows. We talked with her soon after interviewing her daughter.

DOCTOR: We have a very few parents who are coming to us to talk about their very sick children and I know this setup is kind of unusual.

MOTHER: Well, I asked for it.

DOCTOR: What we talked about with your daughter is how she feels and how she looks at death. We were impressed by her calmness and lack of anxiety as long as she is not alone.

MOTHER: She talked much today?

DOCTOR: Yes.

MOTHER: She's in a great deal of pain today and feels very, very bad.

DOCTOR: She talked a lot, much much more than this morning.

MOTHER: Oh, and I was afraid she'd get in here without saying anything.

DOCTOR: We're not keeping you for long, but I would appreciate it if you would allow the young doctors to ask you a few questions.

STUDENT: When you first found out about your daughter's condition, that it was not curable, how did you react to this?

MOTHER: Well, very well.

STUDENT: You and your husband?

MOTHER: My husband wasn't with me at the time and I felt a little bad at the way I found out. We just knew that she was sick, but that was all and so then when I came down to visit her that day, I called to see how she was. The doctor said, "Oh, she's not at all good. I have some bad news for you." He showed me the way to one of the little rooms and he just, quite frankly, said, "Well, she has aplastic anemia and she's not going to get well, that's all." He said, "Nothing can be done, we don't know the cause, we don't know the cure." And so I said, "Well, can I ask you a question?" And he said, "If you want to." I said, "How long does she have, doctor, maybe a year?" "Oh, no, goodness no." And I said, "For this, we're lucky." And that's all he said and so then I had a lot of other questions.

DOCTOR: This was last May?

MOTHER: May, the 26th, uh huh. And he said, "There's a lot of people who have it, it's incurable and that's all there is to it. She'll just have to accept it." And he walked out. I had a hard time finding my way back to her ward and I guess I got lost in one of the halls, trying to go back I got panicky. All the time I just stood there and I thought, "Gee, it means she's not going to live," and I was all wrong and I didn't know how to get back to her. Then I pulled myself together and went back and talked with her. I was afraid at first to go in and tell her how sick she was because I didn't know how I felt and I might go in crying. So I straightened myself up before I went to see her again. But it was quite a shock the way it was presented to me and the fact that I was alone. If he had had me sit down at least and tell me, I think I could have accepted it a little better.

STUDENT: Exactly how did you wish that he would have presented it to you?

MOTHER: Well, if he had waited—my husband was with me every other time and this was the first time I was alone, and if he had called us both in and maybe said, "Well, she has this incurable disease." He could have told it to us frankly, but had a little bit of compassion and needn't seem so hard-hearted. I mean, how he put it, "Well, you're not the only one in the world."

DOCTOR: You know, I've run up against this many times and it hurts. Has it occurred to you that this man might have some difficulties about his own feelings in regard to such situations?

MOTHER: Yes, I've thought this, but it hurts anyway.

DOCTOR: Sometimes the only way they are able to communicate such news is in a cool, detached way.

MOTHER: You're right, too. A doctor can't get emotional about these things and probably should not. But I don't know, there must be better ways.

STUDENT: Have your feelings toward your daughter changed?

MOTHER: No, I'm just real thankful for each day that I have with her, but I hope and pray for a lot more, which isn't right, I know. But no, she was raised with the idea that death can be beautiful and it is nothing to worry about. I know she will be as brave when it happens. Just once have I seen her break down and cry to me, when she said, "Mother, you look worried," and she said, "Don't be worried, I'm not afraid." She said, "My God's waiting for me, he'll take care of me so don't you be afraid." She said, "I'm a little bit afraid, does that bother you?" I said, "No, I think everybody is." I said, "But you just keep up the way you are," I said. "Do you feel like crying? Go ahead and cry, everyone does." She said, "No, there's nothing to cry about." So I mean she had accepted it and we had accepted it, too.

DOCTOR: That was ten months ago, wasn't it?

MOTHER: Yes.

DOCTOR: A very short time ago you had also been given just "twenty-four hours."

MOTHER: Last Thursday the doctor said we were lucky if it was twelve to twenty-four hours. He wanted to give her some morphine to shorten it and make her less painful. We asked him if we could think about it for a minute and he said, "I don't see why you just don't do it and stop the pain." He walked away. We decided therefore it would be better for her to let him go ahead and do it. And so we told the floor doctor that he could tell him that we agreed. We never have seen him since and they have never given her the shot. Then she has had good days and she has real bad ones, but she is slowly getting more of it and she is needing all the things that I have been told that would happen from other patients.

DOCTOR: Where from?

MOTHER: Well, my mother is from P., there are two hundred of these patients and my mother has learned a lot about them. She said towards the end they get so that it hurts to even touch them and it hurts all over. Then she says, even to lift them, their bones break. Now she hasn't wanted to eat for a week or so and all these things begin to happen. Up until the 1st of March, you know, she used to chase the nurses up and down the hall and help them and take water to the other patients, cheer them up.

DOCTOR: So the last month has been the hardest.

STUDENT: Has this changed your relationship with your other children at all?

MOTHER: Oh, no, they used to quarrel all the time and she would quarrel and then she used to say, "Oh, I just hope that this will make it easier." They still quarrel a little bit, but I don't think that they quarrel any more than any other and they never hated each other, but (chuckles) they have been real nice to children.

STUDENT: How do they feel about it themselves?

MOTHER: Oh, they purposely don't baby her. They treat her just like they did before. That is good because it doesn't make her feel sorry for herself and they talk back to her a little bit and so forth. If they have other things to do well they tell her, "I'm not coming to see you this Saturday, I'll be down during the week instead. You understand me, don't you?" And she'd say, "Yeah, have fun." And she'll go along with the idea and each time they come they know that she probably won't be coming home, you know. So they realize and we leave word where we can be reached and get in touch with one another.

DOCTOR: Do you talk with your other children about this possible outcome?

MOTHER: Oh, yes.

DOCTOR: You talk about it open and frankly?

MOTHER: Yes, we do. We have been sort of a religious family. We have devotions every morning, pray before they go to school and I think this has been a great help to them because as a family, especially with teen-agers they've always got some place to go, something to do and we can't seem to get together to sit down and talk over problems and things like that, but they will take this time each morning and bring in family problems. We get things ironed out in these ten or fifteen minutes each morning and it brings us all together. We have talked about it quite a bit and in fact our daughter has made arrangements for her own funeral already.

DOCTOR: Do you want to tell us about that?

MOTHER: Yes, we talked about it. There was a little baby born in our community—in our church, in fact, who is blind. I think she's about six months old and one day my daughter up in the old hospital said, "Mother, I'd like to give my eyes to her when I die." And I said, "Well, we'll see what we can do about that, I don't know if they would take them." I said, "You know we really should talk about things like that, all of us should, because we never know when Daddy and I may be on the road and something may happen to us and you children will be left alone." And she said, "Yes, we should have all these things agreed upon." And she said, "Let's you and I now make it easy for the others. We'll write down what we would like to have done and we'll ask them what they would like to have done." So she made it easy for me and she said, "I'll start and then you tell me." So I just jotted down things that she told me and it made it much easier. But she always does try to make things easy for people.

STUDENT: Did you have any suspicion at all before you were told that it might be an incurable illness? You said your husband had been with you all the other times, this particular time you happened to be alone. Was there any particular reason why he wasn't there?

MOTHER: I try to go to the hospital as much as I can and he was ill. And he has more free time than I ordinarily would. So he was with me most of the time.

STUDENT: Your daughter told us he had been a missionary in S. and you're very active in church work. This was part of the reason for the deep religious background. What was the nature of his missionary work? Why isn't he still in it?

MOTHER: Well, he was a Mormon. And they always paid all his funds, paid all his benefits and everything, and so when we were first married, I went along to church for about a year. Then he started going with me and for seventeen years he went every Sunday with me and the children. About four or five years ago he joined our church and has been a worker—has been in it all that time.

STUDENT: I was wondering since your daughter does have a disease for which the cause and cure are not known, if you've never felt kind of an irrational feeling of guilt?

MOTHER: Yes, we have. Many times we've probed into the fact that I never have given them vitamins. My family doctor kept saying they didn't need it and I kept saying maybe they have, have been taking them, and then I tried to pin it down to all kinds of things. She had an accident back East. They say that could cause it because of the bone. They say any injury to the bone can cause this. But the doctors here say, "No, it would not—it had to be within a few months before." She has had a great deal of pain but she bears up under it so well. No, we always pray "Thy will be done" and we feel that if he wants to take her, he will and if not he'll perform a miracle. But we've almost half given up for a miracle, but they say never give up. We know that the best will be done. And we have asked her—this is another thing. They told us never to tell her. She had a great deal of growing up to do this last year. She's been in with all kinds of women, one who tried to commit suicide, and women who talked about their problems with their husbands and having babies. There isn't a thing she doesn't know and people she hasn't come in contact with. And she's had a great deal to put up with. The one thing she does not like is people trying to hide things from her. She wants to know about everything. So we told her. We talked it over and then when she was so terribly sick last week and we thought that this was the end. The doctor was telling us in the hall about this and she immediately asked, "What did he say, am I going to die now?" And I said, "Well, we're not sure. He said you're very bad." And so she said, "Well, what does he want to give me?" I never did tell her what, I said, "It's a painkiller." She said, "Is it dope, I don't want any dope." I said, "It would help your pain." And she said, "No, I would rather suffer through. I don't want to become a dope addict." I said, "You won't." And she said, "Mother, I'm just amazed at you." And she never did give up, just always keeps on hoping that she will get well.

DOCTOR: Do you want to finish this interview? We have only a few minutes left. Do you want to tell the group how you feel about the hospital treating you as the mother of a dying child. You want to be with her naturally as much as you possibly can. How much help have you gotten?

MOTHER: Well, it was very nice back in the old hospital. They were very friendly; they are much busier in the new one and the service isn't quite as good. They always make me feel like I'm in the way when I'm here, the resident doctor and the intern especially. I'm just in their way. I even get where I hide out down the hall and try to sneak past him. I feel like a thief coming in and going out because they look at me as if to say, "Are you here again?" They just brush past me, you know, don't talk to me. I feel like I'm invading on something, like I shouldn't be here. But I do want to stay here, and the only reason I stay is because my child asked me to and she's never asked me to before. And I try to stay out of the way. In fact, I don't mean to be conceited, but

I think I've helped a lot. They are very short-handed and I know the first two or three nights she was so bad, I don't know what she would have done because the nurses would avoid her and the older lady in the same room. The older lady had a heart attack and cannot even get on a bedpan and I had to help put her on some nights and my daughter would be throwing up and she needed to be washed and cared for and they just wouldn't do it. Somebody has to do it.

STUDENT: Where do you sleep?

MOTHER: In the chair right there. The first night I didn't have a pillow or a blanket or anything. One of the other patients who doesn't sleep with a pillow insisted that I take her pillow and I covered myself with my coat and then the next day I began bringing my own in. I guess I shouldn't tell it, but one of the janitors (chuckles) brings me a cup of coffee now and then.

DOCTOR: Good for him.

MOTHER: I feel like I shouldn't say all this, but I have to get it off my chest.

DOCTOR: I think these things should be brought out. It is important to think about these things and talk about it, not beat around the bush and say everything is fine.

MOTHER: No, as I was saying, the attitude of the doctors and nurses makes such a difference with the patients and family.

DOCTOR: I should hope you had some good experiences, too.

MOTHER: I should say. There's a girl who works at nighttime and they have been taking things and several of the patients complained and nothing was done about it. She is still on the job and so these patients now lay awake at night waiting for her to come in the room because they are afraid of these things being stolen. And when she does come, she's very rude, you know, and extremely mean, and she's a maid. And then the next night a nice, tall colored boy came in to our door and he said, "Good evening. I'm here to make your night more cheerful," and his whole attitude was great. All night long he came when I pushed the bell. He was just wonderful. And the next morning both patients in the room were one hundred percent better and this makes the day so much better.

DOCTOR: Thank you, Mrs. M.
MOTHER: I hope I didn't talk too much.

Following is the interview with Mrs. C., who felt that she could not face her own death because of the pressure of family obligations.

DOCTOR: You said you had so many things that go through your head when you lay in bed alone and think. And so we offered to sit together for a while and just listen. One of your big questions involved your children. Is that correct?

PATIENT: Yes, my biggest concern is my little daughter. I also have three sons.

DOCTOR: They are almost grown up, though, aren't they?

PATIENT: Yes, but I know that children react to very sick parents, especially when it is the mother. You know that these things do have quite a bearing in childhood. I wonder what this might do to her when she grows up like this. When she grows up and looks back at those things.

DOCTOR: What kind of things?

PATIENT: Well, first the fact that her mother has become inactive. Much more inactive than she has ever been before, both in school and church activities. And I am more afraid now of who is taking care of my family. More afraid than when I was at home, even when I was inactive at home. A lot of times it is not known among the friends and nobody wants to talk about it. So I told others, I thought people should know it. And then I wonder if I did the right thing? I wonder if whether I did the right thing in letting my girl know that young, or whether it should have been postponed until later?

DOCTOR: How did you tell her?

PATIENT: Well, children are quite outright in the questions they ask. I was perfectly frank in the way I answered her. But I did it with feelings. I have always had a feeling of hope. A feeling of hope that they might discover something new any day and I still might have a chance. I was not afraid and I feel that she should not be afraid. If the disease ever progressed to a state of hopelessness, that I could not function any more and that I would become too uncomfortable, I was not afraid to still go on. I hope that she was developing and maturing through Sunday school work. If I only knew that she could go on and that she did not feel it was a tragedy. I never, never wanted her to feel that way. I just don't feel that way and that's how I talked with her. Many times I tried to be cheerful with her and she always thinks they are going to fix me up in here. And this time again, she thinks they are going to fix me up in here!

DOCTOR: You still have some hope but certainly not as much as your family has. Is this what you are saying? And it may be the difference of awareness that makes it more difficult.

PATIENT: Nobody knows how long this can still last. I surely have always held on to hope, but this is the lowest I have ever been. The doctors have not revealed anything to me. They have not told me what they have found during the operation. But anybody would know without being told. My weight is down to the lowest it has ever been. My appetite is very poor. They say I have an infection that they have not been able to discover— When you have leukemia, the worst thing that can happen to you is to get an infection on top of it.

DOCTOR: You were upset yesterday when I came to visit you. You had a colon X-ray and you felt like giving somebody a piece of your mind.

PATIENT: Right. You know it is not the big things that count when you are so sick and so weak. It is the little things that count. Why in the world can't they talk with me? Why can't they tell you before they do certain procedures? Why don't they let you go to the bathroom before they take you out of the room like a thing, not like a person?

DOCTOR: What really upset you that much yesterday morning?

PATIENT: It is really very personal, but I just have to tell you. Why don't they supply you with an extra pair of pajamas when you go for this colon X-ray? When you get done you are in an absolute mess. Then you are supposed to sit in a chair and you just don't have any desire to sit in that chair. You know it's going to be a mass of white chalk when you get up, and it's an uncomfortable situation. I thought, well, they are so wonderful to me upstairs there in my room but when they send me down here to X-ray I feel like a number or something, you know. They do these strange things to you and it is very uncomfortable to come back in that state. I don't know how this happens but it seems to happen all the time. I don't think it should happen. I think they should tell you ahead of time. I was very weak and very tired. The nurse that brought me up here thought I could walk and I said, "Well, if you think I can walk I can try." By the time I had all my X-rays and climbing up on the table and everything, I was so weak and tired, I wasn't quite sure I could reach my room.

DOCTOR: That must make you feel angry and frustrated.

PATIENT: I don't get angry too often. I suppose the last time I can remember being angry was when my older son went out and my husband was working. There was no way to lock the house, and, of course, I didn't feel safe to go to sleep with the house unlocked. We are right on the corner. There is a street light on the corner, and I couldn't fall asleep until I knew the house was locked. I had talked to him so much about this and he has been pretty good about calling and letting me know but this night he didn't.

DOCTOR: Your oldest son is a problem child, isn't he? You mentioned yesterday briefly that he has been emotionally disturbed and retarded too, isn't he?

PATIENT: Correct. He has been in a state hospital for four years.

DOCTOR: And he is back home now?

PATIENT: He is home.

DOCTOR: Do you feel that there should be more control over him, and you are a bit worried that he doesn't have enough control, like you over the unlocked house that night?

PATIENT: That is correct, and I feel that I'm the one that's responsible—so much responsible and I can do so little now.

DOCTOR: What happens when you cannot be responsible anymore?

PATIENT: Well, we are hoping that maybe this will open his eyes a little wider because he cannot understand things. He has a lot of good in him but he needs help. He could never manage on his own.

DOCTOR: Who would help him?

PATIENT: Well, there is the problem.

DOCTOR: Can you speculate, do you have people in your house who would help out?

PATIENT: Well, of course, as long as my husband is living he could look after him. But it is a concern because he has to be away from home so many hours working. We have the grandparents there but even then I feel that is altogether unsatisfactory.

DOCTOR: Whose parents?

PATIENT: My husband's father and my mother.

DOCTOR: Are they in good health?

PATIENT: No, they are not in good health. My mother has Parkinson's disease and my father-in-law has a bad heart condition.

DOCTOR: All this in addition to your concerns about your twelve-year-old girl? You have your older son and he is a problem. You have your mother with Parkinson's, who will probably start shaking when she tries to help somebody. Then you have a father on your husband's side who has a heart condition and you are not well. Somebody should be at home to take care of all those people. This I think is what bothers you most.

PATIENT: Right. We try to make friends and hope that the situation would be taken care of. We live from day to day. Each day seems to be taking care of itself, but as far as looking ahead, you cannot help but wonder. You know, with me having this illness on top of everything else. You never know if you should just try to be wise and accepting the situation calmly from day to day or if you should make a drastic change.

DOCTOR: Change?

PATIENT: Yes, there has been a time when my husband said, "a change has to be made." The old folks have to go. One would have to go to my sister, the other would have to go to a nursing home. You just have to learn to be cold, and put your family in an institution. Even my family doctor thinks I should put my son in an institution. And still I cannot accept these things. In the end I went to them and said, "No, I may feel worse if you leave, so you stay. And if it ever has to be, if it does not work out, you just come back again. If you went away it would be worse." I had advised them to come in the first place.

DOCTOR: You would feel guilty if they went to a nursing home?

PATIENT: Well, I would not if it got to the point where it was dangerous for them to go up and down stairs or—I do feel it's getting a little dangerous for my mother around the stove now.

DOCTOR: You have been so used to taking care of other people, it must be tough for you to be taken care of now yourself.

PATIENT: It's a bit of a problem. I have a mother who tries to help me, a mother who is more interested in her children than anything else in the world. That is not always the best thing too, because you should have other interests, you know. She has been entirely interested in her family. That's her life, sewing and doing little things for my sister who lives next door. I'm glad of that because my daughter can go over there. And I'm very happy that my sister lives next door. So my mother goes over there and this is good for her too because it makes a little change for her.

DOCTOR: It makes it easier for everybody. Mrs. C., can you tell us a little more about you. You said that this time you feel the weakest, that you have lost the most weight. When you are in bed, you know, lying there alone, what kind of things do you think about and what helps you most?

PATIENT: Well, coming from the kind of family that I came from and my husband came from, we knew that if we started our marriage we had to have an outer strength besides ourselves. He was a Boy Scout leader and there had been marital problems between his father and mother who eventually separated. This was the second marriage for my father, he had three children. He married a very young waitress and that didn't work out at all. It was really pitiful, these little children were divided around, you know. They didn't come to live with my mother when he married my mother. My father was a very temperamental person, a very high-strung man with not a good disposition. And now I often wonder how did I cope with it. And so when we lived in that area my husband and I met each other in church. We were married. And we knew that to make our marriage we had to have outside strength. We've always felt that way. We've always been active in church work and I started teaching Sunday school when I was sixteen years old. They needed help in the nursery so I did it and I enjoyed it. I taught up until I had the two older boys. I enjoyed it and I often gave devotions in my church and told them what my church meant to me. What my God meant to me, so I think you just don't throw that all overboard when something happens. You go on believing, you know that whatever happens, will happen.

DOCTOR: That's something that helps you now too?

PATIENT: Yes. And when my husband and I talk we know we both feel the same way. As I told Chaplain C., we know that we could never be tired with other people talking about it. I told him also our love is as strong now after twenty-nine years of marriage as it was when we were married. This is another thing that means a lot to me. We have been able, with all our problems, to face them. He's a wonderful man, a very wonderful man!

DOCTOR: You dealt with your problems courageously and well, the hardest perhaps being your son?

PATIENT: We did the best we could. I don't think it's just an opportunity for any parent. You just don't know how to quite deal with it. You think it's stubbornness at first, you just don't know.

DOCTOR: How old was he when you noticed that he had a problem?

PATIENT: Well, you find it quite obvious. They don't ride a tricycle and do not do all the other things that children do. But actually, a mother doesn't want to accept these things. She will find other explanations at first.

DOCTOR: How long did it take you?

PATIENT: Up to my age, but actually when he got into school, into kindergarten, he was a problem to the teacher. He often stuck something into his mouth to attract attention. I began to get reports from the teacher, then I knew definitely that we had a problem with him.

DOCTOR: So you accepted the full facts step by step just as you did with the diagnosis of leukemia. What kind of people in the hospital help you the most with your daily problems?

PATIENT: Every time you run across a nurse who expresses faith, it's a big help. As I say, when I went down to that X-ray yesterday I felt just sort of like a number, you know, and there wasn't anybody who cared very much, especially when I went down the second time. It was late and they were disturbed that they would send a patient down there that late. So they were disturbed all the way around. I knew when she brought me, she was going to put that wheelchair there and disappear, and I'd sit there until someone came out. But one of the girls there told her she shouldn't do that, she should go in and tell them I was there and have them come out. I think she was upset having to go that late with a patient. They were closing up, the technicians were going home and it was late. Little things like this, you know, the cheerfulness of the nurses would help so much.

DOCTOR: What do you think of people who have no faith?

PATIENT: Well, I run across that, too. I run across that with patients here, too. There was a gentleman who was here last time and when he found out what I had he said, "I can't understand, nothing fair in this world, why should you have leukemia, you've never smoked, you never drank, you never did anything like that," you know. He said, "Me, I'm an old man, I did a lot of things I never should have done." It doesn't make any difference. We are not told that we will never have any problems. Our Lord himself had terrific problems to face, so he's the one who teaches us and I am trying to follow him.

DOCTOR: Do you ever think about dying?

PATIENT: Do I think about it?

DOCTOR: Yes.

PATIENT: Yes, I do. I oftentimes think about dying. I don't like the idea of everybody coming to see me because I look so awful. Why does that have to happen? Why can't they just have a little memorial service? You know, I don't like the idea of funerals, you know, maybe that's strange. I just have a repulsion, my body in that casket.

DOCTOR: I am not sure I understand.

PATIENT: I don't like to make people unhappy, like my children, by two or three days of this sort of thing, you know. I thought about that and have done nothing about it. My husband asked me one day when he came in; he said, shall we actually look into this, donating our eyes or donating our bodies? We didn't do it that day, and we still haven't done it because it's one of those things you put off, you know.

DOCTOR: Do you ever talk with anybody about it? Kind of preparing yourself for that time whenever it comes?

PATIENT: Well, as I told Chaplain C., I think for many people there is such a need to lean on somebody, to talk to the chaplain and they want all the answers from him.

DOCTOR: And does he give them the answers?

PATIENT: I think if you understand Christianity, by the time you reach my age you should be mature enough to know that you can reach out and have this yourself because you are going to be by yourself a great many hours. You are alone in illness, because people just can't be with you all the time. You can't have the chaplain with you, you can't have your husband with you, you can't have people with you. My husband is the kind of person who would be with me as much as he could.

DOCTOR: It helps then most to have people with you?

PATIENT: Oh, yes, especially certain people.

DOCTOR: Who are the certain people? You mentioned the chaplain, your husband.

PATIENT: Yes. I enjoy having my pastor coming to visit with me, from my church. There was another young friend of mine about the same age as I am and she's a very fine Christian. She has lost the sight of her eyes. She was in the hospital for several months flat on her back. She accepted it very well. She is the type of person that is forever doing something for somebody else. If they are ill she is visiting them, or she is collecting clothes for the poor or something like that. She wrote me a nice letter the other day and she quoted the 139th Psalm and I really enjoyed getting that. She said, "I wanted you to know you are one of my closest friends." So you look for a person like that and it makes you happy. It's the little things that make you happy. As a whole I think they are very friendly here now. I think I'm a little bit tired, though, about hearing people suffer in the rooms. I hear this and I think, oh, why can't they do something for that person, you know. It's been going on for a long time and you hear them crying out and you fear that maybe they are alone. You have no right to go to their room and talk to them, you just *hear* them, you know. This sort of thing bothers me. The first time I was here I couldn't sleep too well and I thought about it. I thought, well, this can't go on. You're just going to have to get your sleep. So I slept quite well. But I heard two patients crying out that night. It is a thing I hope that I never do. I had a cousin who had cancer not long ago and she was older than I. She was a very wonderful person. She was crippled from birth but she handled it just beautifully. She was in the hospital for a great many months, she never cried out. The last time I visited her was a week before she died. She was a real inspiration. She really was because she was more concerned about me for making the trip over to see her than she was about herself.

DOCTOR: That's the kind of woman you would like to be, hm?

PATIENT: Well, she helped me. I hope I can do it.

DOCTOR: I am sure you can. You have been doing it right here today.

PATIENT: I have one more thing that worries me—one never knows when they get in an unconscious state like that how they are going to react. Sometimes they react differently. I guess it is important that you have confidence in your doctor then, that he can stay with you. Dr. E. is very busy so you just don't talk much with him. Unless he would ask you, you wouldn't bring up a lot of family problems or anything, although I have always felt how much of a bearing do these things have on my health. You know very well that problems can have quite a bearing on your physical health.

CHAPLAIN: That's what you implied the other day that you wondered if the pressures of your family and all the problems there affected your health too.

PATIENT: Yes, because it is true, our son was very bad at Christmastime and in fact his dad took him back to the state hospital. He volunteered to go. He said "I'll pack when we get home from church." Then he got down there and changed his mind and came home. His dad said he told him he wanted to go back home, so he took him home. Usually when this boy comes home this boy will pace back and forth. He can't even sit he is so restless sometimes.

DOCTOR: How old is he?

PATIENT: He's twenty-two. It's okay if you can cope with it and do something about it but when you cannot give him his answers or help him it is a terrific thing, just to talk to him. Not long ago I tried to explain what had happened when he was born and he seemed to understand. I said, "You have an illness like I have an illness and you have the roughest time sometimes. I know you have a terrifically rough time and I know how hard it is for you. In fact I give you a lot of credit for coming out of these rough times and settling down again," you know, and going on. I think he tried harder too, but you really have a mental condition there that you never quite know actually what to do about.

CHAPLAIN: This has been a tension for you. It must tire you, I'm sure.

PATIENT: That's right. I'm sure he's been my biggest problem.

DOCTOR: Your father's first wife had little children and they were kind of distributed and now you have the same question yourself. What is going to happen to them?

PATIENT: My biggest conflict is how can I keep them together, how can I keep from sending them to all sorts of institutions! Well, naturally I feel it will work out. If a person really becomes bedridden then you have an entirely different problem. I may become bedridden again and I say to my husband this will work itself out as the years went by but that hasn't happened. My father-in-law had a very serious heart attack and actually we didn't think he'd do as well as he has. It has been amazing. But he is happy and yet sometimes I wonder if he wouldn't be happier in a situation with other old gentlemen the same age.

DOCTOR: Then you could send him to a nursing home?

PATIENT: Yes, it would not be as hard as he thinks it would be. But he is so proud of being with his son and his wife. He was raised in the town and was in the town all his life.

CHAPLAIN: How old is he?

PATIENT: He is eighty-one.

DOCTOR: He is eighty-one and your mother is seventy-six? Mrs. C., I think we will have to finish because I promised not to make it longer than forty-five minutes. Yesterday you said nobody had talked with you about how your home problems affect you and your thoughts about dying. Do you think this is something that doctors or nurses or anybody else in the hospital should do if the patient so wishes?

PATIENT: It's helpful, very helpful.

DOCTOR: Who should do it?

PATIENT: Well, if you're fortunate enough to have that kind of a doctor, and there are a few, you know, that are going up and are interested in this side of your life. Most of them are purely interested in the medical part of the patient. Dr. M. is very understanding. He has come to see me twice now since I've been here and I appreciate that.

DOCTOR: Why do you think there is such a reluctance?

PATIENT: Well, it's the same thing on the outside world today. How come we don't have more people doing more things that should be done?

DOCTOR: I think we should finish, don't you? Do you have any questions that you would like to ask us, Mrs. C.? We'll be seeing you again anyway.

PATIENT: No. I only hope to get in front of more and more people and tell them about these things that need help. My boy isn't the only one. There's a lot of people in the world and you just try to have someone interested enough in the case so that possibly they could do something for him.

Mrs. C. is similar to Mrs. S., a middle-aged woman for whom death approaches in the midst of a life of responsibilities, caring for a number of dependent people. She has a father-in-law who is eighty-one and who recently had a heart attack, a mother with Parkinson's disease who is seventy-six, a twelve-year-old girl who still needs her mother and may have to grow up "too quickly" as the patient fears, and a twenty-two-year-old nonfunctioning son who goes in and out of state hospitals, for whom she both fears and cares. Her own father left three small children from a previous marriage and the patient worries that she too has to leave all these dependent people now at a time when they need her the most. It is understandable that such family burdens make it extremely difficult to die peacefully until these matters are discussed and some solutions found. If such a patient has no opportunity to share her concerns, she is both angry and depressed. Her anger is perhaps best demonstrated in her indignation about the hospital staff member who feels that she can walk to X-ray, who does not take her needs into consideration, and who is more concerned about the end of the working day than the efficient management of a weak, tired patient who likes to function as long as she can—but not beyond—and who likes to keep her dignity in spite of the unpleasant circumstances.

She describes perhaps best the need for perceptive, understanding people and their influence on the suffering; she sets an example when she allows the old folks to stay at her own home and function as best as they can, rather than sending them off to a nursing home. Also her son, whose presence is barely tolerable but who wishes to stay home rather than to return to the state hospital, is allowed to stay at home and to share as much as he is capable of sharing. In all this struggle to take care of everybody as best as she can, she also communicates the wish to be allowed to stay home and function as long as she can; even if it means being bedridden, her presence there should be tolerated. Her final statement, her wish to get in front of more and more people and let them know the needs of the sick, was perhaps partially fulfilled by this seminar.

Mrs. C. was a patient who wanted to share and accepted help gratefully in contrast to Mrs. L. who accepted the invitation but was unable to share her concerns until much later on, shortly before her death when she asked us to come and visit her.

Mrs. C. continued to do as many things as possible until the question of her emotionally disturbed son was solved. Her understanding husband and her religion helped her and gave her the strength to endure the weeks of suffering. Her last wish, namely, not to be seen "ugly" in the casket, was shared with her husband who understood that Mrs. C. always had a great concern for others. I think this fear of appearing ugly was expressed also in her concerns for the patients she hears crying out loud, "losing their dignity perhaps," and when she fears to lose consciousness and says, "One never knows when they get in an unconscious state . . . how they are going to react. . . . It is important that you have confidence in your doctor then, that he can stay with you. . . . Dr. E. is very busy, so you just don't talk much with him. . . ."

This is not so much a concern for others as it is her fear of perhaps losing control, of becoming indignant when the family problems become too overwhelming and her strength too small.

In a subsequent visit she acknowledged the wish to "scream sometimes"—"Please take over, I just cannot worry for everybody any longer." She was greatly relieved when the chaplain and the social worker intervened and the psychiatrist looked into a possibility of a placement for her son. It was only after all these matters were taken care of that Mrs. C. felt at peace and stopped worrying whether she was seen in the casket or not. That image changed from "looking so awful" to a picture of peace, rest, and dignity which coincided with her final acceptance and decathexis.

The following interview of Mrs. L. will speak for itself. It has been included in this book because she represents the type of patient who can frustrate us the most, since she fluctuates in her willingness to accept help and her denial of any need for help. It is important that we do not impose our services on such patients but remain available to them when they need us.

DOCTOR: Mrs. L., how long now have you been in the hospital?
PATIENT: I came to the hospital the 6th of August.
DOCTOR: That's not the first time, is it?
PATIENT: No, no. I believe it's close to twenty or more times that I've been here.
DOCTOR: When was the first time?
PATIENT: Well, the first time was in 1933 when I had my first baby. But the first time I entered this hospital was in 1955.
DOCTOR: What was it then?

PATIENT: That is when I had my adrenalectomy.

DOCTOR: What did you have your adrenalectomy for?

PATIENT: Because I had a malignancy in the base of my spine.

DOCTOR: In 1955?

PATIENT: Yes.

DOCTOR: So you have had this malignancy for eleven years now?

PATIENT: No, I've had it longer than eleven years. I had one breast removed in 1951. And the second breast was removed in 1954, and the adrenalectomy and the ovaries were removed here in '55.

DOCTOR: How old are you now?

PATIENT: I'm fifty-four, going to be fifty-five.

DOCTOR: Fifty-four. And you have been ill, nearly, as far as you know, since 1951.

PATIENT: That's right.

DOCTOR: Can you tell us how it all started?

PATIENT: Well, I was having a little bit of a family reunion in '51, and I had all of my husband's relatives from out of town. And I went upstairs to clean up and take a bath and I noticed I had a lump on top of my breast. I called my sister-in-law in and asked her if she thought it was anything to worry about. So she said yes, call a doctor and make an appointment, which I did. This was on Friday and I went in to the doctor's office the following Tuesday and on Wednesday I went to the hospital for X-rays. And they told me that it was a malignancy. And by the first of the following week I had surgery, and a breast removed.

DOCTOR: How did you take all that? You were about how old?

PATIENT: I was about thirty—well, close to forty years old. I don't know, everybody thought that I would collapse. They couldn't understand why I was so calm about it. In fact I made fun of the fact. I was hit a couple of times across the hands and the mouth by my sister-in-law for passing the remark that it might be a malignancy when I found the lump. And I took it very lightly. My oldest son took it the worst.

DOCTOR: How old is he?

PATIENT: He was seventeen, not quite seventeen, a few months lacking seventeen. And he stayed home until after I had surgery. Then he went into the service because he was afraid that I would be sick or completely bedridden or something else would happen so he went into the service. But other than that, it didn't bother—the only thing that bothered me was the radiation treatments that I got afterwards.

DOCTOR: How old were your other children? It sounded like there were more.

PATIENT: Yes, I have another boy who is twenty-eight.

DOCTOR: Now?

PATIENT: Now. He was in grammar school at the time.

DOCTOR: You have two boys?

PATIENT: Two boys.

DOCTOR: Your son was really afraid you were going to die.

PATIENT: I think so.

DOCTOR: And he took off.

PATIENT: He took off.

DOCTOR: How did he take it later on?

PATIENT: Well, he has what I tease him about—the "hospital-phobia" because he just can't come to the hospital and see me laying in bed. The only time he has ever come in was when they were giving me a blood transfusion. His father has asked him occasionally to either bring something home or bring something up to me that would be too heavy for him to carry.

DOCTOR: How were you told that you had the malignancy?

PATIENT: Very bluntly.

DOCTOR: Is that good or bad?

PATIENT: It didn't bother me. I don't know how anybody else would take it, but I'd sooner know, that's my version of it. I'd sooner be told than have everybody else know about it. I think you become more susceptible to the fact that everybody is giving you too much attention, you'd figure something's wrong, that's the way I feel about it.

DOCTOR: It would make you suspicious anyway.

PATIENT: I think so.

DOCTOR: And then it was 1951 and now it's 1966 and you have been in the hospital, in and out, about twenty times.

PATIENT: I should say so.

DOCTOR: What do you think you can teach us.

PATIENT: (Laughs) I don't know, I still have a lot to learn.

DOCTOR: What is your physical condition now? I see you have a brace. Do you have difficulties with your spine?

PATIENT: This is my spine. I had a spinal fusion last June, a year ago last June 15th, and I am told that I have to wear the brace continually. Right now I'm in for a little trouble with my right leg. But with the help of the good doctors here in this hospital, why, they'll conquer that for me too.

I had a numbness. I had lost use of it a little bit and had a tingling sensation in the legs, like needles and pins. Yesterday they just disappeared. Now I can move my leg freely and it feels back to normal again.

DOCTOR: Have you had any recurrence of your malignancy?

PATIENT: No, I haven't. I was told that it's nothing to worry about, that it's dormant at the time.

DOCTOR: How long has it been dormant now?

PATIENT: Well, I suspect that it might have been dormant since the adrenalectomy; of course, I don't know too much. If the doctors tell me good news, I let it go at that.

DOCTOR: You like to hear that.

PATIENT: Every time I walk out the door I say to my husband, this is the last time I'm coming back here, I'm not going back anymore. When I went out of here last May 7th, he said it for me so I wouldn't have to say it. But it didn't last long. I was back here the 6th of August.

DOCTOR: You have a smiling face but deep down there is a lot more sorrow and sadness.

PATIENT: Well, I guess you get that way at times.

DOCTOR: How do you take it, to have a malignancy, to have twenty hospitalizations, to have your breasts removed, and the adrenals removed.

PATIENT: And the spinal fusions—

DOCTOR: Spinal fusions, how do you take it all? Where do you get your strengths and what are your concerns?

PATIENT: I don't know, I guess just faith in God and the doctors helps me.

DOCTOR: Which one comes first?

PATIENT: God.

CHAPLAIN: We have talked about that before, and yet even though you have this faith to sustain you, there are times when you feel unhappy.

PATIENT: Oh, yes.

CHAPLAIN: This is something that is hard to avoid, the depression at times.

PATIENT: Yes. I feel a depression, I think, more when I have been alone for any length of time. I think over the past and I think that there is no use laying and thinking about that. It's all behind me. I should think more about the future. When I first came down, and knew that I was going to be operated on for cancer, why, I had these two boys at home, and I prayed that I would be saved just long enough to raise those boys.

DOCTOR: They are big boys now, aren't they? So that worked out all right. (Patient crying)

PATIENT: That's all I need, excuse me, I need a good cry.

DOCTOR: That's all right. I wonder why you said to avoid the depression. Why should you avoid it?

CHAPLAIN: Well, I used a poor word. Mrs. L. and I have talked a lot about how to deal with depression. It's not to be avoided really. It's to be encountered and overcome.

PATIENT: I cannot help but cry sometimes. Sorry—

DOCTOR: No, no, I encourage that.

PATIENT: Oh, you did—

DOCTOR: Yes, I think avoiding it only makes it rougher, doesn't it?

PATIENT: Well, no, I don't. I think you feel worse after you let yourself go, that's my version of it. Because anybody that's in like this as long as I have, why, I think you should be thankful for what's been in the past. You have a lot that many other people haven't had the opportunity of having.

DOCTOR: Would you be referring to the extra time?

PATIENT: The extra time for one thing. I have witnessed that experience in my own family within the last few months. And I feel that I've been very fortunate that these things did not happen to me.

CHAPLAIN: Do you mean the experience of your brother-in-law?
PATIENT: Yes.
CHAPLAIN: He died here.
PATIENT: Yes, the 5th of May.
DOCTOR: What was that experience?
PATIENT: Well, he wasn't sick very long, and he didn't have the opportunity to stay anytime as long as I do. I can't say he was an old man. He had an illness that if he had taken care of it from the beginning—I think that it was sheer neglect on his part, but nevertheless it wasn't that long.
DOCTOR: How old was he?
PATIENT: He was sixty-three.
DOCTOR: What did he have?
PATIENT: He had cancer.
DOCTOR: Well, did he not pay attention to it or what?
PATIENT: He had been ill for about six months before and everybody had told him that he should go to a doctor, go someplace and get care. He would neglect himself until he couldn't care for himself any longer. Then he decided to come in here and ask for help. He and his wife were very perturbed that they couldn't save his life like they saved mine. As I say, he waited until he couldn't stand it any longer.
DOCTOR: Is the extra time a kind of a special time? Different from other time?
PATIENT: No, I can't say it's different. I can't say that because I feel my life is as normal as yours and the chaplain's. I don't feel I'm running on borrowed time nor do I feel that I've got to make more of this time that's left. I figure my time is the same as yours.
DOCTOR: Some people have the feeling that they are living more intensively.
PATIENT: No.
DOCTOR: You know, but that's not true for everybody, you don't share this?
PATIENT: No, no, I know I don't. And I know that we all have a time to go and it's not my time, that's all.
DOCTOR: Have you in any way attempted or even thought about that this is the time to get more ready to die?

PATIENT: No. I just go on from day to day as I've done before.

DOCTOR: Oh. You never even think in terms of how it is and what it means?

PATIENT: No. I've never thought of it.

DOCTOR: Do you think people should? Since we all have to die one day.

PATIENT: Well, it's never really entered my mind to think of preparing myself to die. I think that if the time should come there is something within you that will tell you. I don't feel like I'm ready yet. I think I have a long time.

DOCTOR: Yes, no one knows.

PATIENT: No, but I mean I just figure that I raised those two boys. I'm gonna help look after those grandchildren too.

DOCTOR: You have grandchildren?

PATIENT: Seven of them.

DOCTOR: So you are waiting for them to grow up.

PATIENT: Now I'm waiting for them to grow up and see my great-grandchildren.

DOCTOR: When you are in the hospital, what kind of things help you best?

PATIENT: Oh, I'd be with the doctors a hundred percent if I can.

CHAPLAIN: I think I know one answer to that, too, and that is that you always have a picture of the future, of a goal that you want. You keep saying that all you want is to be able to go home and move around.

PATIENT: That's right. I want to walk again. Which I'm pretty sure I'm gonna do as well as I did many years ago. It's a determination.

DOCTOR: What do you think helped that you didn't let go? You didn't give up?

PATIENT: I just feel that the only one I have left at home now is my husband and he's a bigger baby than all the babies put together. He is diabetic and it has affected his eyes so he can not see too well. We are on disability pension.

DOCTOR: How much can he do?

PATIENT: Well, he can't do too much. His eyesight is poor. He can't see the traffic lights on the street. And last time I was in the hospital he was talking to Mrs. S. and she sat on one side of the bed and she asked him if he could see her. He said he could see her but she was fuzzy so from that I gather that his eyesight is poor. He can see the big headlines in the paper but the second grade headlines he has to use a magnifying glass for and from there on he can't see.

DOCTOR: At home who takes care of whom?

PATIENT: Well, he made a promise with me when I came out of the hospital last October that if I would be his eyes, he would be my feet and that's our plan.

DOCTOR: That's very nice. How has it worked out?

PATIENT: Well, it has worked out pretty good. He makes a mess of the table accidentally, then I do it on purpose so that he thinks that he didn't do it because of his eyesight. If something happens, he should stumble or something, why, I tell him I do it all the time and I got two good eyes so he shouldn't feel bad about it.

CHAPLAIN: He feels bad sometimes?

PATIENT: Oh, yes, it does bother him at times.

DOCTOR: Has he applied—or considered a dog or applied for some training, some mobility training and things like that?

PATIENT: We have a homemaker from the Salvation Army. And the worker has been out to the house. She told him that she was going to see if there was something that they could get for him, as far as help.

DOCTOR: The Lighthouse for the Blind can evaluate his needs, they give mobility training and a cane if necessary.

PATIENT: Well, that would be fine.

DOCTOR: It sounds like at home you are chipping in for each other and each one does what the other one can't do. So you must have a lot of concern about how he's coming along when you are in the hospital.

PATIENT: That's right, I do.

DOCTOR: How is he coming along?

PATIENT: Well, my children have him over for the evening meal. Three times a week we have the homemaker that comes in and she does the cleaning and the ironing. He is able to do the washing. I don't discourage him in anything that he's done. I noticed he has slipped a lot in a lot of things but I tell him it looks good, to keep on doing it, and leaving him in charge.

DOCTOR: You kind of keep telling him things to make him feel good.

PATIENT: I try to.

DOCTOR: Do you do that with yourself too?

PATIENT: I don't try to complain about how I feel. When he asks me how I feel I always tell him I feel great, until I get to the point where I tell him I have to get into the hospital and they said come in. Well, that's about the first that he's learned about it.

DOCTOR: Why, has he ever asked you to do this earlier?

PATIENT: No, I've done it myself because I had a friend that made herself believe that she was real ill. She put herself into a wheelchair. From then on I made up my mind that it has to be pretty bad before I complain. I think that it was a lesson that I learned through her. She went to doctors all over the city to have them agree with her that she had multiple sclerosis. The doctors couldn't find anything wrong with her. Today she is in a wheelchair and she just can't walk. Whether she has got it or not I just don't know, but she has been like this for about seventeen years.

DOCTOR: But that's another extreme.

PATIENT: Yes, but I mean the way she complains continually— And then I have a sister-in-law whose fingernails hurt her and it bothers her to shave her legs and everything else, and I can't stand that constant complaining from the two of them and I have made up my mind that it has to be pretty bad before I'll ever complain.

DOCTOR: Who was like this in your family? Were your parents fighters like that?

PATIENT: My mother just passed away in '49 and the only time I've known her to really be ill is twice. The last time was when she had leukemia, she passed away. My father I don't remember too much, but I only know, what I remember is, that he was sick with the flu during the flu epidemic in 1918 when he passed away. So I can't say too much about my father.

DOCTOR: To complain then is to be equated with passing away

because they both only complained just before they passed away.

PATIENT: That's right, that's right!

DOCTOR: But, you know, there are lots of people who express their aches and pains and don't pass away.

PATIENT: I know that. I have that sister-in-law, the chaplain knows her too.

CHAPLAIN: Another aspect of Mrs. L.'s hospitalization is that she is often looked up to by other patients. And then she finds herself as a kind of a comforter to the others.

PATIENT: Oh, I don't know—

CHAPLAIN: And I sometimes wonder, don't you wish you had someone you could talk to, who could comfort you, instead of them always leaning on you?

PATIENT: I don't feel I need comfort, Chaplain. And I sure don't want pity for anything because I don't feel as if I should be pitied. I feel as if there's nothing been that bad to complain about. Only thing I complain to is my poor doctors.

DOCTOR: You feel sorry for them? You shouldn't pity them either because they don't want pity, do they?

PATIENT: I know they don't want pity but I figure, gee, when they walk out of the rooms and hear everybody's aches and pains, I bet they would really like to take off someplace. The nurses too.

DOCTOR: Sometimes they do.

PATIENT: Well, I don't blame them if they do.

DOCTOR: You say you cooperate with them. Do you ever withhold information because you hate to burden them?

PATIENT: No, no. I figure I'll tell them what's really there and that's the only way they have to work. How can they cure anybody if you don't tell them what's wrong?

DOCTOR: Do you have any feelings of physical discomfort?

PATIENT: I feel wonderful, but I sure wish I could do what I want to do.

DOCTOR: What is it that you would like to do?

PATIENT: Get up and walk and go right straight home and walk all the way.

DOCTOR: And then what?

PATIENT: Well, I don't know what I'd do when I'd get there, probably go to bed. (Laughter) But I feel real good. I don't have any aches or pains at this moment at all.

DOCTOR: And that's been since yesterday?

PATIENT: Well, I had that tingling sensation in my legs up until yesterday and it left. It wasn't bad as far as that goes but I was a little concerned at home because I wasn't able to walk in the last couple of weeks as well as I have previously. I know I was pushing myself which probably, if I had admitted it in the beginning and had called for help and taken care of it, then it wouldn't have gotten to this stage that it was in. But I always think that the next day is going to be better.

DOCTOR: So you wait a bit and hope it disappears.

PATIENT: I wait and wait until I see it isn't getting better. Then I call.

DOCTOR: And you are forced to face it.

PATIENT: I'm forced to face the facts.

DOCTOR: How is it going to be when you are at the end of your days? Will you just be taking it the same way?

PATIENT: I'll wait until that day comes. I hope so. From taking care of my mother before she entered the hospital, I would say that she took it as it came.

DOCTOR: Did she know?

PATIENT: She did not know that she had leukemia.

DOCTOR: No?

PATIENT: The doctors told me that I shouldn't tell her.

DOCTOR: What do you think of that? Do you have any feelings about that?

PATIENT: Well, I felt bad that she didn't know because she was telling the doctor what was wrong with her. And she was, I think, working against the doctors by not knowing. Because she was telling him she had gallbladder trouble and she was doctoring herself for gallbladder trouble and taking medication that would be no good for anybody in her condition.

DOCTOR: Why do you think they didn't tell her?

PATIENT: Well, I don't know, I have no idea. I asked the doctor when he told me what would happen if she knew and he said no, she shouldn't know.

DOCTOR: How old were you then?

PATIENT: Well, I was married then. I was about thirty-seven years old.

DOCTOR: But you did what the doctor told you.

PATIENT: I did what the doctor told me.

DOCTOR: So she died without really knowing or without talking about it.

PATIENT: That's right.

DOCTOR: It's very hard to know then how she took it.

PATIENT: That's right.

DOCTOR: What do you think is easier for a patient?

PATIENT: Oh, think that's very individual. As far as I'm concerned, I'm glad I know what I got.

DOCTOR: Um hm. And your father—

PATIENT: And my father, he knew what he had. He had the flu. I've seen different patients that are ill that didn't know what they had. The chaplain knows the last one. She knew what she had but she didn't know she was going to die. That was Mrs. J. She was putting up a great battle, she was determined she was going home with her husband. Her family kept it from her, how bad she really was, and she didn't suspect anything all along. Maybe to her that was a better way for her to go. I don't know. I think it's according to the individual. I think the doctors would know the best way to handle something like that. I think that they can judge a person best as to how they can take it.

DOCTOR: Then they do it on an individual level?

PATIENT: I think so.

DOCTOR: And you can't generalize. No, we agree that we can't do that. That's what we are trying to do here, to look at each individual and try to learn how we can help this type of individual. And I think you are the kind of fighter who would do as much as you can possibly do till the last day.

PATIENT: I'm gonna do it.

DOCTOR: And then when you have to face it, you'll face it. Your faith has contributed a lot to your being able to smile through this.

PATIENT: I hope so.

DOCTOR: What faith do you belong to?

PATIENT: Well, Lutheran.

DOCTOR: What in your faith helps you most?

PATIENT: I don't know. I can't pinpoint it. I've found a lot of comfort in talking to the chaplain. And I've even called him on the phone to talk to him.

DOCTOR: When you are really having the blues and feeling lonely and nobody around, what kind of things do you do?

PATIENT: Well, I don't know. Anything that comes to my mind, I guess, that has to be done.

DOCTOR: For example?

PATIENT: Well, I've turned on a panel show the last few months on TV and gotten my mind off of myself. That's the only thing. Look at something else or call my daughter-in-law to talk to her and the youngsters.

DOCTOR: On the phone?

PATIENT: On the phone and keeping busy.

DOCTOR: Doing things?

PATIENT: Just to do something to get my mind off myself. And I call the chaplain just for a little moral support once in a while. I don't really talk about my condition to nobody. My daughter-in-law usually gets an idea of when I call that I might be blue or down in the dumps. She'll put one of the youngsters on or she'll tell me something that they did and it's over with by that time.

DOCTOR: I admire your courage for coming in here for this interview. You know why?

PATIENT: No.

DOCTOR: We have a patient every week, and we do this every week, but you are somebody who, I'm finding out now, doesn't really want to talk about it, and you knew that we were going to talk about it. And yet you were willing enough to come.

PATIENT: Well, if I can help somebody else in some way I'm willing to do it. Like I say, as far as my physical condition or health, why, I feel just as healthy as you and the chaplain here. And I'm not sick.

DOCTOR: I just think it is remarkable that Mrs. L. volunteered to come here. You mean to be of some service in a way, or to help us.

PATIENT: I hope so. If I can help somebody else, I'm glad to do it, even though I'm not able to get out and do something. Well— I'm going to be around for a long time. Maybe I'll have a few more interviews. (Laughter)

Mrs. L. accepted our invitation to share some of her concerns but showed a peculiar discrepancy between facing her illness and denying it. It was only after this interview that we were able to understand some of this dichotomy. She offered to come to the seminar not because she wanted to talk about illness or dying but to be of some service while restricted and unable to function outside of her bed. "As long as I function I live," she said at one point. She consoles other patients but is really quite resentful that she cannot lean on somebody's shoulders. She calls the chaplain for a confidential private confession, almost in secret, but admits only briefly during the interview some feelings of occasional depression and need for conversation. She terminates the interview by saying, "I am as well and healthy as you and the chaplain," which means: "I have lifted the veil, now I will cover my face again."

It became evident in this interview that complaining was equated with dying. Both her parents never complained and only admitted to being sick prior to their death. Mrs. L. has to function and keep busy if she wants to live. She has to be the eyes for her visually handicapped husband and helps him deny the gradual loss of his vision. When he has an accident because of his poor vision, she imitates a similar accident to emphasize that this is not related to his illness. When she is depressed she has to talk to someone but should not complain: "People who complain are in a wheelchair for seventeen years!"

It is understandable that progressive illness with all its implications is very difficult to tolerate for a patient who feels so strongly that complaining is necessarily followed by being permanently crippled or dead.

This patient was helped by relatives who allowed her to call up and talk about "other things," by having a television in her room to distract her, later on by little arts and crafts which she was able to do in order to give her a feeling of "still functioning." When the teaching aspects of such interviews are stressed, a patient like Mrs. L. can share a lot of grievances without feeling that she will be labeled a complainer.

CHAPTER XI

Reactions to the Seminar
on Death and Dying

The storm of the last night has crowned this morning
with golden peace.

TAGORE,

from *Stray Birds*, CCXCIII

STAFF REACTIONS

As described earlier, the hospital staff reacted with great resistance, at times overt hostility, to our seminar. At the beginning, it was almost impossible to get permission from the attending staff to interview one of their patients. Residents were more difficult to approach than interns, the latter more resistant than externs or medical students. It appeared that the more training a physician had, the less he was ready to become involved in this type of work. Other authors have studied the physician's attitude toward death and the dying patient. We have not studied the individual reasons for this resistance but have observed it many times.

We have also noticed the change in attitude once the seminar was established and the attending physician had the opinion of either his colleagues or some of the patients who came to the class. Students and hospital chaplains equally contributed to the staff's increased familiarity with our work, and the nurses have perhaps been the most helpful assistants.

It may not be a coincidence that one of the doctors best known for the total care of the dying patient, Cicely Saunders, started her work as a nurse and is now physician attending the terminally ill in a hospital set-up especially designed for their care. She has confirmed that the majority of patients know of their impending death whether they have been told or not. She feels quite comfortable discussing this matter with them, and since she does not need denial she is unlikely to meet much denial in her patients. If they do not wish to talk about it, she certainly respects their reticence. She emphasizes the importance of the doctor who can sit and listen. She confirms that most of her patients then take the opportunity to tell her (more often than the other way around!) that they knew what was happening, resentment and fear being almost nonexistent at the end. "More important still," she says, "the staff who has chosen to do such work should have had the opportunity to think deeply about it and to find their satisfaction in a different sphere from the usual aims and activities of hospitals. If they themselves believe in and really enjoy such work, they will help the patient more by their attitude than by any words."

Hinton was equally impressed by the insight and awareness the terminally ill patients demonstrated and the courage they showed in facing their death, which almost always came quietly. I give these two examples because I think they reflect as much about these authors' attitudes as they say about the reactions of their patients.

Among our staff we have found two subgroups of physicians who were able to listen and talk calmly about cancer, impending death, or the diagnosis of a usually fatal illness. They were the very young in the medical profession who either had experienced the death of a person close to them and worked through this loss or who had attended the seminar over a period of several months; the other, smaller group were older physicians, who—we presume this only—grew up a generation ago in an environment which used fewer defense mechanisms and fewer euphemisms, faced death more as a reality, and trained doctors in the care of the terminally ill. They were trained in the old school of humanitarianism and are successful now as physicians in a more scientific world of medicine. They are the doctors who tell their patients about the seriousness of their illness without taking away all hope. These physicians have been helpful and supportive both to their patients and to our seminar. We have had less contact with them, not only because they are the exceptions but also because their patients were comfortable and rarely required a referral.

Approximately nine out of ten physicians reacted with discomfort, annoyance, or overt or covert hostility when approached for their permission to talk to one of their patients. While some of them used the patient's poor physical or emotional health as a reason for their reluctance, others flatly denied having any terminally ill patients under their care. Some expressed anger when their patients asked to talk to us, as if it reflected their inability to cope with them. While only a few flatly refused, the great majority regarded it as a special favor to us when they finally allowed an interview. It has only changed slowly to a situation in which they are coming to ask us to see one of their patients.

Mrs. P. is an example of the turmoil that such a seminar can cause among physicians. She was greatly disturbed about many aspects of her hospitalization. She felt in great need to express her concerns and desperately tried to find out who her doctor was. She happened to be hospitalized at the end of June when there is a big turnover of hospital staff and hardly came to know her "crew" when they left to be replaced by another group of young doctors. One of the newcomers, who had previously attended the seminar, noticed her dismay, but he was unable to spend any time with her as he was busily trying to get to know his new supervisors, his new ward and duties. When I approached him with the request to interview Mrs. P., he quickly consented. A few hours after the seminar, his new supervisor, a resident, cornered me in a busy hallway and angrily and loudly reproached me for seeing this lady, adding that "this is the fourth patient in a row that you have taken from my ward." He did not feel the least embarrassed about bringing out his complaints in front of visitors and patients; it did not bother him either to talk quite disrespectfully to a senior member of the faculty. He was clearly enraged about the implication and about the fact that other members of his team quickly gave permission without asking him first.

He did not wonder why so many of his patients had difficulties in coping with their illness, why his team avoided asking him, and why it was impossible for his patients ever to bring up such concerns. The same physician told his interns later on that they were henceforth not allowed to talk to any of their patients about the serious aspect of their illness nor were they allowed to have them talk to us. In the same meeting he mentioned the respect and admiration he had for the seminar and for our work with the terminally ill—but he himself wanted no part in it and that included his patients, most of whom had an incurable illness.

Another physician called the moment I entered my office after an especially moving interview. I had half a dozen visiting priests and nursing supervisors in my office when a loud voice yelled through the telephone and said something to the effect of, "How do you have the nerve to talk to Mrs. K. about dying when she does not even know how sick she is and may go home once more?" When I finally came to my senses, I explained to him the content of our interview, namely, that this woman asked to talk to someone who was not involved in her immediate treatment. She wanted to share with someone in the hospital that she knew that her days were numbered. She was not yet able to acknowledge this in its full meaning. She asked us to reassure her that her own physician (the one I had on the telephone!) would somehow give her a cue when her end was near and that he would not play a hiding game with her until it was too late. She had the greatest confidence in him and was very uncomfortable that she had not been able to convey to him her awareness of the seriousness of her condition.

When this doctor heard what we were actually doing (which was in great contrast to his suppositions!), he became more curious than angry and finally consented to listen to the tape of Mrs. K.'s interview, which was actually a plea from his own patient to him.

The visiting clergy could not have gotten a better learning experience than the actual interruption by this angered doctor, who showed them the displaced effect that such a seminar can provoke.

Early in my work with dying patients I observed the desperate need of the hospital staff to deny the existence of terminally ill patients on their ward. In another hospital I once spent hours looking for a patient capable to be interviewed, only to be told that there was no one fatally ill and able to talk. On my walk through the ward I saw an old man reading a paper with the headline "Old soldiers never die." He looked seriously ill and I asked him if it did not scare him to "read about that." He looked at me with anger and disgust, telling me that I must be one of those physicians who can only care for a patient as long as he is well but when it comes to dying, then we all shy away from them. This was my man! I told him about my seminar on death and dying* and my wish to interview someone in front of the students in order to teach them not to shy away from these patients. He happily agreed to come, and gave us one of the most unforgettable interviews I have ever attended.

In general, the physicians have been the most reluctant in joining us in this work, by referrals at first and then by attending the seminar. Those who have done either have contributed a great deal, and once they joined they usually continued to do so in increasing involvement. It may take both courage and humility to sit in a seminar which is attended not only by the nurses, students, and social workers with whom they usually work, but in which they are also exposed to the possibility of hearing a frank opinion about the role they play in the reality or fantasy of their patients. Those who are fearful of hearing how others see them will naturally be reluctant to attend such a meeting—aside from the fact that we are talking about a topic which is usually taboo and not talked about with patients and staff publicly. Those who have come to such seminars have always been amazed how much

---

*I used to give such a seminar as an introduction to psychiatry before I began my present work, which is described in this book.

they can learn from the patient and the opinion and observations of others and have come to appreciate it as an unusual learning experience which gave them both insight as well as encouragement in pursuing their work.

It is the first step which is the most difficult with physicians. Once they opened the door, listened to what we were actually doing (rather than speculating on what we might be doing), or actually attended a seminar, they were almost sure to continue. We have had over two hundred interviews over a period of almost three years. During all this time we have had physicians from abroad, from Europe, from the East and the West Coast of the United States attending the seminars on their way through Chicago, but we have had only two members of the faculty from our own University honor us with their presence. I guess it is easier to speak about death and dying when it concerns someone else's patient and we can look at it as we view a stage play rather than be actual participants in the drama.

The nursing staff were more divided in their responses. Originally they met us with similar anger and often quite inappropriate remarks. Some referred to us as vultures and made it clear that our presence was unwarranted on their ward. There were others, though, who greeted us with relief and anticipation. Their motivations were manifold. They were angry at certain doctors for the way and manner they conveyed the seriousness of an illness to their patients; they were angry at them for avoiding the issue or for leaving them out during rounds altogether. They were angry at the many unnecessary tests they ordered as a substitute for spending time with them. They sensed their own impotence in the face of death and when they became aware of the doctor's similar feelings, it angered them out of proportion. They blamed them for their inability to acknowledge that there was nothing else to be done for a given patient and for ordering tests solely to prove that somebody was doing something for them. They were bothered by the discomfort and lack of organization in regard to family members of such patients and were naturally much less able to avoid them than the doctors. Their empathy and exposure to the patients were greater, they felt, but also their frustrations and limitations.

Many nurses felt a great lack of training in this area and had little instruction as to their role in the face of such crisis. They acknowledged their conflicts with more ease than the physicians, and they extended themselves often beyond expectations to attend at least part of the seminar while one of their colleagues guarded the ward. Their attitudes changed much more quickly than those of the doctors, and they opened up in the discussions without hesitation once they realized that frankness and honesty were more valued than socially expected kind words about their attitude toward patients, family members, or members of the treatment team. When one of the doctors was able to say that a patient almost moved him to tears, the nurses were quick to acknowledge that they avoided entering the woman's room in order to avoid the picture of her small children on the nightstand.

They were quickly able to express their real concerns, conflicts, and coping mechanisms when their statements were used to understand a given conflictual situation rather than to judge them. They were equally free in supporting a doctor who had the courage to hear his patient's opinion about himself and they soon learned to point out when he became defensive, as well as to look at their own defensiveness.

There was one ward in the hospital where the terminally ill patients seemed to remain alone much of the time. The nursing supervisor arranged for a meeting with her nursing staff in order to understand the specific problems. We all met in a small conference room and each nurse was asked what she thought about the role of the nurses vis-à-vis a terminally ill patient. An older nurse broke the ice and expressed her dismay about "the waste of time spent on these patients." She pointed out the reality of the shortage of nursing staff and the "absolute absurdity of wasting the precious time on people who cannot be helped any longer."

A younger nurse then added that she always felt very bad when "these people die on me," and yet another one was especially angry when "they died on me while others members of the family were present" or she had "just shaken the pillow." Only one out of twelve nurses felt that dying patients, too, needed their care, and while there was not very much that they were able to do, they could at least make them physically comfortable. The whole meeting was a courageous expression of their dislike for this kind of work mixed with a sense of anger, as if these patients committed an angry act against them by dying in their presence.

The same nurses have come to understand the reasons for their feelings, and now perhaps they can react to their terminally ill patients as suffering human beings who need good nursing care more than their healthier roommates.

Gradually their attitude has changed. Many of them have taken over the role we used to play in the seminar. Many of them feel quite comfortable now when a patient asks them a question in regard to his future. They are much less afraid to spend time with a terminally ill patient and they do not hesitate to come and sit with us to share some of their problems with an especially troubled person and difficult relationship. At times they bring relatives to us or to the chaplain's office, and they organize nurses' meetings to discuss different aspects of total patient care. They have been both students and teachers to us and have contributed a great deal to the seminar. Most credit has to be given to the administrative and supervisory staff who have supported the seminar from the beginning and who have even made arrangements to have the floors covered while others were given the time to attend the interview and discussion.

The social workers, occupational therapists, and inhalation therapists, though fewer in number, have equally contributed and made this a truly interdisciplinary workshop. Volunteers have visited our patients later on and functioned as readers to those too handicapped to open a book. Our occupational therapists have helped many of our patients with little arts and crafts projects as a means of showing them that they can still function on some level. Of all the staff involved in this project, the social workers appeared to have the least apprehension in dealing with the crisis. It may be that the social worker is so busy taking care of the living that she does not have to really deal with the dying. She is usually concerned with the care of the children, the financial aspects of the care, a nursing home perhaps, and last but not least, with the conflicts of the relatives, so that a death may be less threatening to her than to those members of the helping profession who deal directly with the terminally ill and whose care is terminated when the patient dies.

A book on the interdisciplinary study of the care of the terminally ill would not be complete without a word about the role of the hospital chaplain. He is the one who is often called when a patient is in a crisis, when he is dying, when his family has difficulty in accepting the news, or when the treatment team wishes to have him play the role of the mediator. During the first year I did this work without the assistance of the clergy. Their presence has changed the seminar a great deal. The first year was incredibly difficult for many reasons. Neither my work nor I were known and thus met with much understandable resistance and reluctance aside from the difficulties inherent in this undertaking. I had no resources nor did I know the staff well enough to know whom to approach and whom to avoid. It required hundreds of miles of walking through the hospital and by trial and error finding out the hard way who was approachable and who was not. If it had not been for the overwhelmingly good response from the patients, I might have long ago given up.

It was at the end of a fruitless search that I ended up in the chaplain's office one night, exhausted, frustrated, and looking for help. The hospital chaplain then shared with me his own problems with these patients, his own frustrations, and need to have some help, and we joined forces from then on. He had a list of the critically ill available and had previous contact with many of the seriously ill patients; thus the search ended and it became a matter of choosing the most needy.

Among all of the many chaplains, ministers, and rabbis and priests who have attended the seminar, I have seen few who avoided the issue or who showed as much hostility or displaced anger as I have seen among other members of the helping professions. What amazed me, however, was the number of clergy who felt quite comfortable using a prayer book or a chapter out of the

Bible as the sole communication between them and the patients, thus avoiding listening to their needs and being exposed to questions they might be unable or unwilling to answer.

Many of them had visited innumerable very sick people but began for the first time, in the seminar, really to deal with the question of death and dying. They were very occupied with funeral procedures and their role during and after the funeral but had great difficulties in actually dealing with the dying person himself.

They often used the doctor's orders "not to tell" or the ever existing presence of a family member as an excuse for not really communicating with the terminally ill patients. It was in the course of repeated encounters that they began to understand their own reluctance in facing the conflicts and thus their use of the Bible, the relative, or the doctor's orders as an excuse or rationalization for their lack of involvement.

The most touching and instructive change in attitude, perhaps, was presented by one of our theology students who had attended the classes regularly and who seemed deeply involved in this work. One afternoon he came to my office and asked for a meeting alone. He had gone through a week of utter agony and confrontation with the possibility of his own death. He had developed enlarged lymph glands and was asked to have a biopsy taken in order to evaluate the possibility of a malignancy. He attended the next seminar and shared with the group the stages of shock, dismay, and disbelief he had gone through—the days of anger, depression, and hope, alternating with utter anxiety and fear. He vividly compared his attempts to cope with the crisis with the dignity and pride he had seen in our patients. He described the comfort of his wife's understanding and shared with us the reactions of his young children who overheard some of their discussions. He was able to talk about it in a very real sense and made us aware of the difference between being an observer and being the patient himself.

This man will never use empty words when he meets a terminally ill patient. His attitude has not changed because of the seminar but because he himself had to face the possibility of his own death at a time when he just learned how to cope with the impending death of those in his care.

We have learned from the staff that the resistance to such an undertaking is tremendous, the displaced hostility and anger hard to accept at times, but these attitudes can be changed. Once the group understood the reasons for their defensiveness and learned to face the conflicts and analyzed them, they were able to contribute not only to the patient's well-being but also to the growth and understanding of the other participants. Where the obstacle and fear is great, the need is equally great. It may be for this reason that the fruit of our work tastes so much better now because it took so much hard soil to dig and so much care to plant the ground.

STUDENTS' REACTIONS

Most of our students entered the course not knowing what to expect exactly or because they heard from others certain aspects appealing to them. Most of them felt that they had to face "real patients" before having the responsibility of their care. They knew that the interviews would be conducted behind a one-way mirror and that it served for many students as a "getting used to" process before they would have to sit and face an actual patient.

A great many of the students (so we learned later during the discussion) signed up because of some unresolved conflicts in their own life regarding the death of a loved or ambivalent figure, and a few came because they wanted to learn interviewing techniques. Most of them said they came in order to learn more about the complex problems of dying; only a few of them really meant it. Many a student came to the first interview quite self-confident, only to leave the room before the end of the interview. Many students had to make several attempts before they were able to sit through both interview and discussion, and then they were still shaken up when a patient requested to have the session in the audience room rather than behind the mirror.

It took three or more sessions until they became comfortable discussing their own reactions and feelings in front of the group, and many of them discussed their responses long after the day was over. There was one student who constantly picked up some minor details of the interview, challenging an argument among the group until other participants wondered if that, too, was perhaps his way of avoiding the real issue, namely, the patient's impending death. Others were able to talk only about the medical-technical problems and management and became quite uncomfortable when the social worker mentioned the agony of the young husband and the small children. When a nurse spoke up and questioned the rationale of certain procedures and tests, the medical students quickly identified with the doctor who had ordered them, and came to his defense. It was another medical student who then wondered whether he would react the same way if the patient were his father and he was the one who could give the orders. Suddenly the students of the different disciplines began to realize the magnitude of problems that some doctors are faced with, and they began not only to appreciate the role of the patient better but also the conflicts and responsibility of the different members of the treatment team. A growing respect and appreciation for each other's role began soon to be experienced, which enabled the group truly to share their problems on an interdisciplinary level.

From an original feeling of helplessness, impotence, or sheer fright, they developed a sense of group mastery of the problems with a gradual and increasing awareness of their own role in this psychodrama. Each one of them was forced to deal with the relevant questions; he had to get involved or else someone in the group would point out his avoidance to him. And so each one in his own way tried to face his own attitude toward death and gradually made himself and the group familiar with it. Since each one in the group went through the same painful but gratifying process, it became easier for the individual members, just as in group therapy one's problem-solving may help another face his own conflicts and learn how to better deal with it. Openness, honesty, and acceptance made it possible to experience what each member brought to this group.

PATIENTS' REACTIONS

In great contrast to the staff, the patients responded favorably and overwhelmingly positively to our visits. Less than 2 percent of the questioned patients flatly refused to attend the seminar, only one patient out of over two hundred did not ever talk about the seriousness of her illness, problems resulting from her terminal illness, or fears of dying. This type of patient is described in more detail (Chapter III, on denial).

All other patients welcomed the possibility of talking with someone who cared. Most of them tested us first in one way or another, to assure themselves that we were actually willing to talk about the final hours or the final care. The majority of patients welcomed a breakthrough of their defenses, were relieved when they did not have to play a game of superficial conversation when deep down they were so troubled with real or unrealistic fears. Many of them reacted to the first meeting as if we had opened a floodgate: they poured out all their bottled-up feelings and responded with great relief after such a meeting.

Some patients postponed the confrontation for a while only to ask us the next day or the following week to come and sit with them. It is well for those who are trying to do this kind of work to remember that a "rejection" by such a patient does not mean, "No, I do not want to talk about it." It means only, "I am not ready now to open up or to share some of my concerns." If visits are not discontinued after such a rejection but are renewed, the patient will give the cue when he is ready to talk. As long as the patients know that there is someone available when they are ready, they will call at the right time. Many of these patients have later on expressed their appreciation for our patience and shared with us the struggles they had within themselves before they were able to put them into words.

There will be many patients who never use the word death or dying but they talk about it all the time in disguised ways. A perceptive therapist can answer their questions or concerns without using the avoided words and still be of great help to such a patient. Numerous examples are given in the descriptions of Mrs. A. and Mrs. K. (in Chapters II and III).

If we ask ourselves what is so helpful or so meaningful that such a high percentage of terminally ill patients are willing to share this experience with us, we have to look at the answers they give when we ask them for the reasons of their acceptance. Many patients feel utterly hopeless, useless, and unable to find any meaning in their existence at this stage. They wait for doctors' rounds, for an X-ray perhaps, for the nurse who brings the medication, and the days and nights seem monotonous and endless. Then, into this dragging monotony a visitor comes who stirs them up, who is curious as a human being, who wonders about their reactions, their strengths, their hopes and frustrations. Someone actually pulls a chair up and sits down. Someone actually listens and does not hurry by. Someone does not talk in euphemisms but concretely, in straightforward, simple language about the very things that are uppermost in their mind—pushed down occasionally but always coming up again.

Someone comes who breaks the monotony, the loneliness, the purposeless, agonizing waiting.

Another aspect which is perhaps more important is the sense that their communications might be important, might be meaningful at least to others. There is a sense of service at a time when these patients feel that they are of no earthly use to anybody anymore. As more than one patient put it: "I want to be of some use to somebody. Maybe by donating my eyes or my kidneys, but this seems so much better, because I can do it while I am still alive."

Some patients have used the seminar to test their own strength in peculiar ways. They have used it to preach to us, to tell us about their faith in God and their readiness to accept God's will while fear was written all over their face. Others who had a genuine faith which enabled them to accept the finality of their life have been proud to share this with a group of young people in the hope that a little of it may rub off. Our opera singer with the malignancy of her face asked to come to our class as a last performance, a last request to sing for us before returning to her ward where they were ready to pull her teeth before radiation treatment.

What I am trying to say is that the response was unanimously positive, the motivations and reasons different. A few patients may have wished to decline but were concerned that such a rejection might affect their future care. A certainly much higher percentage used it to ventilate their anger and rage at the hospital, the staff, the family, or the world in general for their isolation. To live on borrowed time, to wait in vain for the doctors to make rounds, lingering on from visiting hours to visiting hours, looking out of the window, hoping for a nurse with some extra time for a chat . . . this is the way many terminally ill patients pass their time. Is it then surprising when such a patient is intrigued by a strange visitor who wants to talk to her about her own feelings, her own reaction to this state of affairs? Who wants to sit and share some of the fears, fantasies, wishes she thinks of during those lonely hours? Maybe it is this alone, a little attention, a little "occupational therapy," a break in the monotony of things, a little color to the whiteness of the hospital wall, that this seminar offers to these patients. Suddenly they are all dressed up, put in a wheelchair, asked if their response can be tape-recorded, and aware that a group of interested people are watching. It may just be this attention that helps and that brings a little sunshine, meaning, and perhaps hope into the life of the terminally ill patient.

Probably the best measure of the patient's acceptance and appreciation of this type of work is the fact that they all welcomed us during the remainder of their hospitalization during which time the dialogue continued. The majority of patients who were discharged maintained their contact on their own initiative by phone calls at times of crisis or of important happenings. Mrs. W. called me to share with me her feelings of great relief that her physicians Drs. K. and P. had called on her at home to check about her well-being. Her wish to share the good news with us is perhaps an indication of the closeness and intimacy of such an informal but meaningful relationship. She said, "If I were on my death bed and I would see either one of them, I am sure I would die smiling!" This shows how meaningful such relationships can become and how little expressions of care can become the most important communications.

Dr. B. was described in similar terms by Mr. E. who said, "I was so desperate about the lack of human care, I was ready to sign out. The interns came all day long and stuck me in my veins. They did not care if the bed and the pajamas were a mess. Then one day Dr. B. came and before I knew it he pulled a needle out. I did not even feel it, he did it so tenderly. Then he put a bandage on—this never happened before—and told me which way to pull it off, so it wouldn't hurt!" Mr. E. (a young father of three small children who had acute leukemia) said that this was the most meaningful thing that happened to him during his ordeal.

The patients respond often with almost exaggerated appreciation to someone who cares and who takes a little time out. They are deprived of such kindnesses in a busy world of gadgets and numbers and it is not surprising, then, that a little touch of humanity elicits such an overwhelming response.

In a time of uncertainty, of the hydrogen bomb, of the big rush and the masses, the little small, personal gift may again become meaningful. The gift is on both sides: from the patient in the form of the help, inspiration, and encouragement he may give to others with a similar predicament; from us in the form of our care, our time, and our wish to share with others what they have taught us at the end of their lives.

The last reason perhaps for patients' good response is the need of the dying person to leave something behind, to give a little gift, to create an illusion of immortality perhaps. We acknowledge our appreciation for their sharing with us their thoughts about this taboo topic, we tell them that their role is to *teach* us, to help those who follow them later on, thus creating an idea that something will live perhaps after their death, an idea, a seminar in which their suggestions, their fantasies, their thoughts continue to live, to be discussed, become immortal in a little way.

A communication has been established by the dying patient who attempts to separate himself from human relationships in order to face the last separation with the fewest possible ties, yet is unable to do this without help from an outsider who shares some of these conflicts with him.

We are talking about death—the subject of social repression—in a frank, uncomplicated manner, thus opening the door for a wide variety of discussions, allowing complete denial if this seems to be necessary or open talk about the patient's fears and concerns if the patient so chooses. The fact that *we* don't use denial, that we are willing to use the words death and dying, is perhaps the most welcomed communication for many of our patients.

If we attempt to summarize briefly what these patients have taught us, the outstanding fact, to my mind, is that they are all aware of the seriousness of their illness whether they are told or not. They do not always share this knowledge with their doctor or next of kin. The reason for this is that it is painful to think of such a reality, and any implicit or explicit message not to talk about it is usually perceived by the patient and—for the moment—gladly accepted. There came a time, however, when all of our patients had a need to share some of their concerns, to lift the mask, to face reality, and to take care of vital matters while there was still time. They welcomed a breakthrough in their defenses, they appreciated our willingness to talk with them about their impending death and unfinished tasks. They wished to share with an understanding person some of their feelings, especially the ones of anger, rage, envy, guilt, and isolation. They clearly indicated that they used denial when the doctor or family member expected denial because of their dependency on them and their need to maintain a relationship.

The patients did not mind so much when the staff did not confront them with the facts directly, but they resented being treated like children and not being considered when important decisions were made. They all sensed a change in attitude and behavior when the diagnosis of a malignancy was made and became aware of the seriousness of their condition because of the changed behavior of the people in their environment. In other words, those who were not told explicitly knew it anyway from the implicit messages or altered behavior of relatives or staff. Those who were told explicitly appreciated the opportunity almost unanimously except for those who were told either crudely in hallways and without preparation or follow-up, or in a manner that left no hope.

All of our patients reacted to the bad news in almost identical ways, which is typical not only of the news of fatal illness but seems to be a human reaction to great and unexpected stress: namely, with shock and disbelief. Denial was used by most of our patients and lasted from a few seconds to many months as some of our included interview examples reveal. This denial is never a total denial. After the denial, anger and rage predominated. It expressed itself in a multitude of ways as an envy of those who were able to live and function. This anger was partially justified and enforced by the reactions of staff and family, at times almost irrational and a repetition of earlier experiences, as the example of Sister I. shows. When the environment was able to tolerate this anger without taking it personally, the patient was greatly helped in reaching a stage of temporary bargaining followed by depression, which is a stepping-stone towards final acceptance. The following diagram demonstrates how these stages do not replace each other but can exist next to each other and overlap at times. The final acceptance has been reached by many patients without any external help, others needed assistance in working through these different stages in order to die in peace and dignity.

No matter the stage of illness or coping mechanisms used, all our patients maintained some form of hope until the last moment. Those patients who were told of their fatal diagnosis without a chance, without a sense of hope, reacted the worst and never quite reconciled themselves with the person who presented the news to them in this cruel manner. As far as our patients are concerned, all of them maintained some hope and it is well for us to remember this! It may come in form of a new discovery, a new finding in a research laboratory, a new drug or serum, it may come as a miracle from God or by the discovery that the X-ray or pathological slide really belongs to another patient. It may come in form of a naturally occurring remission, as Mr. J. so eloquently describes (in Chapter IX), but it is this hope that should always be maintained whether we can agree with the form or not.

Though our patients greatly appreciated sharing their concerns with us and talked freely about death and dying, they, too, gave their signals when to change the topic, when to turn to more

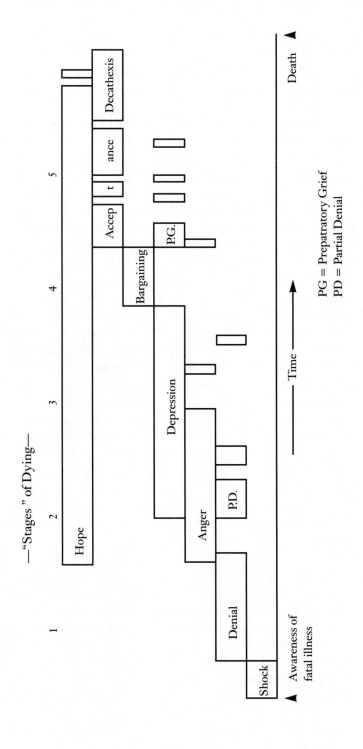

—"Stages" of Dying—

Shock

Denial

Anger   P.D.

Depression

Bargaining

Accep t ance   Decathexis

Hope

P.G.

1   2   3   4   5

Awareness of fatal illness

◄——— Time ———►

Death

PG = Prepatratory Grief
PD = Partial Denial

cheerful things again. They all acknowledged that it was good to ventilate their feelings; they also had the need to choose the time and the duration for this.

Earlier conflicts and defense mechanisms allow us to predict to a certain degree what defense mechanisms a patient will use more extensively at the time of this crisis. Simple people with less education, sophistication, social ties, and professional obligations seem in general to have somewhat less difficulty in facing this final crisis than people of affluence who lose a great deal more in terms of material luxuries, comfort, and number of interpersonal relationships. It appears that people who have gone through a life of suffering, hard work, and labor, who have raised their children and been gratified in their work, have shown greater ease in accepting death with peace and dignity compared to those who have been ambitiously controlling their environment, accumulating material goods, and a great number of social relationships but few meaningful interpersonal relationships which would have been available at the end of life. This has been described in more detailed an example in Chapter IV on the stage of anger.

Religious patients seemed to differ little from those without a religion. The difference may be hard to determine, since we have not clearly defined what we mean by a religious person. We can say here, however, that we found very few truly religious people with an intrinsic faith. Those few have been helped by their faith and are best comparable with those few patients who were true atheists. The majority of patients were in between, with some form of religious belief but not enough to relieve them of conflict and fear.

When our patients reached the stage of acceptance and final decathexis, interference from outside was regarded as the greatest turmoil and prevented several patients from dying in peace and dignity. It is the signal of imminent death and has allowed us to predict the oncoming death in several patients where there was little or no indication for it from a medical point of view. The patient responds to an intrinsic signal system which tells him of his impending death. We are able to pick up these cues without really knowing what psychophysiological signals the patient perceives. When the patient is asked, he is able to acknowledge his awareness and often communicates it to us by asking us to sit down *now*, since he knows that tomorrow will be too late. We should be keenly aware of such insistence on the part of our patients, as we may miss a unique chance to listen to them while there is still time.

Our interdisciplinary seminar on the study of terminally ill patients, has become an accepted and well-known teaching approach, attended weekly by up to fifty people of different backgrounds, disciplines, and motivations. It is perhaps one of the few classes where hospital personnel meet informally and discuss the total patient need and care from different angles. In spite of the increasing number of attending students, the seminar often resembles a group therapy session, in which the participants speak freely about their own reactions and fantasies in relation to the patient and thus learn something about their own motivations and behavior.

Medical and theology students get academic credit for this course and have written meaningful papers about this topic. In short, it has become a part of the curriculum of many students who encounter the terminally ill patients early in their careers in order to be ready to care for them less defensively when the responsibility is theirs. Older general practitioners and specialists have visited the seminar and contributed through their practical experience outside of a hospital set-up. Nurses, social workers, administrators, and occupational therapists have added to the interdisciplinary dialogue, and each discipline has taught the other something about their professional roles and struggles. There has developed a much greater mutual understanding and appreciation, not only through the exchange of shared responsibilities but mainly perhaps through our mutual acceptance of a frank expression of our own reactions, our own fears and fantasies. If a doctor can admit that he had gooseflesh while listening to a certain patient, then his nurse can feel more comfortable sharing her innermost feelings about the situation.

One patient expressed the changed atmosphere perhaps most

eloquently. She had called us during a previous hospitalization expressing her dismay and anger about the loneliness and isolation she experienced on a given ward. She had an unexpected remission and called upon us a second time when she was rehospitalized. She had a room on the previous ward and wished to come to the seminar again in order to share with us her surprise that the atmosphere was a different one altogether. "Imagine!" she said, "it happens now that a nurse comes into my room and actually takes some time and says, 'Feel like talking?' " We have no proof that it is actually the seminar and the nurses' greater comfort that brought about this change, but we too have noticed the changes on this specific ward where we have an increasing number of referrals from doctors, nurses, and other terminally ill patients.

The greatest change is perhaps the fact that we are asked for consultations by staff for themselves, a sign of increasing awareness of their own conflicts which may interfere with the best management of the patient. Lately we have also received requests from terminally ill patients and their family members outside the hospital set-up to find some tasks for them in the framework of the seminar in order to give meaning to their own life and to others in similar circumstances.

Maybe instead of cryo-societies we should develop societies for dealing with the questions of death and dying, to encourage a dialogue on this topic and help people to live less fearfully until they die.

A student wrote in a paper that the most amazing aspect of this seminar was perhaps that we talked so little about death itself. Was it Montaigne who said that death is just a moment when dying ends? We have learned that for the patient death itself is not the problem, but dying is feared because of the accompanying sense of hopelessness, helplessness, and isolation. Those who have attended the seminar and given thought to these things, expressed their feelings freely and experienced that something can be done, not only face their patients with less anxiety but also feel more comfortable about the possibility of their own death.

CHAPTER XII

Therapy with
the Terminally Ill

Death belongs to life as birth does.
The walk is in the raising of the foot as in the laying
of it down.

TAGORE,

from *Stray Birds*, CCLXVII

From the foregoing it is evident that the terminally ill patient
has very special needs which can be fulfilled if we take the
time to sit and listen and find out what they are. The most
important communication, perhaps, is the fact that we let him
know that we are ready and willing to share some of his concerns. To work with the dying patient requires a certain maturity which only comes from experience. We have to take a
good hard look at our own attitude toward death and dying
before we can sit quietly and without anxiety next to a terminally ill patient.

The door-opening interview is a meeting of two people who
can communicate without fear and anxiety. The therapist—
doctor, chaplain, or whoever undertakes this role—will
attempt to let the patient know in his own words or actions that

he is not going to run away if the word cancer or dying is mentioned. The patient will then pick up this cue and open up, or he may let the interviewer know that he appreciates the message though the time is not right. The patient will let such a person know when he is ready to share his concerns, and the therapist will reassure him of his return at an opportune time. Many of our patients have not had more than just such a door-opening interview. They were, at times, hanging onto life because of some unfinished business; they cared for a retarded sister and had found no one to take over in case of their death, or they had not been able to make arrangements for the care of some children and needed to share this worry with someone. Others were guilt-ridden about some real or imagined "sins" and were greatly relieved when we offered them an opportunity to share them, especially in the presence of a chaplain. These patients all felt better after "confessions" or arrangements for the care of others and usually died soon after the unfinished business was taken care of.

Rarely an unrealistic fear prevents a patient from dying, as earlier exemplified in the woman who was "too afraid to die" because she could not conceive of "being eaten up alive by the worms" (Chapter IX). She had a phobic fear of worms and at the same time was quite aware of the absurdity of it. Because it was so silly, as she herself called it, she was unable to share this with her family who had spent all their savings on her hospitalizations. After one interview this old lady was able to share her fears with us and her daughter helped her with arrangements for a cremation. This patient too died soon after she was allowed to ventilate her fears.

We are always amazed how one session can relieve a patient of a tremendous burden and wonder why it is so difficult for staff and family to elicit their needs, since it often requires nothing more but an open question.

Though Mr. E. was not terminally ill, we shall use his case as a typical example of a door-opening interview. It is relevant because Mr. E. presented himself as a dying man as a consequence of unresolved conflicts precipitated by the death of an ambivalent figure.

Mr. E., an eighty-three-year-old Jewish man, was admitted to the medical service of a private hospital because of severe weight loss, anorexia, and constipation. He complained of unbearable abdominal pains and looked haggard and tired. His general mood was depressed and he wept easily. A thorough medical work-up was negative, and the resident finally asked for a psychiatric opinion.

He was interviewed in a diagnostic-therapeutic interview with several students present in the same room. He did not mind the company and felt relieved to talk about his personal problems. He related how he had been well until four months before admission when he suddenly became "an old, sick, and lonely man." Further questioning revealed that a few weeks before the onset of all his physical complaints he lost a daughter-in-law and two weeks before the onset of his pains his estranged wife died suddenly while he was on a vacation out of town.

He was angry at his relatives for not coming to see him when he expected them. He complained about the nursing service and was generally displeased with the care he received from anybody. He was sure that his relatives would come immediately if he could promise them "a couple of thousand dollars when I die," and he elaborated at length about the housing project in which he lived with other old people and the vacation trip they all were invited to attend. It soon became evident that his anger was related to his being poor and that being poor meant that he had to take the trip when it was planned for his place of residence, i.e., he had no choice in the matter. On further questioning it became clear that he blamed himself for having been absent when his wife was hospitalized and tried to displace his guilt on the people who organized the vacation.

When we asked him if he did not feel deserted by his wife and was just unable to admit his anger at her, an avalanche of bitter feelings poured out in which he shared with us his inability to understand why she deserted him in favor of a brother (he called him a Nazi), how she raised their only son as a non-Jew, and finally how she left him alone now when he needed her the most! Since he felt extremely guilty and ashamed about his negative feeling towards the deceased, he displaced his feelings on the relatives and nursing staff. He was convinced that he had to be punished for all those bad thoughts and that he had to endure much pain and suffering to alleviate his guilt.

We simply told him that we could share his mixed feelings, that they were very human and everybody had them. We also told him bluntly that we wondered if he could not acknowledge some anger at his former wife and express it in further brief visits with us. He answered to this, "If this pain does not go away I will have to jump out of the window." Our answer was, "Your pain may be all those swallowed feelings of anger and frustration. Get them out of your system without being ashamed and your pains will probably go away." He left with obviously mixed feelings but did ask to be visited again.

The resident who accompanied him back to his room was impressed with his slumped posture and took notice of it. He reinforced what we had said in the interview and reassured him that his reactions were very normal, after which he straightened up and returned in a more erect posture to his room.

A visit the next day revealed that he had hardly been in his room. He had spent much of the day socializing, visiting the cafeteria, and enjoying his food. His constipation and his pain was gone. After two massive bowel movements the evening of the interview, he felt "better than ever" and made plans for his discharge and resumption of some of his former activities.

On the day of discharge, he smiled and related some of the good days he had spent with his wife. He also told of the change in attitude towards the staff "whom I have given a hard time" and his relatives, especially his son whom he called to get acquainted a bit better, "since both of us may feel lonely for a while."

We reassured him of our availability should he have more problems, physical or emotional, and he smilingly replied that he had learned a good lesson and might face his own dying with more equanimity.

The example of Mr. E. shows how such interviews may be beneficial to people who are not actually ill themselves, but—due to old age or simply due to their own inability to cope with the death of an ambivalent figure—suffer a great deal and regard their physical or emotional discomforts as a means of alleviating guilt feelings for suppressed hostile wishes toward dead persons. This old man was not so much afraid to die as he was worried about dying before he had paid for his destructive wishes toward a person who had died without having given him a chance "to make up for it." He suffered agonizing pains as a means of reducing his fears of retribution and displaced much of his hostility and anger onto the nursing staff and relatives without being aware of the reasons for his resentment. It is surprising how a simple interview can reveal much of this data and a few statements of explanation, as well as reassurance that these feelings of love and hate are human and understandable and do not require a gruesome price, can alleviate much of these somatic symptoms.

For those patients who do not have a simple and single problem to solve, short-term therapy is helpful, which again does not necessarily require the help of a psychiatrist, but an understanding person, who has the time to sit and listen. I am thinking of patients like Sister I., who was visited on many occasions and who received her therapy as much from her fellow patients as she did from us. They are the patients who are fortunate enough to have time to work through some of their conflicts while they are sick and who can come to a deeper understanding and perhaps appreciation of the things they still have to enjoy. These therapy sessions, like the brief psychotherapy sessions with more terminally ill patients, are irregular in time and occurrence. They are individually arranged depending on the patient's physical condition and his ability and willingness to talk at a given time; they often include visits of just a few minutes to assure them of our presence even at times when they do not wish to talk. They continue even more frequently when the patient is in less comfort and more pain, and then take the form of silent companionship rather than a verbal communication.

We have often wondered if group therapy with a selected group of terminally ill patients is indicated, since they often share the same loneliness and isolation. Those who work on wards with terminally ill patients are quite aware of the interactions that go on between the patients and the many helpful statements that are made from one very sick patient to another. We are always amazed how much of our experiences in the seminar are communicated from one dying patient to another; we even get "referrals" of one patient from another. We have noticed patients sitting together in the lobby of the hospital who have been interviewed in the seminar, and they have continued their informal sessions like members of a fraternity. So far we have left it up to the patients how much they choose to share with others, but we are presently looking into their motivation for a more formal meeting, since this seems to be desired by at least a small group of our patients. They include those patients who have chronic illnesses and who require many rehospitalizations. They have known each other for quite a while and not only share the same illness but they also have the same memories of past hospitalizations. We have been very impressed by their almost joyful reaction when one of their "buddies" dies, which is only a confirmation of their unconscious conviction that "it shall happen to thee but not to me." This may also be a contributing factor why so many patients and their family members, like Mrs. G. (Chapter VII), get some pleasure in visiting other perhaps more seriously ill patients. Sister I. used these visits as an expression of hostility, namely, to elicit patients' needs and to prove to the nursing staff that they were not efficient (Chapter IV). By helping them as a nurse, she could not only temporarily deny her own inability to function, but she could also express her anger at those who were well and unable to serve the sick more effectively. Having such patients in a group therapy set-up would help them understand their behavior and at the same time help the nursing staff by making them more accepting of their needs.

Mrs. F. was another woman to be remembered as she started informal group therapy between herself and some very sick young patients, all of whom were hospitalized with leukemia or Hodgkin's disease, from which she had suffered for over twenty years. During the past few years she had an average of six hospitalizations a year, which finally resulted in her complete acceptance of her illness. One day a nineteen-year-old girl, Ann, was admitted, frightened of her illness and its outcome and unable to share this fear with anyone. Her parents had refused to talk about it, and Mrs. F. then became the unofficial counselor for her. She told her of her sons, her husband, and the house she had taken care of for so many years in spite of the many hospitalizations, and finally enabled Ann to ventilate her concerns and ask questions relevant to her. When Ann was discharged, she sent another young patient to Mrs. F. and so a chain reaction of referrals began to take place, quite comparable to group therapy in which one patient replaces another. The group rarely consisted of more than two or three people and remained together as long as the individual members were in the hospital.

THE SILENCE THAT GOES BEYOND WORDS

There is a time in a patient's life when the pain ceases to be, when the mind slips off into a dreamless state, when the need for food becomes minimal and the awareness of the environment all but disappears into darkness. This is the time when the relatives walk up and down the hospital hallways, tormented by the waiting, not knowing if they should leave to attend the living or stay to be around for the moment of death. This is the time when it is too late for words, and yet the time when the relatives cry the loudest for help—with or without words. It is too late for medical interventions (and too cruel, though well meant, when they do occur), but it is also too early for a final separation from the dying. It is the hardest time for the next of kin as he either wishes to take off, to get it over with; or he desperately clings to something that he is in the process of losing forever. It is the time for the therapy of silence with the patient and availability for the relatives.

The doctor, nurse, social worker, or chaplain can be of great help during these final moments if they can understand the family's conflicts at this time and help select the one person who feels most comfortable staying with the dying patient. This person then becomes in effect the patient's therapist. Those who feel too uncomfortable can be assisted by alleviating their guilt and by the reassurance that someone will stay with the dying until his death has occurred. They can then return home knowing that the patient did not die alone, yet not feeling ashamed or guilty for having avoided this moment which for many people is so difficult to face.

Those who have the strength and the love to sit with a dying patient in the *silence that goes beyond words* will know that this moment is neither frightening nor painful, but a peaceful cessation of the functioning of the body. Watching a peaceful death of a human being reminds us of a falling star; one of a million lights in a vast sky that flares up for a brief moment only to disappear into the endless night forever. To be a therapist to a dying patient makes us aware of the uniqueness of each individual in this vast sea of humanity. It makes us aware of our finiteness, our limited lifespan. Few of us live beyond our three score and ten years and yet in that brief time most of us create and live a unique biography and weave ourselves into the fabric of human history.

> *The water in a vessel is sparkling; the water in the sea is dark.*
>
> *The small truth has words that are clear; the great truth has great silence.*
>
> TAGORE,
> from *Stray Birds*, CLXXVI

Bibliography

Abrams, R. D., and Finesinger, J. E. "Guilt Reactions in Patients with Cancer," *Cancer*, Vol. VI (1953), pp. 474–482.

Aldrich, C. Knight. "The Dying Patient's Grief," *Journal of the American Medical Association*, Vol. 184, No. 5 (May 4, 1963), pp. 329–331.

Alexander, G. H. "An Unexplained Death Coexistent with Death Wishes," *Psychosomatic Medicine*, Vol. V (1943), p. 188.

Alexander, Irving E., and Alderstein, Arthur M. "Affective Responses to the Concept of Death in a Population of Children and Early Adolescents," in *Death and Identity*, ed. Robert Fulton. New York, John Wiley & Sons, Inc., 1965.

Allport, Gordon. *The Individual and His Religion*. New York, The Macmillan Company, 1950.

Anderson, George Christian. "Death and Responsibility: Does Religion Help?" *Psychiatric Opinion*, Vol. III, No. 5 (October, 1966), pp. 40–42.

Anthony, Sylvia. *The Child's Discovery of Death*. New York, Harcourt, Brace & Co., 1940.

Aponte, Gonzaol E., M.D. "The Enigma of 'Bangungut,' " *Annals of Internal Medicine*, Vol. 52 (June, 1960), No. 6, pp. 1258–1263.

Aring, Charles D., M.D. "A Letter from the Clinical Clerk," *Omega*, Vol. I, No. 4 (December, 1966), pp. 33–34.

Aronson, G. J. "Treatment of the Dying Person," in *The Meaning of Death*, ed. Herman Feifel. New York, McGraw-Hill Book Co., 1959.

"Aspects of Death and Dying." Report, *Journal of the American Medical Woman's Association*, Vol. 19, No. 4 (June, 1964).

Ayd, Frank J., Jr. "The Hopeless Case," *Journal of the American Medical Association*, Vol. 181, No. 13 (September 29, 1962), pp. 1099–1102.

Bach, Susan R. von. "Spontanes Malen Schwerkranker Patienten," *Acta Psychosomatica* (Basle) (1966).

Bakan, David. *The Duality of Human Existence*. Chicago, Rand, McNally & Co., 1966.

————. *Disease, Pain and Sacrifice*. Chicago, The University of Chicago Press, 1968.

Barber, T. X. "Death by Suggestion, a Critical Note," *Psychosomatic Medicine*, Vol. XXIII (1961), pp. 153–155.

Beach, Kenneth, M.D., and Strehlin, John S., Jr., M.D. "Enlisting Relatives in Cancer Management," *Medical World News* (March 10, 1967), pp. 112–113.

Beecher, Henry K., M.D. "Nonspecific Forces Surrounding Disease and the Treatment of Disease," *Journal of the American Medical Association*, Vol. 179, No. 6 (1962), pp. 437–440.

Beigner, Jerome S. "Anxiety as an Aid in the Prognostication of Impending Death," *American Medical Association Archives of Neurology and Psychiatry*, Vol. LXXVII (1957), pp. 171–177.

Bell, Bertrand M., M.D. "Pseudo-Terminal Patients Make Comeback." *Medical World News* (August 12, 1966), pp. 108–109.

Bell, Thomas. *In the Midst of Life*. New York, Atheneum Publishers, 1961.

Bettelheim, Bruno. *The Empty Fortress*. New York, Free Press, 1967.

Binswanger, Ludwig. *Grundformen und Erkenntnis des Menschlichen Daseins*. 2d Ausgabe Zurich, Max Niehaus, 1953.

Bluestone, Harvey, M.D., and McGahee, Carl L., M.D. "Reaction to Extreme Stress: Death by Execution," *American Journal of Psychiatry*, Vol. 119, No. 5 (1962), pp. 393–396.

Bowers, Margaretta K. *Counseling the Dying*. New York, Thomas Nelson & Sons, 1964.

Brodsky, Bernard, M.D. "Liebestod Fantasies in a Patient Faced with a Fatal Illness," *International Journal of Psychoanalysis*, Vol. 40, No. 1 (January–February, 1959), pp. 13–16.

————. "The Self-Representation, Anality, and the Fear of Dying," *Journal of the American Psychoanalytic Association*, Vol. VII, No. 1 (January, 1959), pp. 95–108.

Brody, Matthew, M.D. "Compassion for Life and Death," *Medical Opinion and Review*, Vol. 3, No. 1 (January, 1967), pp. 108–113.

Cannon, Walter B. "Voodoo Death," *American Anthropology*, Vol. XLIV (1942), p. 169.

Cappon, Daniel. "Attitudes Of and Towards the Dying," *Canadian Medical Association Journal*, Vol. 87 (1962), pp. 693–700.

Casberg, Melvin A., M.D. "Toward Human Values in Medical Practice," *Medical Opinion and Review*, Vol. III, No. 5 (May, 1967), pp. 22–25.

Chadwick, Mary. "Notes Upon Fear of Death," *International Journal of Psychoanalysis*, Vol. 10 (1929), pp. 321–334.

Chernus, Jack, M.D. "Let Them Die with Dignity," *Riss*, Vol. 7, No. 6 (June, 1964), pp. 73–86.

Choron, Jacques. *Death and Western Thought*. New York, Collier Books, 1963.

————. *Modern Man and Mortality*. New York, The Macmillan Company, 1964.

Cohen, Sidney, M.D. "LSD and the Anguish of Dying," *Harper's Magazine* (September, 1965), pp. 69–78.

Comfort, Alex, M.D., D.Sc. "On Gerontophobia," *Medical Opinion and Review,* Vol. III, No. 9 (September, 1967), pp. 30–37.

Conference on the Care of Patients with Fatal Illness, The New York Academy of Sciences, February 15–17, 1967.

Cooper, Philip. "The Fabric We Weave," *Medical Opinion and Review,* Vol. III, No. 1 (January, 1967), p. 36.

Cutler, Donald R., Ph.D. "Death and Responsibility: A Minister's View," *Psychiatric Opinion,* Vol. III, No. 4 (August, 1966), pp. 8–12.

Deutsch, Felix. "Euthanasia: A Clinical Study," *The Psychoanalytic Quarterly,* Vol. V (1936), pp. 347–368.

———, ed. *The Psychosomatic Concepts in Psychoanalysis.* New York, International Universities Press, 1953.

Deutsch, Helene. *The Psychology of Women.* 2 vols. New York, Grune & Stratton, 1944–45.

Dobzhansky, Theodosius. "An Essay on Religion, Death, and Evolutionary Adaptation," *Zygon—Journal of Religion and Science,* Vol. I, No. 4 (December, 1966), pp. 317–331.

Draper, Edgar. *Psychiatry and Pastoral Care.* Englewood Cliffs, N.J., Prentice-Hall, Inc., 1965.

Easson, Eric C., M.D. "Cancer and the Problem of Pessimism," *Ca—a Cancer Journal for Clinicians,* American Cancer Society, Inc., Vol. 17 No. 1 (January–February, 1967), pp. 7–14.

Eaton, Joseph W., Ph.D. "The Art of Aging and Dying," *The Gerontologist,* Vol. IV, No. 2 (1964), pp. 94–100.

Eissler, K. R. *The Psychiatrist and the Dying Patient.* New York, International Universities Press, 1955.

Evans, Audrey E., M.D. "If a Child Must Die . . ." *New England Journal of Medicine,* Vol. 278 (January, 1968), pp. 138–142.

Farberow, Norman L., ed. *Taboo Topics.* New York, Atherton Press, 1963.

Feifel, Herman. "Attitudes Toward Death in Some Normal and Mentally Ill Populations," in *The Meaning of Death,* ed. Herman Feifel. New York, McGraw-Hill Book Co., 1959, pp. 114–130.

———. "Is Death's Sting Sharper for the Doctor?" *Medical World News* (October 6, 1967), p. 77.

Feifel, Herman, Ph.D. and Heller, Joseph, M.D. "Normality, Illness, and Death." Paper, Third World Congress of Psychiatry, Montreal, Canada, June, 1961, pp. 1–6.

Feinstein, Alvan R. *Clinical Judgment.* Baltimore, Williams & Wilkins Co., 1967.

Fenichel, Otto. *The Psychoanalytic Theory of Neurosis.* New York, W. W. Norton & Co., 1945.

Finesinger, Jacob E., Shands, Harley C., and Abrams, Ruth D. "Managing the Emotional Problems of the Cancer Patient," *Clinical Problems in Cancer Research*, Sloan-Kettering Institute for Cancer Research (1952), pp. 106–121.

Fischer, Roland, Ph.D. "The Unity of Life and Time," *Omega*, Vol. II, No. 1 (March, 1967), pp. 4–10.

Fletcher, Joseph. *Morals and Medicine*. Boston, Beacon Press, 1960.

Foster, Zelda P. L. "How Social Work Can Influence Hospital Management of Fatal Illness," *Social Work* (Journal of the National Association of Social Workers), Vol. 10, No. 4 (October, 1965), pp. 30–35.

Freud, Sigmund. *Beyond the Pleasure Principle*. New York, Liveright Publishing Corp., 1950.

———. *Civilization and Its Discontents*. (1930). *The Complete Psychological Works of Sigmund Freud*, Standard Edition, ed. James Strechy. London, Hogarth Press, 1961, Vol. XXI, pp. 59–145.

———. *Inhibitions, Symptoms, and Anxiety*. (1926). *The Complete Psychological Works of Sigmund Freud*, Standard Edition, ed. James Strechy. London, Hogarth Press, 1961, Vol. XX, pp. 77–175.

———. *On Transcience*. (1916). *The Complete Psychological Works of Sigmund Freud*, Standard Edition, ed. James Strechy. London, Hogarth Press, 1961, Vol. XIV, pp. 303–308.

———. *Thoughts for the Times on War and Death*. (1915). *The Complete Psychological Works of Sigmund Freud*, ed. James Strechy. London, Hogarth Press, 1961, Vol. XIV, pp. 273–302.

Fromm, Erich. *Escape From Freedom*. New York, Henry Holt & Co., 1941.

———. *Man For Himself*. New York, Henry Holt & Co., 1947.

Fulton, Robert, ed. *Death and Identity*. New York, John Wiley & Sons, Inc., 1966.

Gaines, Renford G. *Death, Denial, and Religious Commitment*. D. Min. thesis, Meadville Theological School (Chicago), 1968.

Garner, Fradley. "Doctors' Need to Care More for the Dying," *American Journal of Mental Hygiene*.

Garner, H. H., M.D. *Psychosomatic Management of the Patient with Malignancy*. Springfield, Ill., Charles C. Thomas.

Gartley, W., and Bernasconi, M. "The Concept of Death in Children," *Journal of Genetic Psychology*, Vol. 110 (March, 1967), pp. 71–85.

Ginsberg, R. "Should the Elderly Cancer Patient Be Told?" *Geriatrics*, Vol. IV (1949), pp. 101–107.

Ginsparg, Sylvia, Moriarty, Alice, and Murphy, Lois B. "Young Teenagers' Responses to the Assassination of President Kennedy: Relation to Previous Life Experiences," in *Children and the Death of a President*, ed. Martha Wolfenstein and Gilbert Kliman. Garden City, N.Y., Doubleday & Company, Inc., Anchor Books, 1966.

Glaser, Barney G. "The Physician and the Dying Patient," *Medical Opinion and Review* (December, 1965), pp. 108–114.

Glaser, Barney G., and Strauss, Anselm L. *Awareness of Dying.* Chicago, Aldine Publishing Co., 1965.

Green, M., and Solnit, A. J. "Psychologic Considerations in the Management of Deaths on Pediatric Hospital Services," Part 1, "The Doctor and the Child's Family," *Pediatrics,* Vol. XXIV (1959), pp. 106–112.

—— "The Pediatric Management of the Dying Child," Part 2, "The Child's Reaction (vica) Fear of Dying," in *Modern Perspectives in Child Development.* New York, International Universities Press, Inc., pp. 217–228.

Grollman, Rabbi Earl A., D.D. "Death and Responsibility," *Psychiatric Opinion,* Vol. III, No. 6 (December, 1966), pp. 36–38.

Hackett, T. P., and Weisman, A. D. "Predilection to Death: Death and Dying as a Psychiatric Problem," *Psychosomatic Medicine,* Vol. 23 (May–June, 1961), pp. 232–256.

——. "The Treatment of the Dying." Unpublished paper, Department of Psychiatry, Harvard University Medical School, 1962.

Hamovich, Maurice B. "Parental Reactions to the Death of a Child." Unpublished paper, University of Southern California, September 19, 1962.

Haroutunia, Joseph. "Life and Death Among Fellowman," in *The Modern Vision of Death,* ed. Nathan A. Scott, Jr. Richmond, Va., John Knox Press, 1967.

Hicks, William, M.D. and Robert S. Daniels, M.D. "The Dying Patient, His Physician and the Psychiatric Consultant," *Psychosomatics,* Vol. IX (January–February, 1968), p. 47–52.

Hinton, J. M. "Facing Death," *Journal of Psychosomatic Research,* Vol. 10 (1966), pp. 22–28.

——. *Dying.* Baltimore, Penguin Books, 1967.

Hofling, Charles K., M.D. "Terminal Decisions," *Medical Opinion and Review,* Vol. II, No. 1 (October, 1966), pp. 40–49.

Howland, Elihu S., M.D. "Psychiatric Aspects of Preparation for Death." Paper read at meeting of the Wisconsin State Medical Society, Milwaukee, Wisconsin, May, 1963.

Irwin, Robert, and Weston, Donald L., M.D. "Preschool Child's Response to Death of Infant Sibling," *American Journal of Diseases of Children,* Vol. 106, No. 6 (December, 1963), pp. 564–567.

Jackson, Edgar Newman. *Understanding Grief: Its Roots, Dynamics and Treatment.* New York, Abingdon Press, 1957.

Jonas, Hans. *The Phenomenon of Life.* New York, Harper & Row, Inc., 1966.

Jones, Ernest. "Dying Together," in *Essays in Applied Psychoanalysis,* Vol. I, London, Hogarth Press, 1951.

——. "The Psychology of Religion," in *Essays in Applied Psychoanalysis,* Vol. II. London, Hogarth Press, 1951.

Kalish, Richard A., Ph.D. "Death and Responsibility: A Social-Psychological View." *Psychiatric Opinion,* Vol. 3, No. 4 (August, 1966), pp. 14–19.

Kast, Eric, M.D. "LSD and the Dying Patient," *Chicago Medical School Quarterly*, Vol. 26 (Summer, 1966), pp. 80–87.

Kastenbaum, Robert, Ph.D. "Death and Responsibility: Introduction" and "A Critical Review," *Psychiatric Opinion*, Vol. 3, No. 4 (August, 1966), pp. 5–6, 35–41.

Katz, Alfred H., D.S.W. "Who Shall Survive?" *Medical Opinion and Review*, Vol. III, No. 3 (March, 1967), pp. 52–61.

Klein, Melanie. "A Contribution to the Theory of Anxiety and Guilt," *International Journal of Psychoanalysis*, Vol. 29, No. 114 (1948), pp. 114–123.

Knudson, Alfred G., Jr., M.D., Ph.D., and Natterson, Joseph M., M.D. "Observations Concerning Fear of Death in Fatally Ill Children and Their Mothers," *Psychosomatic Medicine*, Vol. XXII, No. 6 (November–December, 1960), pp. 456–465.

————. "Practice of Pediatrics—Participation of Parents in the Hospital Care of Fatally Ill Children," *Pediatrics*, Vol. 26, No. 3, Part 1 (September, 1960), pp. 482–490.

Kramer, Charles H., and Dunlop, Hope E., R.N., "The Dying Patient," *Geriatric Nursing* (September–October, 1966).

LeShan, L., and LeShan, E. "Psychotherapy in the Patient with a Limited Life Span," *Psychiatry*, Vol. 24 (November, 1961), p. 4.

Lieberman, Morton A., Ph.D. "Psychological Correlates of Impending Death: Some Preliminary Observations," *Journal of Gerontology*, Vol. 20, No. 2 (April, 1965), pp. 181–190.

"Life in Death." Editorial, *New England Journal of Medicine*, Vol. 256, No. 16 (April 18, 1957), pp. 760–761.

Lifton, Robert J. *Challenges of Humanistic Psychology*, 2 vols., ed. James F. T. Bugental. New York, McGraw-Hill Book Co., 1967.

Malino, Jerome R. "Coping with Death in Western Religious Civilization," *Zygon—Journal of Religion and Science*, Vol. I, No. 4 (December, 1966), pp. 354–365.

"Management of the Patient with Cancerphobia and Cancer," *Psychosomatics*, Vol. V, No. 3 (1964), pp. 147–152.

Mathis, James L., M.D. "A Sophisticated Version of Voodoo Death," *Psychosomatic Medicine*, Vol. 26, No. 2 (1964), pp. 104–107.

McGann, Leona M. "The Cancer Patient's Needs: How Can We Meet Them?" *Journal of Rehabilitation*, Vol. XXX, No. 6 (November–December, 1964), p. 19.

Meerloo, Joost, A.M. "Psychological Implications of Malignant Growth: A Survey of Hypothesis," *British Journal of Medical Psychology*, Vol. XXVII (1954), pp. 210–215.

————. "Tragic Paradox of the Nuclear Death Wish," Abbott Pharmaceutic Co., pp. 29–32.

Menninger, Karl. *Man Against Himself.* New York, Harcourt, Brace & Co., 1938.

Moellendorf, Fritz. "Ideas of Children About Death," *Bulletin of the Menninger Clinic*, Vol. III, No. 148 (1939).

Morgenthau, Hans. "Death in the Nuclear Age," in *The Modern Vision of Death*, ed. Nathan A. Scott, Jr. Richmond, Va., John Knox Press, 1967.

Moritz, Alan R., M.D. "Sudden Deaths," *New England Journal of Medicine*, Vol. 223, No. 20 (November 14, 1940), pp. 798–801.

Mueller, Ludwig. *Ueber die Seelenverfassung der Sterbenden.* Berlin, Springerverlag, 1931.

Nagy, Maria H. *The Meaning of Death.* New York, McGraw-Hill Book Co., 1965.

Natanson, Maurice, Ph.D. "Death and Mundanity," *Omega*, Vol. I, No. 3 (September, 1966), pp. 20–22.

Negovskii, V. A. "The Last Frontier," in *Resuscitation and Artificial Hypothermia*, trans. from Russian by Basil Haigh, *Hospital Focus* (December, 1962).

Norton, Janice, M.D. "Treatment of the Dying Patient," *The Psychoanalytic Study of the Child*, Vol. XVIII (1963), pp. 541–560.

O'Connell, Walter, Ph.D. "The Humor of the Gallows," *Omega*, Vol. I, No. 4 (December, 1966), pp. 31–33.

Ostrow, Mortimer, M.D. "The Death Instincts: A Contribution to the Study of Instincts," *International Journal of Psychoanalysis*, Vol. XXXIX, Part 1 (1958), pp. 5–16.

Parkes, C. Murray, M.D. "Grief as an Illness," *New Society*, Vol. IX (April 9, 1964).

———. "Effects of Bereavement on Physical and Mental Health: A Study of the Medical Records of Widows," *British Medical Journal*, Vol. II (August 1, 1964), pp. 274–279.

Patton, Kenneth. "Science, Religion and Death," *Zygon—Journal of Religion and Science*, Vol. 1, No. 4 (December, 1966), pp. 332–346.

Peabody, Francis Weld, M.D. "The Care of the Patient," *Journal of the American Medical Association* (1927).

Pfister, Oskar. "Schockenden und Schockphantasien bei Hoechster Lebensgefahr," *Internationale Zeiting fuer Psychoanalyse*, Vol. 16 (1930), p. 430.

Piaget, Jean. *The Language and Thought of the Child.* 3rd edition. London, Routledge and Kegan Paul, 1959.

"Prognosis in Psychiatric Disorders of the Elderly: An Attempt to Define Indicators of Early Death and Early Recovery," *Journal of Mental Science*, Vol. 102 (1956), pp. 129–140.

"Progress Against Cancer, 1966," in *Care of the Leukemia Patient.* Washington, D.C., National Advisory Council, U.S. Department of Health, Education, and Welfare, 1966, p. 33.

Rheingold, Joseph C. *The Fear of Being a Woman.* New York, Grune & Stratton, 1964.

———. *The Mother, Anxiety, and Death: The Catastrophic Death Complex.* Boston, Little, Brown & Co., 1967.

Richmond, Julius B., and Waisman, Harry A. "Psychological Aspects of Management of Children with Malignant Diseases," *American Journal of Diseases of Children*, Vol. 89, No. 1 (January, 1955), pp. 42–47.

Richter, Curt P., Ph.D. "On the Phenomenon of Sudden Death in Animals and Man," *Psychosomatic Medicine*, Vol. XIX, No. 103 (1957), pp. 191–198.

Rosenblum, J., Ph.D. *How to Explain Death to a Child.* International Order of the Golden Rule, 1963.

Ross, Elisabeth K., M.D. "The Dying Patient as Teacher: An Experiment and An Experience," *Chicago Theological Seminary Register*, Vol. LVII, No. 3 (December, 1966).

———. "Psychotherapy with the Least Expected," *Rehabilitation Literature*, Vol. 29, No. 3 (March, 1968), pp. 73–76.

Rothenberg, Albert, M.D. "Psychological Problems in Terminally Cancer Management," *Cancer*, Vol. XIV (1961), pp. 1063–1073.

Rydberg, Wayne D. "The Role of Religious Belief in the Suicidal Crisis." Unpublished B.D. dissertation, Chicago Theological Seminary, June, 1966.

Sandford, B. "Some Notes on a Dying Patient," *International Journal of Psychiatry*, Vol. 38 (1957).

Saul, Leon J., M.D. "Reactions of a Man to Natural Death," *Psychoanalytic Quarterly*, Vol. 28 (1959), pp. 383–386.

Saunders, Cicely, M.D., O.B.E. *Care of the Dying.* London, Macmillan & Co., Ltd., 1959.

———. "Death and Responsibility: A Medical Director's View," *Psychiatric Opinion*, Vol. III, No. 4 (August, 1966), pp. 28–34.

———. "The Management of Terminal Illness," *Hospital Medicine* Part I, December, 1966, pp. 225–228; Part II, January, 1967, pp. 317–320; Part III, February, 1967, pp. 433–436.

———. "The Need for Institutional Care for the Patient with Advanced Cancer," in *Anniversary Volume.* Madras, Cancer Institute, 1964, pp. 1–8.

———. "A Patient," *Nursing Times* (March 31, 1961).

———. "The Treatment of Intractable Pain in Terminal Cancer," *Proceedings of the Royal Society of Medicine*, Vol. 56, No. 3 (March, 1963), pp. 191–197.

———. "Watch With Me," *Nursing Times* (November 25, 1965).

Scherzer, Carl J. *Ministering to the Dying.* Englewood Cliffs, N.J., Prentice-Hall, Inc., 1963.

Shands, Harley C. "Psychological Mechanisms in Cancer Patients," *Cancer*, Vol. IV (1951), pp. 1159–1170.

Shepherd, J. Barrie. "Ministering to the Dying Patient," *The Pulpit* (July–August, 1966), pp. 9–12.

Simmons, Leo W. "Aging in Primitive Societies: A Comparative Survey of Family Life and Relationships," *Law and Contemporary Problems* (Duke University School of Law), Vol. 27, No. 1 (Winter, 1962).

————. "Attitudes Toward Aging and the Aged: Primitive Societies," *Journal of Gerontology*, Vol. I, No. 1 (January, 1946), pp. 72–95.

Sperry, Roger. "Mind, Brain and Humanist Values," in *New Views of the Nature of Man*, ed. John R. Platt. Chicago, University of Chicago Press, 1965.

Spitz, Rene. *The First Year of Life*. New York, International Universities Press, 1965.

Stinnette, Charles R. *Anxiety and Faith*. Greenwich, Conn., Seabury Press, Inc., 1955.

Stokes, A. "On Resignation," *International Journal of Psychosomatics* Vol. XLIII (1962), pp. 175–181.

Strauss, Richard H., M.D. "I Think, Therefore:" *Perspectives in Biology and Medicine* (University of Chicago), Vol. VIII, No. 4 (Summer, 1965), pp. 516–519.

Sudnow, David. *Passing On*. Englewood Cliffs, N.J., Prentice-Hall, Inc., 1967.

"Telling the Relatives," *Hospital Medicine*, I (April, 1967).

Tichauer, Ruth W., M.D. "Attitudes Toward Death and Dying among the Aymara Indians of Bolivia," *Journal of the American Medical Women's Association*, Vol. 19, No. 6 (June, 1964), pp. 463–466.

Tillich, Paul. *The Courage To Be*. New Haven, Conn., Yale University Press, 1952.

"Time, Perspective, and Bereavement." *Omega*, Vol. I, No. 2 (June, 1966).

Treloar, Alan E., Ph.D. "The Enigma of Cause of Death," *Journal of the American Medical Association*, Vol. 162, No. 15 (December 8, 1956), pp. 1376–1379.

Verwoerdt, Adriaan, M.D. "Comments on: 'Communication with the Fatally Ill,' " *Omega*, Vol. II, No. 1 (March, 1967), pp. 10–11.

————. "Death and the Family," *Medical Opinion and Review*, Vol. I, No. 12 (September, 1966), pp. 38–43.

Verwoerdt, Adriaan, M.D., and Wilson, Ruby. "Communication with Fatally Ill Patients," *American Journal of Nursing*, Vol. 67, No. 11 (November, 1967), pp. 2307–2309.

Von Lerchenthal, E. "Death from Psychic Causes," *Bulletin of the Menninger Clinic*, Vol. XII, No. 31 (1948).

Wahl, Charles W. "The Fear of Death," *ibid.*, Vol. XXII, No. 214 (1958), pp. 214–223.

————, ed. *Management of Death and the Dying Patient Book: Dimensions in Psychosomatic Medicine*. Boston, Little, Brown & Co., 1964, pp. 241–255.

Walters, M. "Psychic Death: Report of a Possible Case," *Archives of Neurology and Psychiatry*, Vol. 52, No. 1 (1944), p. 84.

Warbasse, James Peter. "On Life and Death and Immortality," *Zygon—Journal of Religion and Science*, Vol. I, No. 4 (December, 1966), pp. 366–372.

Warner, W. Lloyd. *The Living and the Dead: A Study of the Symbolic Life of Americans*, Vol. V of *The Yankee City Series*, ed. Cornelius Crane. New Haven, Conn., Yale University Press, 1959.

Weisman, Avery D. "Birth of the Death-People," *Omega*, Vol. I, No. 1 (March, 1966), pp. 3–4. (Newsletter distributed by Cushing Hospital, Framingham, Mass.)

————. "Death and Responsibility: A Psychiatrist's View," *Psychiatric Opinion*, Vol. 3, No. 4 (August, 1966), pp. 22–26.

Weisman, Avery D., and Hackett, Thomas P. "Denial as a Social Act," in *Psychodynamic Studies on Aging: Creativity, Reminiscing, and Dying*, ed. Sidney Levin and Ralph J. Kahana. New York, International Universities Press, 1967.

Weiss, Soma, M.D. "Instantaneous 'Physiologic' Death," *New England Journal of Medicine*, Vol. 223, No. 20 (November 4, 1940), pp. 793–797.

Wentz, Walter Yeeling Evans. *Das Tibetanische Totenbuch*. Zurich, Rascher Verlag, 1953.

Westburg, Granger E. *Good Grief*. Rock Island, Ill., Augustana Book Concern, 1961.

Wieman, Henry N. *The Source of Human Good*. Carbondale, Ill., Southern Illinois University Press, 1946.

Wolf, Stewart F., Jr., M.D. "Once Lifesaving 'Dive Reflex' Said to Cause Sudden Death." Report, 19th Annual Meeting of the California Academy of General Practice, *Hospital Tribune* (January 15, 1968), p. 18.

Woolf, Kurt, M.D. "Fear of Death Must Be Overcome in Psychotherapy of the Aged." Report delivered at meeting of Gerontological Society. *Frontiers of Hospital Psychiatry* (1966), p. 3.

Zilboorg, Gregory. "Differential Diagnostic Types of Suicide," *Archives of Neurology and Psychiatry*, Vol. 35, No. 2 (February 1936), pp. 270–291.

————. "Fear of Death," *Psychoanalytic Quarterly*, Vol. 12 (1943), pp. 465–475.